Vincent Brome was educated at Streatham Gram
He started writing professionally at 21, and has
including as feature writer, as editor at Menu a
and as propagandist at the Ministry of Information during World War II.
He has written over thirty books including novels, biographies, literary
and historical studies, and plays for radio and television. His novels
The Embassy and The Surgeon were international bestsellers, and have been
translated into eleven languages. Brome has travelled very widely, and was
present in Hungary during the 1956 uprising, an experience on which he
based his novel The Revolution.

He has been a regular contributor to radio, newspapers and magazines
including The Observer, The Times and Sunday Times, The Guardian, The Spectator and
The New Statesman (UK), and The Nation and The New York Times (USA). He lives
in Central London.

VINCENT BROME

FREUD
AND HIS
DISCIPLES

HOUSE OF
STRATUS

This edition published in 2000 by House of Stratus, an imprint of Stratus Holdings plc, 24c Old Burlington Street, London, W1X 1RL, UK.

www.houseofstratus.com

Typeset, printed and bound by House of Stratus.

A catalogue record for this book is available from the British Library.

ISBN 1-84232-030-0

CONTENTS

INTRODUCTION

Freud, said by his critics to be dead, has suddenly come alive again in television form. No less than two series of programmes, one proposed for Channel Four and another from BBC 2 unfold his life story. The BBC 2 series dramatises his life but does not give detailed documentary evidence. This book is a companion volume for either series for anyone who wishes to read the fascinating story of the development, quarrels and defections of the psycho-analytic movement.

It spells out in detail the development of Freud's early circle which involved all the leading psycho-analytic pioneers from Fliess, Stekel, Ferenczi and Adler, to Jung, Abraham and Jones. Each of these personalities becomes a key figure in one or other of the television series but here the emphasis is on the underlying documentary truths, and the relevant parts of Freudian theory. However, by its very nature, the narrative unfolds in these pages with the ease and pace of a story.

The general significance of Freud's work is treated with the respect it deserves, but highly controversial personal issues are not evaded. Did Freud sleep with his sister-in-law Minna Bernays? How strong was the homosexual streak in his relations with Fliess and Jung? What was the truth about Jung's defections from Freud's circle? Was Jung anti-Semitic and therefore consciously or unconsciously hostile to Freud? These and many other questions are dealt with here on a basis which creates a counterpoint between the book and the television versions.

The full sources of this book, personal, published and unpublished would make tedious reading by their very length and complexity, but wherever necessary the sources of all major facts are given. Suffice it to say that a wealth of material has been tapped including the mass of Jones' papers which he accumulated for his biography of Freud, the unpublished correspondence between Jones and Freud, and the author's personal knowledge of some of the figures involved.

For the rest I must acknowledge my debt to Ernest Jones' biography of Freud and the Hogarth Press and Mrs Ernest Jones for permission to quote from *The Life and Work of Sigmund Freud*. Thanks also to Collins and Routledge Kegan Paul for permission to quote from C J Jung's *Memories, Dreams, Reflections*. I am also grateful to Dr Marian C Putnam for allowing me to quote from her father's correspondence.

PROLOGUE

The casual traveller arriving in Vienna in the year 1909 would have seen a beautiful city clustering around the Danube with all the external appearance of an imperial city, capital of an Empire of fifty million souls. The fashionable cafés teeming with that very special life which reinforced the legend of Viennese graciousness had an unmistakable gaiety, but surface impressions did not survive close scrutiny. The Blue Danube was, on too many occasions, not blue, the rituals of high-society balls and dinner parties could not smother the underlying callousness of the people, and the prosperity of the middle-class Viennese reflected in the monumental buildings erected down the Ringstrasse in the last quarter of the nineteenth century, did not conceal a rabid anti-Semitism. Since Mozart's time aristocratic baroque had given place to a commercial and industrial centre where electric trams crashed through crowded noisy streets to the discomfort of its rapidly multiplying population.

In the year 1909 two men destined to become internationally famous figures lived simultaneously in Vienna, each totally unaware of the other's presence. They occupied different quarters of the city but their daily life frequently took them into identical streets to sit occasionally in the same cafés. One man spoke of his stay in Vienna as "five years in which I had to earn my daily bread, first as a casual labourer, then as a painter of trifles".[1] An impoverished young man up from the country, he described his life vividly: "He loiters about and is hungry. Often he pawns or sells the last of his belongings. His clothes begin to get shabby — with the increasing poverty of his outward appearance he descends to a lower social level."[2] The second, less spectacular person, did not suffer quite such extreme physical hardship but

iii

there were different reasons why he too hated the city: "I have hardly been back...for three days and already I am overcome by the bad mood of the Vienna surroundings. It is a misery to live here."³ "I hate Vienna almost personally..."⁴

In one sense, the two men epitomized the opposing forces of demagoguery and reason, of political violence and the cool detachment of the scientific method. At a deeper level they interlocked in a racial struggle which was to horrify the world and finally to split it asunder. Adolf Hitler was still groping in the embittered mists of class hatred, hunger and anti-Semitism for the vision which would reveal his destiny as the leader of the German people, and Sigmund Freud was unmistakably one of the very Jews whose extermination became his dedicated purpose. In 1909, they went their separate ways without communication, but before the story was done one finally impinged on the other. For the moment, Freud lived with loathing in a narrow-minded city where one economic crisis followed another, and a tired sadness was mistaken by the romantic for Viennese charm. Freud expressed his envy of the lively and progressive spirit which seemed to him to be stirring in Berlin under Kaiser Wilhelm II. Compared to Vienna, where Burgermeister Lueger was openly anti-Semitic, and professional, academic and civil service circles reflected his intolerance, Berlin seemed to Freud a haven of liberalism.

Ironically, Hitler in these early years carried over his hatred of men in long caftans, wearing black sidelocks, into the very field of sexuality which became the chosen speciality of Sigmund Freud. "The black-haired Jewish youth lies in wait for hours on end, satanically glaring at and spying on the unsuspicious girl whom he plans to seduce, adulterating her blood and removing her from the bosom of her own people..." He was haunted by "the nightmare vision of the seduction of hundreds of thousands of girls by repulsive, crooked-legged Jew bastards".⁵

Freud in 1909 was 53, a man living in a brilliant intellectual ferment as he probed deeper and deeper into the mysteries of the human psyche. The power of his presence gave the illusion of height to his person although he was, in fact, barely five feet seven inches, and his flashing eyes and fine moustaches added a panache which marked him out in any company. Hitler was a bare twenty years old, a pale, harassed young man whose closest associate, a tramp called Reinhold Hamisch, described him as thin, fanatical, with a black beard and large staring eyes.

Beyond the superficial coincidence of living in the same city, lay the deeper one of anti-Semitism, which right up until his break with Jung was to haunt Freud and to stay deeply buried in that repository of profound human experience which he had discovered and named – the unconscious.

NOTES
1.   *Mein Kampf*. Adolf Hitler, p. 32.
2.   *Ibid.*, p. 35.
3.   Letter to Fliess, 22 September 1898.
4.   Letter to Fliess, 11 March 1900.
5.   *Mein Kampf*. Adolf Hitler, p. 273.

Chapter One

The Fliess–Freud Episode

Any examination of the history of that brave band of men who formed the first psycho-analytic group in Vienna, would be incomplete without a careful analysis of Freud's initial quarrel with his old friend Wilhelm Fliess which began long before Freud had reached the height of his powers and fame.

A brief recapitulation of well-known facts is a necessary preliminary to more detailed examination. Two years younger than Freud, Fliess was a nose and throat specialist who practised in Berlin, and at the outset his capacity for bold, imaginative speculation allied to "a fascinating personality" strongly attracted Freud. Two, at least, of Freud's relationships with men – Fliess and Ferenczi – were of a passionate kind, but in the case of Fliess a whole nexus of interrelated fixations and motives gave it a special intensity. As Ernest Jones himself wrote in his biography of Freud: "For a man of nearly middle age, happily married and having six children, to develop a passionate friendship for someone intellectually his inferior and for him to subordinate for several years his judgement and opinions to those of that other man...is unusual." [1]

The two men first met in Vienna when Fliess attended Freud's lectures on the "anatomy and mode of functioning of the nervous system". During the discussions which followed, Freud found himself powerfully attracted by the flashing personality of Fliess and his brilliant conversation. His first letter to Fliess had an interesting ambiguity. He begins by saying that the letter was "occasioned by professional matters" but immediately added: "I must however confess to begin with that I have hopes of continuing the intercourse

1

with you, and that you have left a deep impression on me which could easily tempt me to say outright in what category of men I would place you."

The friendship between them slowly developed and from 1893 onwards they corresponded at regular intervals, gradually abandoning formal modes of address for Christian names. So strong was Freud's attachment, even at this early stage, that he wanted to name one of his children Wilhelm, but the next two children turned out to be girls. Both men came from the Jewish middle class, and followed closely similar careers as young medical specialists, but Fliess took a much easier path than Freud by marrying a rich Viennese wife. The teachings of the Helmholtz school of physics and physiology formed their scientific background, but Fliess quickly revealed a predilection for wildcat speculation which at first fascinated Freud and made palatable hypotheses he would have scorned later in life.

Struggling to explain why Freud should so far demean himself as to become subservient to a mediocre mind, Ernest Jones in his biography admits that "the extreme dependence he displayed towards Fliess...up to the age of 45, has almost the appearance of delayed adolescence". He then qualifies the statement with that kind of Freudian thinking which sometimes justifies the charge of psycho-analytic double-talk. "The self-depreciation of his capacities and his achievements he so often voiced in the correspondence with Fliess sprang not from an inner weakness but from a terrifying strength, one he felt unable to cope with alone." So now, Freud was unable to cope with his own strength. It seems just as probable that in the natural process of maturation he reached that stage when lack of experience generated uncertainties, and he became the victim of a seething pool of fermenting ideas, any one of which, he felt, was likely to be brought sharply to heel by scientific scrutiny. Such a stage alone would explain the self-depreciation, and this in turn would become a safeguard against the possible failure of his ideas.

Another factor which Jones brilliantly analyses obviously influenced Freud deeply. In psycho-analytic terms, Freud played out with a number of people – Fliess among them – his love–hate relationship with his father. First he had been forced to leave his famous teacher Brucke, and then Meynert – who did so much to defend his talents in early days – withdrew because he could not countenance Freud's interest in hysteria and hypnotism. As the sexual revelation tightened its grip on him towards the end of the eighties, Freud turned to his old teacher Breuer for support and temporarily Breuer assumed the attributes of the father-figure until Freud found it difficult to induce him to complete his chapter for *Studien über Hysterie*. After its publication this relationship, too, broke down. Fliess resembled Breuer to the extent that they shared Helmholtz's view that biological and medical science should aim "to describe their findings in terms of physics and ultimately mathematics"; but Fliess had one supreme advantage over Breuer. He did not recoil from sexuality as a basis of human behaviour. Indeed he made it the key to his work. "Not merely", as Jones wrote, "was his syndrome, when functional, due to sexual disturbances, but it was his sexual periods, one male, the other female, that were to explain all the phenomena of life and death." If the two men appeared to proceed professionally hand in hand, later experience was to undermine any such interpretation but, for the moment, Freud endowed Fliess with the combined powers of mentor, father-figure and passionate friend, and developed an exaggerated belief in his scientific originality.

In the light of modern knowledge, some of the propositions put forward by Fliess which so fascinated Freud now seem ludicrous and once again the evidence points to some hidden emotional tie which must have inhibited Freud's scientific scepticism. Fliess drew his theory of periodicity in life from the two facts that menstruation occurred once a month and sexual desire seemed to fluctuate according to some unknown rhythm. Among a multiplicity of "daring" hypotheses he put forward the proposition that there was a tendency towards periodicity in all the vital activities of life – which might seem a defensible proposition – and that some relationship could be established between the mucous membrane of the nose and sexual life – which seemed highly eccentric. These two hypotheses were linked together by the fact that the mucous membrane swells "with genital excitement or during menstruation", and that the nose contains erectile tissue.

In an extraordinary passage of mathematical nonsense very much in line with the general fashion of introducing mathematics into biology, Fliess excitedly announced to Freud one day that he had found the master key to the general law of periodicity in the two numbers 28 and 23, one derived from the timing of the normal menstrual cycle and the other from the interval between periods. Implicit in these hypotheses was a third one, over which the two men finally came to blows because it represented a probability much less subject to mathematical or imaginative mumbo-jumbo. All human beings, Fliess said, were bisexual and Stekel later claimed to have anticipated what, in a quite different manner, Jung formulated as the anima and animus. Nothing if not grandiose, Fliess employed his magic numbers to interpret the stages of growth, the dates of illnesses, the date of death, the sex of infants before birth and, reaching out into the universe, sought to explain with the same key a connection between astronomical movements and the creation of living organisms. It was all a mystical abuse of numbers which subsequently fell to pieces in his hands. Excluding the bisexuality theory, many of Fliess' elaborate

3

patterns of periodicity have long since been discredited, but Freud at the outset took them very seriously.

It has to be emphasized that Freud, at this stage, was a very different person from the bold, confident, creative man who came to dominate the Wednesday circle in Vienna with such inflexible purpose. Unaware of his true powers, not knowing how to measure himself against men like Fliess and needing above all a substitute for Breuer, he came to Fliess' work with an uncritical admiration which was sometimes fulsome. He wrote to him on 26 August 1898:

"Yesterday the glad news reached me that the enigmas of the world and of life were beginning to yield an answer, news of a successful result of thought such as no dream could excel." Whether Fliess would reach the final goal in the short or long run Freud said, was irrelevant, because he felt sure the path was open to him.

Simultaneously with his reverence for Fliess' work he made his own demands on him. He expected Fliess to listen to, and comment on, every detail of his work from casebook histories to theoretical explanations. That Fliess, in his turn, greatly admired the work of Freud is clear from Freud's letter of 74 July 1894, where he says: "Your praise is nectar and ambrosia to me."

Unfortunately, Freud misunderstood, at the outset, the precise nature of Fliess' sexual etiology, but slowly it dawned on him that there was little of his own earthy preoccupation with the physiological facts of sex in the mathematical conjuring tricks which Fliess performed. The very fact of a proliferating cloud of figures protected Fliess against the attacks which Freud presently faced, since numerology was much more respectable than sex and the more extravagant mathematical flights were only open to the initiate.

A portent of the differences which were to occur later, can be seen in Freud's letter to Fliess dated 1 January 1898: "It interests me that you should take it so much amiss that I am still unable to accept your interpretation of left-handedness..."[2] This he added was due to the neurosis in himself. Turning to Fliess' theory of bisexuality he found this highly significant for his own work but in the third paragraph of the letter he asked: "What becomes of the femininity of the left half of a man if the latter includes a testicle (and the corresponding lesser male sexual organs) just as the right half does?"[3]

By 7 August 1901 all doubts about bisexuality had vanished and he wrote: "My next book as far as I can see will be called Bisexuality in Man. It will tackle the root of the problem and say the last word which it will be granted me to say on the subject — the last and the deepest." Not unexpectedly this annoyed Wilhelm Fliess. It was one thing to change his view about bisexuality, and quite another to speak as if the idea had just occurred to him in all its original freshness independently of Fliess.

The final clash between the two came in the summer of 1900 at Achensee. It is better to describe it in the words of Fliess who has been given scant opportunity to put his point of view in other accounts:

> "I often met Freud for scientific discussions. These took place in Berlin, Vienna, Salzburg, Dresden, Nuremberg, Breslau and Achensee. Freud reacted to my contribution to the discussion with a violence that was at first inexplicable, because I attributed unlimited importance to periodic occurrences even for the psyche while we were discussing Freud's observations on his patients; in particular, I represented them as being effective even for those psychopathic manifestations which Freud was attempting to cure by analysis. I pointed out that neither sudden relapses nor sudden improvements should be laid at the door of analysis. I demonstrated my argument with various observations. In the ensuing discussion I thought I noticed some personal animosity arising from envy in Freud's attitude to me. Freud had said to me once, on an earlier occasion in Vienna: 'It is a good thing that we are friends. I would die of envy if I heard that anyone else in Berlin was making such discoveries.' In my astonishment, I repeated this remark to my wife and also to the wife of the Court band-leader, Frau Schalk, née Hopfen, who is at present in Vienna and who will gladly verify my statement."[4]

Fliess went on to say that as a result of this exchange he quietly withdrew from his relationship with Freud and ceased to correspond with him. He added, very pointedly, that Freud heard no more from him about his scientific findings. Fliess next described how Freud made the acquaintance of a man called Swoboda and treated him for a neurotic condition. "During this treatment Swoboda became acquainted with the fact of persistent bisexuality which, as Freud himself states, has, since I talked to him, come to be regularly discussed in the course of his psycho-neurotic treatment."

The sequel is best understood from a letter of Fliess to Freud dated 20 July 1904:

Dear Sigmund,
A book by Weininger has come to my attention in which I find, to my astonishment, my ideas on bisexuality and the consequent kind of sexual attraction − feminine men attract masculine women and vice versa − expounded in the first biological section. I see from one of the quotations that Weininger was in contact with Swoboda − your pupil −

[before the publication of his book] and I hear that the two men were very close friends. I have no doubt that Weininger obtained knowledge of my ideas through you and that there was an abuse of other people's property on his part. What do you know about it? I beg you to give me a candid answer (to my Berlin address, as I am leaving here on the evening of the 23rd).

Best wishes,

Wilhelm[5]

Freud opened his reply to this letter with the words "I too believe that the late Weininger broke into private property with a key he picked up by chance. That is all I know about it."

He then admitted that he had mentioned bisexuality to Swoboda, as a necessary part of his treatment. The question of bisexuality frequently arose in treatment, he said, and much later Swoboda, talking over Weininger's sexual problems with him, had mentioned the word, whereupon Weininger "clapped his hand to his forehead and rushed home to write this book". Giving the narrative a somewhat false air of objectivity Freud added: "I am not, of course, in a position to judge whether or not this...is accurate."

There followed a long diversion on the possibility that Weininger might have discovered the idea from other sources "since it has played a part in the literature of the subject for some time". Swoboda insisted, Freud said, that he had given Weininger no further help and indeed was in no position to enlighten him beyond that point, because all Freud had ever disclosed to him was the recurrence in treatment of a strong "streak of homosexuality in every neurotic".

There followed the statement that Swoboda did not come to Freud as a pupil but as a patient who was seriously ill. "I have had no part in his 'discovery' which does seem to infringe your ideas. I did not read his book before publication." Freud added that in his own new book – three treatises on sexual theory – he was avoiding bisexuality as far as possible, but there were two points where it seemed inescapable. "I will remember to put a note to the effect that I was made aware of the importance of this discovery by your remarks on the subject." Fliess replied:

Berlin, 26.7.1904

Dear Sigmund,

Obviously what Oskar Rie told me, in all innocence, when I mentioned Weininger, was incorrect. He said that Weininger had been to you with his manuscript and you, after examining it, had advised him against publication, because the contents were rubbish. In that case, I would have thought that you would have warned both him and myself of the theft. Weininger clearly did not agree with you that he could have found the idea of persistent and inevitable bisexuality – not just bisexual constitution – elsewhere, for he declares on page 10 that the idea in this form is completely new. I would be very grateful if you would give me the references to the other sources you mention (Krafft-Ebing...etc.) so that I can look them up easily. I am not very well read in the literature of the subject...

I was not aware until today, when I read your letter, that you make use of the theory of persistent bisexuality in treatment. The first time we spoke of it was in Nuremberg, when I was in bed and you were telling me the history of the sick woman who kept dreaming of giant snakes. You were very struck with the idea that in the case of a woman there could be undercurrents from the male part of her psyche. That made your resistance in Breslau to the acceptance of bisexuality in the psyche seem all the more surprising. In Breslau I also discussed with you the fact that there were so many left-handed husbands of my acquaintance, and I evolved a theory of left-handedness which agrees with Weininger's in all details (and Weininger knew nothing about left-handedness). Of course, you rejected the left-handedness idea and forgot our bisexual conversation a long time ago as you frankly admit...

I did not know that the discussion of bisexuality is necessary in treatment. Nor did I realize that Dr Swoboda was your patient...

We might have asked for a better reason for our correspondence than this debate over a plagiarist. Let us hope that the future will bring us one.

Best wishes,

Wilhelm[6]

Freud's reply was ambiguous. "I see that you have more right on your side than I originally thought," he began, and then came a tangled reference to forgetting how he had "complained about Swoboda as a pupil". It now emerged that he had in fact read the manuscript of the Weininger book before publication, but "the manuscript I had in my hands certainly read quite differently from the published book". He openly regretted that he had "handed over Fliess' ideas through Swoboda" and proceeded to apply psycho-analytic interpretations to his behaviour. "Together with my own attempt to steal this idea from you I can understand my behaviour towards W and my subsequent loss of memory."

7

Next came a paragraph which further infuriated Fliess: Freud did not think that he would have cried – Stop thief! First "it would not have done any good, for the thief could perfectly well maintain it was his own idea, secondly you cannot take out a patent on ideas."

Worse was to follow. Freud now made a long and laboured attempt to justify his lapse of memory instead of cutting the whole exchange short. The history of the derivation of ideas is charged with deception, unconscious plagiarism and straight forward forgetfulness. Inevitably, no one man conceives a revolutionary scientific proposition in total isolation. The derivative hinterland is highly populated and intermarriage occurs between the most unexpected ideas. Freud repeated this explanation in his defence: "In my eyes you have always been the originator of the theory of bisexuality (1900),[7] [but] I'm afraid that if you look through the literature you will find that many have run you very close." Unfortunately, Freud said, he could not immediately back up this claim and fell back on the obvious explanation: "As for the names I gave you, I find that I have not brought the right books with me to give you any clearer references." However he would certainly find them in the *Psychopathia Sexualty* of Krafft-Ebing.

Once more Freud qualified his early confession and insisted that he had given Swoboda *no details* of what Fliess had communicated to him. Then came this: "I have often secretly reproached myself, as I now do openly, with my generosity or rather carelessness in making free with your property." However, stealing, he said, was not nearly such a simple matter as Weininger seemed to imagine. No one would take his scissors and paste book too seriously and it could do very little harm to Fliess.

The letter closed with yet another unfortunate remark. Having more or less admitted, with tortuous qualification, that he had given away the idea of a colleague, he concluded: "It is, however, not my fault if you only find the time and inclination to write to me on such a trivial matter."

Trivial matter! It may have seemed so to Freud. It certainly was not trivial to Fliess. Their correspondence ended abruptly on this note.

In *Die Traumdeutung*[8] Freud relates a dream which occurred to him about this time, without seeing the associations. "The idea of plagiarism – of appropriating whatever one can, even though it belongs to someone else – clearly led on to the second part of the dream in which I was treated as though I were the thief who had for some time carried on his business of stealing overcoats in the lecture rooms."[9]

Another event now complicated the situation. Weininger, a brilliant but disturbed person, suddenly committed suicide, leaving his library and papers to his friend Swoboda. Inspired by his inheritance, Swoboda himself produced a book in 1904 called *The Periods of the Human Organism in their Psychological and Biological Significance*. In 1905 he followed this with a post doctoral thesis entitled *Studies Towards a Foundation of Psychology*, in which he played the mathematical game with even more comic elaboration than Fliess. Once again his two books dealt with periodicity in life but now Fliess' 28/23-day periods became hour periods. Swoboda's theory took into account the fluctuation of plus or minus 1 day which appeared in Fliess' original work and a correspondence developed between them. Swoboda was very perturbed when Fliess, quite unaware of the shock he would cause, said that he had overcome the plus and minus fluctuation in a new book which he, in turn, was about to publish.

In 1906 Fliess at last published his book with another ambitious title, *The Course of Life: A Foundation for an Exact Biological Study*, and his quarrel with Freud suddenly flared up again and came to a head. A man known as the Royal Librarian, Richard Pfenning, an admirer of Fliess, took it on himself to make public what he believed to be a case of sheer plagiarism, attacking Weininger and Swoboda directly, and Freud indirectly. He published a pamphlet, obviously inspired by Fliess, which outlined the ideas of bisexuality and periodicity and examined their history.[10]

Pfenning gave a much more detailed account of the relationships between Freud, Weininger and Swoboda, than Fliess and quoted a passage from Freud's *The Psychopathology of Everyday Life* in which he spoke of bisexuality and said: "It is painful to have to surrender one's originality in this way."[11]

Not even this satisfied the vengeful Pfenning: "It is not our task", he said, "to criticize the way that Professor Freud made use of his friendship for Fliess. It is enough that after disputing that Swoboda was his pupil and maintaining his careful silence on the main point at issue – that is his knowledge of Weininger's work before publication – his confession has a candour which can only be called – cynical."

Meanwhile, Fliess himself had decided to publish a pamphlet telling the world the final truth about his quarrel with Freud and this revealed one quite new aspect. "I received an unexpected letter from Freud in which he asked me to work on a new journal and I refused." In this letter, dated 26 April 1904, the following passage occurred. "You will have received a book from Dr Swoboda the intellectual originator of which I am in many respects although I wouldn't like to be the author."[12]

Fliess commented: "These letters show Freud as the *spiritus rectus* who had not only known about the forbidden use of someone else's property...but in fact had made this possible himself and yet he made no objection and warned neither Weininger nor myself."[13]

9

Swoboda now wrote an answer to Pfenning entitled *The Public Utility of Research and the Selfish Researcher*. When this failed to have much effect he tried to sue Fliess and Pfenning for defamation of character, but the case never came before the courts because the law did not deal with scientific plagiarism.

Freud reappeared once more with a letter dated January 1906 to Karl Krauss, editor of *Die Fackel*. He explained that Dr Fliess of Berlin had published a pamphlet attacking O Weininger and H Swoboda, accusing them of blatant plagiarism. Both were young authors and Dr Fliess "mishandled" them "in a most cruel fashion". "...The credibility of the wretched publication may be judged by the fact that I myself, a friend of Fliess for many years, am accused of being the one who gave the information to Weininger and Swoboda..."

So now, once again, he was denying responsibility in the matter. Freud also spoke of the "overbearing presumption of Fliess' brutal personality", words which he was later to re-echo about Jung.

Another letter went to Magnus Hirschfeld, editor of *Jahrbuch für sexuelle Zwischenstufen*. It described Pfenning's pamphlet as "a disgusting scribble which among other things casts absurd aspersions on me". What, in fact, we have to deal with, he went on, is the "phantasy of an ambitious man who in his loneliness has lost the capacity to judge what is right and what is permissible". It was very hard, Freud said, to use such language about a man who had been his intimate friend for twelve years "and thereby provoke him to further insults", but he had no choice in the matter.

Very much later, when the dust of what threatened to become a feud had subsided, Freud acknowledged Fliess' work on periodicity, but did not connect it with theories of his own of a comparable kind. Similarly, in his *Three Essays*, he referred once more to bisexuality and strove to prove his claim that there were many predecessors who had anticipated Fliess. Unfortunately, as Jones points out, he bases this on the date of Fliess' book (1906) instead of on the date of his "actual discovery". Taking the discovery date as the measure, only two of the five predecessors Freud quoted remain to challenge Fliess. As for his indebtedness to Fliess, he still maintained that he had observed bisexual impulses in his own work – which was probably true.

Three possibilities emerge from this preliminary battle. First, did Freud suffer, like the common run of men, from a capacity to forget inconvenient conversations; second, did he find it hard to acknowledge originality in others; and third, were some of his relationships with men of a very passionate nature?

NOTES
1. *Sigmund Freud: Life and Work*: Ernest Jones, Vol. I, p. 316.
2. *The Origins of Psycho-Analysis*: Sigmund Freud, p. 242.

3.   *Ibid.*
4.   *In eigener Sadie:* Wilhelm Fliess, pp. 16–17.
5.   *In eigener Sadie:* Wilhelm Fliess, pp. 21–22
6.   *In eigener Sadie:* Wilhelm Fliess, pp. 22–22.
7.   In reality since the spring of 1897.
8.   *The Interpretation of Dreams:* Sigmund Freud, Vol. I, p. 205.
9.   *The Interpretation of Dreams:* Vol. I, p. 205.
10. *Wilhelm Fliess und seine Nachentdecker:* Richard Pfenning, 1900.
11. *The Psychopathology of Everyday Life:* Sigmund Freud, p. 43.
12. *In eigener Sache:* Wilhelm Fliess, p. 18.
13. *Ibid.*, p. 23.

Chapter Two

The Formation of the Wednesday Circle

By the year 1900 Freud was already a seasoned lecturer, despite the hostility of so many professional circles in Vienna, and it was Fritz Wittels who went to one of his early lectures at the psychiatric clinic of the General Hospital, and left a vivid description of the experience. The audience turned out to be scanty and scarcely filled the first three rows of the echoing hall, but Freud spoke without notes for nearly an hour, and held his small audience enthralled. A brief pause while he took the "feeling of the meeting" and then he plunged in again and another hour went by. He looked younger than forty-six and spoke swiftly and vigorously. His "black hair, slightly grizzled, was smooth and parted on the left side. His beard...was small and trimmed to a fine point." His eyes, "dark brown and lustrous", made a quick penetrating scrutiny of anyone who asked questions before he answered. One characteristic marked him down to Wittels as a man who spent long hours working alone in his study. His slender figure "had the student's stoop".

His lecture dealt with the shortcomings of traditional psychology and speaking of Wundt, Freud referred to the battle in Ariosto's *Orlando Furioso*, where the head of a giant is smitten off but he remains too busy to notice, and goes on fighting. Wundt was rather like that warrior, Freud said. "We cannot help thinking that the old psychology has been killed by my dream doctrine, but the old psychology is quite unaware of the fact and goes on teaching as usual."

At the end of the lecture a group of admirers left the hospital with Freud and accompanied him "in triumph through the courtyards as far as the Alser

Strasse. On the way from the lecture hall to the street we always made ourselves as conspicuous as possible. Freud was generally in a cheerful mood. There he usually took a cab to his home where he would play a game of cards."[1]

It is worth recording that Dr Fritz Wittels, who subsequently underwent considerable depreciation at the hands of certain psycho-analytic historians, remained a devoted admirer of Freud all his life. As a doctor–teacher he had an alert and active mind, as a writer he could be very evocative and – scientific work apart – he published many books, among them a number of original and successful novels.[2]

The first beginnings of the Vienna Psycho-Analytical Society can be traced back to the year 1902 when Freud sent postcards to four comparatively unknown men suggesting that they might care to form a small coterie which met at his home once a week to discuss psycho-analytic work. These four men were Adler, Kahane, Reitler and Stekel. Of the four, only two were to survive as famous names, and one of these, Stekel, was in fact responsible for putting the idea of a weekly meeting into Freud's mind. Many other remarkable men quickly became associated with the group, from Federn and Otto Rank to Sandor Ferenczi and Hanns Sachs, and the small handful of four or five members quickly rose by 1908 to twenty-two, but it was unusual for more than ten members to attend any one meeting.

For the previous ten years Freud had suffered from intellectual loneliness "which the warm contact of his family and social life only partly alleviated". A case can be made out to show that his academic career was not so difficult as Jones suggested. His papers easily achieved publication where others faced constant rejection, but there were certainly anti-Semitic professors in Vienna, who deliberately overlooked his outstanding gifts, preferring gentile mediocrity to Jewish brilliance.

Now, at 46, when the Wednesday meetings first began, he had behind him a number of distinguished books, including The Interpretation of Dreams, published in the last year of the nineteenth century and generally regarded by Freudians as his greatest work. He was also at the height of his remarkable powers, a man constantly throwing out brilliant hypotheses and steadily gathering an intellectual momentum which was to carry him into the highest clouds of clinical discovery and philosophic speculation. Among the men who joined the Wednesday meetings four very contradictory personalities immediately concern this book, first among them Alfred Adler. According to Ernest Jones, Alfred Adler was a "morose and cantankerous person, whose behaviour oscillated between contentiousness and sulkiness. He was evidently very ambitious and constantly quarrelling with the others over points of priority in his ideas."[3]

That, in fact, represented only one side of his character. Unlike Freud he had the marks of a typical Viennese intellectual whose day seemed impossibly barren if it had not taken him deeply into the café life of Vienna and involved him in one or more arguments for which a display of wit was obligatory.

> "To a Viennese – and Adler was a Viennese to the last drop of his blood – his café was a place where he felt most alone… Here he could be warm and comfortably concentrated or relaxed, silent or garrulous at will. Here he could look through his business correspondence in peace, read or write letters in private, sustain himself and pay for his right of entry by drinking the best coffee in the world… At these times whole groups met for animated discussions, tables were linked together…"[4]

There were personal factors at work which explain why the image of a brilliantly sociable Adler was sometimes qualified by the other cantankerous Adler described by Jones. Politically a man of the left he was not far left enough to satisfy his wife but too far left to please powerful friends in high places. His mercurial nature could not easily accept the discipline of party membership and he once said to a friend seeking political advice: "Don't join things." Dogmatic Marxists were anathema to him and there were times when his wife fell into this category. By the time he met Freud he was in person a stout, active, little man with a fine sweep of brow and eyes which flashed one moment with twinkling laughter and the next fell into a challenging stare. He could be endearing, affectionate, arrogant, infuriating by turns and was certainly a man of moods. See him posing with his wife and first child for a photograph, and the drainpipe collar, the long drooping moustaches, the pince-nez glasses, and the waistcoat with long watch-chain hung across a comfortable stomach give the impression of a correct, family doctor of the early twentieth century. Mrs Adler standing at his side has a much more challenging air. Presently she had to face a situation which contradicted the message of the photograph. "For [Mrs Adler] knew now that she must face essential loneliness," Adler's biographer, Phyllis Bottome, wrote. "Her husband was swallowed up in his work nor was she able to follow him, as she had once hoped, into all his developments… It was…Adler's psychology that took him away from Raissa…"

According to Mrs Bottome, Adler's first encounter with Freud occurred in print. While Viennese medical circles poured steadily greater scorn on Freud's theories and a vicious element became more deliberate in their attacks, Adler wrote to the *Neue Freie Presse*, defending a man whose ideas had at once fired his imagination. "Freud was much touched by it and sent Adler the famous postcard thanking him for his defence and asking him to join the discussion circle of psycho-analysis."[5] It seems pretty certain that Adler did not, in fact, write any such letter to the *Neue Freie Presse* because even the historian of the Adlerian Society has failed to find it.[6] Hence the famous postcard, if it existed, must have omitted the still more famous thanks.

It was in Freud's home at 19 Berggasse that the discussion circles began on Wednesday evenings and slowly developed until they involved Adler, Wittels, Wilhelm Stekel, Paul Federn, Otto Rank, Edward Hitschmann and later Carl Jung. The Berggasse opened off Vienna's historic junk-market, the Tandelmarkt, and ended at the Votivkirche, a Gothic cathedral which dominates one of the most ornamental squares of Vienna. It deserved its name Hill Street because part of it became a steep hill, but No. 19 was on a fairly level stretch in a quiet and respectable section.

The Wednesday evenings were not carefully planned or organized in the first place. Members of the group would drift into Freud's waiting-room after supper and range themselves round a long table. The door leading from the waiting-room into the study was always left open and they could glimpse the collection of statuettes, mostly Egyptian, on Freud's desk, the famous couch with the armchair behind it, and the walls lined with book shelves.

Freud would enter the room briskly when the company had assembled and black coffee and cigars were served by Mrs Freud. A hardened smoker, Freud sometimes consumed twenty cigars in a day and he invariably smoked throughout the evening. What the atmosphere must have been like with four, five or six other people all smoking cigars it is not difficult to imagine, but when Freud presented a paper himself, excitement overwhelmed any concern for the atmosphere. According to Wittels, the doctor who played an important role as a popular expositor of psycho-analysis in these early days, Freud would "begin by enunciating his main contentions categorically, so that they were apt to repel".[7] Then the charm of his words and personality would work their magic as he illustrated every argument with such a wealth of evidence that disgruntlement diminished and in many cases melted away.

Wittels believed that Freud's motive for organizing the Wednesday circle was "to have his own thoughts passed through the filter of other trained intelligences. It did not matter if the intelligences were mediocre. Indeed he had little desire that these associates should be trained persons of strong individuality... The realm of psycho-analysis was his idea and his will, and he welcomed anyone who accepted his views. What he wanted was to look into the kaleidoscope lined with mirrors that would multiply the images he introduced into it."⁸ This was exaggerated. Freud's motives were mixed, as will presently appear, but a genuine desire to distil from discussion fresh insights into psycho-analysis and to pass propositions through the fire of argument also played a part.

To these meetings came Wilhelm Stekel, a dashing young doctor with wide Slav eyes, a pointed beard, bow-tie and a curly brimmed hat. He had read one day an article by Freud, which referred to the work of Stekel: "It appears certain that our children are exposed to sexual aggressions much more frequently than one would expect... In the last few weeks I came across a study written by Dr Stekel in Vienna which deals with Coitus in Children..."⁹

Stekel wrote to Freud saying that he had a sexual problem of his own about which he would like to consult him and ten days later he was walking up and down Freud's consulting-room at No. 79, his nervous energy making it impossible for him to lie on the famous couch. Not unexpectedly Freud recommended a course of psycho-analysis.

"My treatment lasted not more than eight sessions. I told Freud my life history and he expressed his surprise about the fact that I had so few repressions. In one of my dreams he found what he termed a mother fixation. I could not believe it. The few incestuous dreams I had before, appeared to me as normal human manifestations..."¹⁰

Stekel consulted Freud at a time when his marriage had reached that critical point which he himself described as "the period when the couple begins to weary of each other, and develop a craving for outside company". At the very beginning of his marriage, his wife had become anxious about his small income and had reproached him one day because a colleague earned far more than he did. Stekel looked at her in astonishment and protested that he earned enough for their modest requirements. Some months later, she asked him for something beyond his immediate means and he said: "You see things are getting better and better. Wait until I earn a little more money." To his horror she responded by losing her temper, pouring abuse over his head and calling him a miser. Momentarily, the scene sank into the background and was forgotten but it remained fixed at an unconscious level and he now told Freud that "many things that happened later may have been due to a desire to avenge this unwarranted insult".

There followed a period when his wife stopped playing duets with him, a form of spiritual communication which he found deeply satisfying, and seemed to prefer the "society of garrulous, illiterate women". He was "forced to accompany her to coffee houses where he played cards in order to avoid the boring gossip. But I must confess that playing cards served as a mental narcotic; it afforded escape from the gradually emerging dissonance of our marriage."

Thus when Stekel first met Freud, his marriage had reached a critical stage, "he had some sexual problems" of his own, and many other complications threatened the comfortable routine of his everyday life. From verbal evidence among those who knew him and from hints in the autobiography, it seems highly probable that for a period of two years Stekel suffered from that not uncommon complaint, psychological impotence. As he commented at one point: "One day I was no longer a man. I tried everything to overcome my weakness but I failed."[11]

Whether Freud "cured" him of this trouble is not clear, but by now Stekel was deeply involved with Freud, and he became a regular member of the Wednesday evening group. According to Stekel these first meetings were full of an exciting sense of discovery. "A spark seemed to jump from one mind to the other, and every evening was like a revelation. We were so enthralled...that we decided new members could be added to our circle only by unanimous consent. The new ones came: Paul Federn and Edward Hitschmann, later Isidor Sadger..."

Privately, Stekel's developing interest in psycho-analysis distressed his wife, because he wanted to free himself from general practice in order to specialize in psychiatry and she believed that this threatened them with penury. The study of psychology either bored or angered her and she once said to her husband: "I can't go along with you in this matter, it's like a swindle." Mrs Stekel was, in the estimation of her friends, a fine woman with many virtues, but she suffered from a commonplace aptitude for hen-pecking her husband.

As he tried to disengage himself from his old practice and told each patient that he no longer accepted telephone calls, she ignored this ruling and continued to take messages. She would break into his study, where, exhausted from a day's work among the unfamiliar hazards of psychiatry, he sought sanctuary in the evenings, and aggressively thrust under his nose a slip of paper on which were recorded the symptoms and condition of a former patient.

He would point out that the patient had been told twenty times to find another doctor and she would raise her voice to demand: "Is this an example of your humanity? Are you a physician or aren't you? Will you let your patients down?"

"There are many other physicians who will be glad to help them," Stekel answered, but she insisted – quite accurately – "They want only you. They have confidence in you."[12]

As Stekel wrote in his autobiography: "What could I do? After a hard day's work, I had to go on visiting many patients." The process of ridding himself of these faithful adherents became a nightmare, and time and again it required cruel determination to fight the dictates of his conscience before he could steel himself to refuse a man who said: "I don't want anyone else… I don't care how long I wait."

These complications were growing around Dr Stekel when he became a member of the Wednesday circle, partly to escape the tensions of home life, but much more insistently because here was a group of like-minded men with the brilliant Freud at their centre, pioneering the psychiatric world in which he desired to immerse himself.

It was much later that Carl Gustav Jung appeared for the first time one Wednesday evening, not as a fully-fledged member of the circle but as a guest of Freud. A tall, powerfully built man with brilliantly alive eyes and steel-rimmed spectacles, his face was said to be unpaintable since its planes were always changing. Jung had first intended to become an archaeologist but he transferred, in the University of Basle, to the medical faculty, and between the years 1900 and 1909, his deep interest in psychiatry became an overwhelming preoccupation. He first encountered the work and person of Sigmund Freud as physician to the Psychiatric Clinic of the University of Zurich. In 1903 he married the beautiful daughter of a conservative Swiss family and began a long, conventionally successful marriage which produced four daughters and a son, with little outward sign of the neurotic disturbances which tormented other members of the Wednesday Circle.

As early as 1900, he had read The Interpretation of Dreams, and laid the book aside without fully grasping what a pioneering work it represented. He was just 25 years old, an earnest, truth-seeking person, still groping in the mists of so many possibilities for the precise direction which his own career should follow. "I lacked the experience to appreciate Freud's theories," he later wrote. "Such experience did not come until later."

In 1903 he once more took up The Interpretation of Dreams and now, unexpectedly, he found a coincidence between his own and Freud's work, which was at first exciting and then disturbing. He had frequently encountered the mechanism of repression in his own word-association experiments. Repeating a list of words a patient would confront one which produced silence, a stumbling reply, or an obvious evasion and Jung came to understand that these words touched some repressed and unpleasant memory – what he called a psychic lesion or conflict. Now, in The Interpretation of Dreams, Freud described a similar process in the mechanism of dreams and excited Jung's imagination afresh.

19

Academic life still strongly attracted Jung at this time and he was about to complete a paper intended to advance his university career, but Freud was definitely *persona non grata* in the academic world and any connection with him would have been damaging in scientific circles. "Important people...mentioned him surreptitiously, and at congresses he was discussed only in the corridors, never on the floor. Therefore the discovery that my association experiments were in agreement with Freud's theories was far from pleasant to me."[13]

What followed needs some emphasis because it became very significant in the relationship which developed between Freud and Jung. One day, Jung recorded, "the devil whispered to me that I would be justified in publishing the results of my experiments and my conclusions without mentioning Freud".[14] At the very outset, it is clear that a sense of rivalry existed on Jung's part and a conflict arose over the ethics of priorities. Simultaneously the voice of what Jung refers to as his "second personality" spoke to him again saying: "If you do a thing like that, as if you had no knowledge of Freud it would be a piece of trickery. You cannot build your life on a lie." Whereupon, it seems, the devil stopped whispering in his ear, the prowling person who wanted to exploit the very repression with which Jung's discoveries were so concerned, capitulated, and Jung became an open partisan, fighting for Freud.

There are some odd features in this account. It is quite normal in scientific circles for men to be familiar with research undertaken internationally by colleagues in the same field or to stumble on related ideas without wishing to suppress the work of another. Why, instead of deciding to mention Freud in his own paper, did Jung suddenly swing to the opposite extreme and become a crusading spirit on behalf of his would-be rival? Psychologically there are obvious explanations which will recur later. For the moment, Jung certainly spoke out on behalf of Freud when a lecturer discussed obsessional neuroses and deliberately avoided mentioning Freud's name.

It was the occasion of a Congress in Baden-Baden in May 1906, when Aschaffenburg vigorously denounced Freud's method as wrong in most cases, objectionable in many, superfluous in all, and completely immoral anyway. In 1907, this duel was repeated at the First International Congress of Psychiatry and Neurology in Amsterdam. Freud himself had been invited to attend but he wrote to Jung: "They were evidently looking forward to my having a duel with Janet... I hate gladiator fights in front of the noble mob and find it hard to agree to an unconcerned crowd voting on my experiences."[15] Freud was, in fact, away on holiday when the Congress took place and, suddenly overcome with a qualm of conscience that someone should be fighting his cause in his place, he sat down and wrote another letter to Jung. "I don't know whether you will be lucky or unlucky but I should like to be with you just now, enjoying the feeling that I am no longer alone." If Jung needed any encouragement, he "could tell [him] about [his] long years of honourable but painful loneliness". These years began, Freud said, as soon as he glimpsed the new world of sexual pathology, when even his closest friends failed to understand what he was trying to do and he reached a point where he himself wondered whether he was "in error". In later storms and difficulties he clung to The Interpretation of Dreams "as to a rock in the breakers", until he reached the calm certainty that this was his chosen path and waited for a voice from the outside world which would respond. When it came, he now wrote to Jung, "It was yours!"

Later, Jung prepared a paper for the Münchener Medizinische Wochenschrift replying to Aschaffenburg and dealing in detail with Freud's theory of the neuroses.[16] This promptly brought letters from two German professors who warned him that his academic career would be in jeopardy if he continued defending Freud.

Jung replied: "If what Freud says is the truth I am with him. I don't give a damn for a career if it has to be based on the premise of restricting research and concealing truth."[17]

Accepting Freud's general description of neuroses from the out set, Jung did not entirely agree with the sexual basis of Freud's theories. Correspondence between them began in 1906 when Jung sent Freud his Diagnostische Assoziationsstudien (Studies in Word Association, 1918) and continued until 1913 when the final clash occurred.

Jung's first meeting with Freud took place in 1907, a year when many distinguished guests came as visitors to the Wednesday evening meetings. Among them were Max Eitingon on 30 January, C G Jung and L Binswanger on 6 March, and A A Brill and Ernest Jones on 6 May 1908.

Jung, in fact, met Freud alone before he joined the Wednesday Circle. He had sent Freud a copy of his Psychology of Dementia Praecox and Freud suggested that Jung should call on him if he happened to be in Vienna. It was a cold, blustering 27th day of February in the same year, 1907, which brought Jung to Freud's house at one o'clock in the afternoon.[18] According to Ernest Jones: "He had much to tell Freud and to ask him, and with intense animation he poured forth in a spate for three whole hours. Then the patient, absorbed listener interrupted him with the suggestion that they conduct their discussion more systematically..."

Ernest Jones told me that Freud regarded the first meeting with Jung as very important because he had seldom encountered a man with such wide-ranging knowledge, and such a lively sympathy for the mechanism of neuroses. There was also an intellectual dynamism which injected tremendous verve into their talk, and above all, Jung's unrestrained imaginative flow captivated Freud. According to Jung, Freud "was the first man of importance I had encountered: in my experience up to that time no one else could compare with him". As a result their talk became a marathon exchange which ran on, with brief breaks, for thirteen hours, and but for sheer exhaustion, might still have continued twenty-four hours later. The two giants of psycho-analysis had met and grappled for the first time in that academic atmosphere which permitted fierce discussion without rancour.

At the outset Jung tried to introduce qualifications into sexual motivation, but Freud said that as his evidence widened, he would find himself in agreement with the Viennese school. In retrospect Jung recalled that a peculiar passion informed every sentence which Freud uttered concerning sex. "There was no mistaking the fact", he wrote, "that Freud was emotionally involved in his sexual theory to an extraordinary degree. When he spoke of it, his tone became urgent, almost anxious, and all signs of his normally critical and sceptical manner vanished..."[19]

Jung made no allowance for the double impact of Freud's passionate temperament and the magnitude of his "discovery", heightened in turn by the twin forces of anti-Semitism and the scorn, if not open abuse, of Viennese medical circles.

A flood of passionate language came naturally to Freud whenever he was deeply moved, and now, freshly challenged by a neopyhte, the result was not as Jung implied a display of compulsive intolerance. Jung applied to Freud's personality phrases from his own philosophy which Freud would have found irrelevant and distasteful. "A strange, deeply moved expression came over his face, the cause of which I was at a loss to understand. I had a strong intuition that for him, sexuality was a sort of *numinosum*." A glossary attached to Jung's reminiscences defines the word numinosum as meaning the "inexpressible, mysterious, terrifying, directly experienced and pertaining only to the divinity".[20]

Sex for some people was certainly directly experienced; for others it became terrifying and for some mysterious, but not even Freud, who believed that it permeated and dictated large areas of human experience, saw it as "pertaining only to the divinity". From the outset Jung attempted to convert Freud's preoccupation with sex into religious channels which made him explicable in his own terms.

Meanwhile, the Wednesday evening group had reached numbers uncomfortably large for Freud's waiting room and they changed the meeting place to a room in the College of Physicians. Here, in 1907, came Max

Eitingon, a medical student who had turned away from orthodox medicine to the new psychological theories. He consulted Freud about a severe case which puzzled him and Freud took him walking through the streets of Vienna while they talked. During the next few evenings the walks were repeated and became in effect a brilliantly condensed peripatetic training in psycho-analysis which left Eitingon physically breathless and intellectually dazzled. As Ernest Jones later remarked in the biography: "I remember the swift pace and rapid spate of speech on such walks. Walking fast used to stimulate the flow of Freud's thoughts but it was, at times, breathtaking for a companion who would have preferred to pause and digest them... Such was the first training analysis..."

Another visitor, Sandor Ferenczi, came from Budapest and had already experimented with hypnotism. When he first read The Interpretation of Dreams, Ferenczi turned away from it with a shrug of the shoulders, but Dr Stein, a friend who knew Freud slightly, persuaded him to read the book again, and on the second reading, he suddenly saw it in a quite new light. He wrote to Freud who immediately replied, and presently Ferenczi and Dr Stein travelled to Vienna to meet Freud. Ferenczi's animation, his lively, speculative mind and capacity for quick laughter, attracted Freud and they became close friends. Thus another member was drawn into the circle and duly accepted as a fully fledged disciple.

Hanns Sachs, a wealthy literary man, first met Freud as early as 1904 and left a vivid description of entering the long courts and narrow doorways of the Aligemeine Krankenhaus (General Hospital) one dark winter evening to attend a course of Freud's lectures. Sachs had read The Interpretation of Dreams and found it so electrifying that he determined to meet the author. Careful enquiries led him to the Psychiatric Clinic of the General Hospital in Vienna. "When I had seen the hall before, it was in plain daylight and all the benches had been crowded with students. Now the windows were dark and the only light came from a few bulbs suspended above the table and chair of the lecturer..."

A man full of shyness and timidity in the face of any new adventure, Sachs had persuaded his cousin, a medical student, to accompany him, but when Freud entered the room, panic over took him and he whispered an excuse and half rose to leave. At the last moment he changed his mind again and sat down once more. Freud he described as a "middle-aged gentleman who wore a short, dark-brown beard, slender and of medium size. He had deep-set and piercing eyes and a finely shaped forehead, remark ably high at the temples."[21] Freud pointed to a row of ten chairs which formed a semicircle in front of the benches very close to where he stood and said, politely: "Won't you come nearer and be seated, gentlemen?"

"My shyness, which he waved aside at our first meeting, disappeared, and with it went, bit by bit, many other inhibitions and inner obstacles that had been standing in my way. Of course I attended faithfully every one of the successive lectures." [22]

Sachs' first visit to No. 19 Berggasse occurred in the spring of 1907. Freud received him with a characteristic combination of warmth and scepticism, and they quickly fell into literary discussion, mutually praising the great Swiss poet and novelist Conrad Ferdinand Meyer. Again Sachs gave this description of the house at 19 Berggasse:

"The office consisted of a dark little ante-room and three chambers — waiting-room, the room for seeing patients and the study library behind. Each room had but one window opening on to a courtyard in the middle of which stood a tall and beautiful tree. None of the rooms got much light or sunshine. They were comfortably furnished in the taste and style of middle-class homes in the eighties... Only the study had a strong individual note which was due not to the style of furniture but to the full bookshelves that covered the walls almost to the ceiling and to the glass cases which contained Freud's collection of antiques." [23]

When, in the following winter, the Psycho-Analytical Society was formed, Sachs applied to Dr Adler, then President, for admission, giving Freud as a reference. By now, the meetings had overflowed into the big room belonging to the Medizinische Doktoren-Kollegium (College of Physicians) which the group rented for one evening a week. "We new members were naturally somewhat diffident at the beginning and did not take part in the discussion until Freud said, 'We won't be divided into an Upper House that does all the talking and a Lower House that plays the part of a passive listener.' Thus the ice broke and loosened our tongues." [24]

The scene was now set for the full-scale formulation of the International Psycho-Analytical Association, but very soon came a circular letter from Freud to all members of the group which Jones interpreted as an illustration of "Freud's delicacy and considerateness".

The letter was dated 22 September 1907, from Rome:

"I wish to inform you that I propose at the beginning of this new working year to dissolve the little Society which has been accustomed to meet every Wednesday at my home and immediately afterwards to call it to life again." This extraordinary procedure needed explanation, and Freud went on to give the reasons for circularizing members which he quite rightly thought might seem superfluous. He claimed that the circular simply took into account "the natural changes in human relationships", which made it possible that some people now reacted differently to the group's work, because, as he put it, their "interest in the subject is exhausted or their leisure time and mode of life are no longer compatible with attendance".

Nowhere, explicitly, did Freud say that his letter gave anyone who disagreed with the general philosophy and aims of the group an opportunity to resign because he only wanted true sympathizers to remain in the group: i.e. people who accepted the basic tenets of psycho-analysis as he conceived them. Instead, he described the dissolving and reorganizing of the Society as "re-establishing the personal freedom of each individual and making it possible for him to stay apart from the Society without in any way disturbing his relations with the rest of us..."

Ambiguities in the letter may have been unconscious, but what the letter, in fact, seemed to establish was not freedom inside the group, but freedom to resign and stay outside the group. It could easily be read as the first call to discipline and loyalty, and it was as if Freud, suddenly aware of the possibility of rebellion, had decided to forestall any actual uprising by a warning to the faithful disguised as a gentlemanly gesture. The tolling of the muezzin bell calling the faithful to prayer might be muffled, but the sophisticated ear could detect it on the air.

NOTES
1. *Sigmund Freud*: Fritz Wittels, p. 130.
2. *The International Journal of Psycho-Analysis*: Vol. 32: iv: 325: 1951.
3. *Sigmund Freud: Life and Work*: Ernest Jones, Vol. I, p. 147.
4. *Alfred Adler*: Phyllis Bottome, pp. 43–44.
5. *Alfred Adler*: Phyllis Bottome, p. 57.
6. *Journal of Individual Psychology*: Vol. 18, pp. 125–35, November 1962.
7. *Sigmund Freud*: Fritz Wittels, p. 134.
8. *Sigmund Freud*: Fritz Wittels, p. 134.
9. Etiology of Hysteria (Wiener Klin-Rundschau, 1896).
10. *Autobiography of Wilhelm Stekel*: p. 91.
11. *Autobiography of Wilhelm Stekel*: p. 77.
12. *Autobiography of Wilhelm Stekel*: p. 124.
13. *Memories, Dreams, Reflections*: C G Jung (recorded and edited Aniela Jaffé), p. 145.
14. *Ibid.*
15. April 1907.
16. Eng. trans.: *Freud's Theory of Hysteria: a Reply to Aschaffenburg in Freud and Psycho-Analysis*. (*Collected Works*, Vol. 4.)
17. *Memories, Dreams, Reflections*: C G Jung, p. 146.

18. This is Jung's version. According to Jones the meeting took place at 10 o'clock on Sunday morning. *Sigmund Freud: Life and Work:* Ernest Jones, Vol. II, p. 36.
19. *Memories, Dreams, Reflections:* C G Jung, p. 147.
20. *Ibid.*
21. *Freud, Master and Friend:* Hanns Sachs, pp. 40–41.
22. *Ibid.*
23. *Freud, Master and Friend:* Hanns Sachs, p. 49.
24. *Ibid.*, p. 50.

Chapter Three

Resistance to Psycho-Analysis

Ernest Jones believed that the world had lived through three periods of organized prejudice during which persecution became the natural weapon of irrational dogmas. The first period he called *odium theologicum*, when religious intolerance made life unbearable for thousands of people; the second replaced that with *odium sexicum* when sex became the new devil to be hounded by every possible means, and the third was *odium politicum*, when deviation from the party line represented ultimate corruption. Freud and his small band of followers, talking their sexual heresies during the Wednesday evenings, lived under the shadow of *odium sexicum*.

In public this had already made itself felt, sometimes with cunning, sometimes obliquely, but often with a vicious frankness which employed street-corner vituperation. Freud was publicly cut in the streets of Vienna. Once a man came up to him and said: "Are you Dr Freud?" Freud admitted it. "Then let me tell you what a dirty-minded filthy old man you are."[1] Hardened by abuse Freud smiled and turned away.

In America, Dr Allen Starr, specialist in nervous diseases, created a sensation at a crowded meeting of the Neurological Section of the Academy of Medicine in New York. Dr Starr warned his fellow physicians that they should be careful before accepting a theory which depended for its existence on the environment of the man who had originated it. "I knew Doctor Sigmund Freud well in Vienna", he said.

"Vienna is not a particularly moral city and working side by side with
Freud in the laboratory all through one winter, I learned that he enjoyed
Viennese life thoroughly. Freud was not a man who lived on a
particularly high plane. He was not self-repressed. He was not an ascetic.
I think his scientific theory is largely the result of his environment and
of the peculiar life he led."[2]

The only difficulty about this statement was that Freud could not recollect the
appearance of a Dr Allen Starr anywhere in his life.

As the "Wednesday Society" grew into the Vienna Psycho-Analytic Society
and that in turn became the International Psycho-Analytical Association,
professional vituperation swelled the growing chorus of abuse. It was at a
congress of German neurologists and psychiatrists in 1910 that Professor
Weygandt became very angry, banged his fist on the table and shouted: "This
is not a topic for discussion at a scientific meeting; it is a matter for the
police." In a letter to Freud dated 16 February 1911 Sandor Ferenczi said that
when he read a paper before the Medical Society of Budapest one of the
audience stood up and denounced Freud's work as pure pornography written
by a man who should have been in the hands of the police, if not in prison.

The personal abuse of Freud achieved the characteristics of a vendetta on
more than one occasion. During the Neurological Congress in Berlin towards
the end of 1910, a famous neurologist, Professor Oppenheim, rose and
proposed, in a voice charged with emotion, that they should boycott any
institution where Freud's views were accepted. The meeting almost cheered
this statement and the hall re-echoed to that kind of enthusiasm which
belonged to politics rather than science. The Directors of Sanatoria each in
turn disclaimed Freud, as if they were desperately anxious to clear themselves
of any charge of guilt by association, and Professor Raimann, as Assistant at
the Psychiatric Clinic in Vienna, declared that it was their duty not merely
to boycott Freud's teachings, but to "seek out the enemy in his lair", and to
publicize all those cases where psycho-analysis had treated patients
unsuccessfully. Raimann developed his vendetta against Freud over a period of
twelve years and at one time privately expressed his view that "any man who
concentrates his attention so exclusively on sex must be some sort of pervert
and there was no doubt that behind his carefully built-up and over-respectable
façade, Freud must be just that".[3] As Ernest Jones later wrote: "He pursued
Freud unrelentingly from 1904 to 1916 when Freud at last protested to his
chief, Wagner-Jauregg, who put a stop to the invective."[4]

There were actual professional casualties from persecution and eventually Ernest Jones himself became a victim. "I was forced to resign a neurological appointment in London for making inquiries into the sexual life of patients." Worse still, one morning in 1906, Jones received a summons from Dr Kerr, the head of his department, to "meet him at a certain school for mental defectives". When Jones arrived there, he was confronted with a charge from two small children that he had behaved indecently towards them while carrying out a speech test. Dr Kerr wanted to persuade the headmistress to forget the whole matter, but she remained adamant, and he had no alternative but to report the details to the Education Committee. The members of the Committee had no desire to envelop their activities in a cloud of scandal but a moment of panic drove them to place the whole case in the hands of the police.

The following afternoon, two plain-clothes detectives arrived at Jones' house and one of them dramatically exclaimed: "Doctor, there are two ways out of this room, the door and the window; I hope you will choose the door." Brushing aside melodramatic comment, Jones asked to be allowed to take something to read, and they were nonplussed when he selected Nietzsche's *Thus Spake Zarathustra*.

That night a young Harley Street physician, still wearing his professional frock-coat, sat alone on the stone bench of a cell whose equipment lacked anything resembling a pillow, while outside, the evening papers did their best to arouse salacious interest in the case. For two months, Ernest Jones lived on the edge of an abyss because if he were committed for trial and pleaded not guilty even an acquittal would not efface the stain of the charge.

In the end, the magistrate decided that the evidence was too flimsy and dismissed the case. Later, he went to the trouble of sending Jones a sympathetic letter in which he said how dangerously easy it was to set the whole machinery of the law in action to answer a charge based on nothing more serious than a child's fantasy.

In London, New York, Vienna and Berlin the wave of opposition to Freud's theories brought first attacks, then vendettas and sometimes professional dismissal. When Abraham read a paper on the erotic aspects of family relationships before the Psychiatrische Verein, the same Professor Oppenheim delivered a furious out burst which mounted to an outright attack on "such monstrous ideas". Privately, he declared that Abraham should be struck off the medical registers for propagating such filth.

It was against this steadily mounting opposition, criticism and outright attack, that the small Society which encompassed the Wednesday meetings, grew into the International Psycho-Analytical Association, and now external friction and opposition, slowly found a counterpart in internal dissension.

It is possible to trace what was being said in the Viennese Society, before Adler's spectacular defection, since the actual Minutes have been preserved. The Society acquired a salaried secretary during 1906, in the person of Otto Rank, author of *The Trauma of Birth*. Rank was one of forty-two members from six different countries who attended the first historic meeting of the International Psycho-Analytical Association at Salzburg in 1908. From 1906 onwards, he duly recorded, on large sheets of paper, in neat, crabbed handwriting, the protocols of the scientific meetings while the "attendance lists and communications" were kept in a small black book. The quality of the discussions varied from the brilliant to the dull, from the logically exact to the emotionally confused, and Rank did not attempt to make a verbatim record which would have been impossible in longhand. Instead, he took extensive notes while the discussions were actually in progress and edited the notes afterwards. A certain amount of confusion was inevitable with this primitive technique. Some papers were condensed to notes which make them unintelligible, and others are discussed without being named. Moreover, it was possible for each member to read and correct his personal record, a process which could lead to important deletions. As the years advance, the Minutes become less and less satisfactory, until it needs considerable imaginative powers to deduce precisely what is being said. The records do not cover the very early years, but begin in 1906 and continue until the Wednesday meetings became part of the activities of the Vienna Psycho-Analytic Society.

In order to see the subsequent quarrels in perspective it is worth dipping back into the Minutes to read what was being said immediately prior to the early frictions. Freud, for instance, had a high opinion of Stekel's abilities in these early days and he listened with admiration to many another member of the circle, subsequently doomed to suffer severe criticism and final exile.

On 27 November 1907, Dr Stekel presented two cases of anxiety hysteria which were summarized by Rank thus:

"The first case is that of a typesetter, twenty-four years of age, who wishes to be freed from his manifold nervous complaints by means of hypnosis. He is an onanist who masturbates mostly with sadistic fantasies (beating little boys on the nude buttocks). He himself traces his sadistic inclinations to his father's habit of beating him and his two sisters on the buttocks and then forcing them to urinate in front of him..."

The second case concerned a famous concert singer who lost her voice. "She believed that she was suffering from cancer of the throat partly because her father had died of cancer of the rectum but Stekel discovered psychic motives for losing her voice."

The significant point in the subsequent notes is Freud's constant approval of the work of Dr Stekel. As one Minute says: "Prof. Freud first expresses his appreciation of Stekel's psycho-analytic skills and then adds a few critical observations."

Similarly, Fritz Wittels, a man of great charm and gusto, who came to be regarded as the *enfant terrible* of the group, but finally vanished from the scene in a cloud of obscurity, also received Freud's approval in these early days. During the meeting on 10 April 1907 Freud listened very carefully to what was called a "presentation" by Dr Wittels, in which he proffered explanations of the motives of certain female assassins. Freud's final speech is summarized in the Minutes:

"Freud emphasizes that the speaker in an ingenious manner (and with personal complexes) has said something very serious. He has exposed the psychology of the assassin quite correctly: in his opinion it is the suppressed erotism which puts the weapon in the hands of these women. Every act of hate issues from erotic tendencies."

Every act of hate issues from erotic tendencies – it was one of those all-embracing assumptions which characterized these primitive days of psycho-analysis when vast matters were crushed into preconceived categories without a qualm.

Among the more distinguished members of the Wednesday circle Stekel and Adler had become close friends and both planned to write books, a hazardous procedure in the face of the critical habits which the circle presently developed. In due course Stekel completed a book dealing with dreams and dream symbols, and a special Wednesday evening was set aside to discuss the work. Stekel believed that man's nature was composed of negative and positive elements, "like the current of electricity", and each component implied its opposite, desire being matched by disgust, love by hate, the will to power by the will to submission. He complained bitterly that "later Bleuler described this fact as 'ambivalence', a term that was accepted by everybody, whereas previously they had laughed at my discovery and given me the nickname 'Stekel with his Bipolarity'." 'Whatever sense of fun sometimes broke into the Wednesday meetings, Stekel certainly seemed to be singled out for attention, especially by the always witty Hitschmann. On the fateful

Wednesday evening when his book was to be scrutinized in depth, he set out for Freud's home in some trepidation. He had special reason to fear not only Hitschmann but "a very gifted physician, Tausk, a former judge, who had broken down on the occasion of his maiden speech to the circle". Stekel wrote: "Tausk had spoken on Philosophy and Psycho-analysis, promising to build a bridge between the philosophers and Freud. He had started off excellently but in the middle of the speech he became confused and was unable to finish. I tried to save the situation and continued the lecture extemporaneously."[5]

It is difficult to imagine a more tactless move. A sensitive and sympathetic man might have tried to fill the silence with some relevant discussion, but when Stekel deliberately underlined Tausk's inadequacies by continuing the lecture in his place, he invited trouble. Now, on this special Wednesday evening, Tausk savagely criticized Stekel's new book, examining every chapter ruthlessly. He also "spoke at length about mistakes in grammar in the preface".

Following Tausk's attack, one by one, the members of the circle spoke, and as their criticism mounted without relief, Stekel became very depressed. Almost everyone belittled the book and at last there were only two members left to speak – Freud and Adler. "Even Freud failed me," Stekel said. Adler alone spoke in favour of the book and Adler, as Stekel pointedly remarked, was "my friend at that time".

It was the privilege of the author to have the last word and this, according to Stekel, is what he finally said.

"Mr Chairman and gentlemen. An architect built a new house: he was very proud of the arrangement of the rooms and the corridors... He invited his colleagues to inspect the house and was eager to listen to their opinion. The first colleague noticed that the lavatory was not big enough, the second repeated the same criticism and so on to the last. 'But, gentlemen,' cried the desperate architect, 'the daring staircase, the arrangement of the rooms, every room well-lit, the façade...' But all they spoke about was the lavatory."[6]

Stekel did not wait for any further comment, but walked out of the room. According to Stekel, Freud, "who had not uttered one word of praise during the critical meeting", later accepted "many of my findings". He also claimed that Freud had once confessed to him that every new conception offered by others found him resistant and unreceptive. "Sometimes he required two weeks to overcome such resistance."

Whatever Freud's precise reaction this was a small rehearsal of bigger rifts to come.

NOTES
1. Verbal evidence from Ernest Jones.
2. *New York Times*: 5 April 1912.
3. Verbal evidence from Ernest Jones.
4. *Sigmund Freud: Life and Work*: Ernest Jones, Vol. II, p. 122.
5. *Autobiography of Wilhelm Stekel*: pp. 130–3.
6. *Autobiography of Wilhelm Stekel*: pp. 133–4.

Chapter Four

The First Troubles

Although Freud constantly protested that he disliked holding prominent positions where it might be necessary to "rule" other people, he could not escape evoking in his followers all those infantile complexes which drove them to try to win his favour as a father-figure. The circle, in fact, became an enlarged example of the Oedipal situation which Freud had so profoundly analysed. Whether he liked it or not, he was, for a time, the undisputed Father and many among his disciples clamoured to become his favourite child. The economic motive for currying Freud's favour was, as Jones points out, equally strong. Men like Stekel had deliberately abandoned their ordinary practice to take up psychological medicine and Freud had at his disposal a surplus of patients which he could pass on to anyone in the circle.

After a prolonged period of intellectual and social isolation, Freud could not afford to be too particular about new recruits to the Wednesday gatherings and although most were serious-minded physicians with a bent for psychological medicine, some were too temperamental, neurotic and in other cases, eccentric, to become ideal disciples. Men like Stekel suffered from quite serious psychological troubles which culminated, in his case, in a prolonged bout of impotence. The clash of personalities became steadily more marked as time went on, and Jones later commented: "the atmosphere grew more and more unpleasant".

Freud had remarked to Jung at the very first Congress of the International Psycho-Analytical Association in Salzburg, "I am certainly not fitted for the role of leader", but now, with leadership forced on him he revealed conflicting characteristics. His diplomatic skill in modifying both his own demands and those of rivals was married to a determined effort to remain scientifically detached. Time and again his cool voice and calming influence broke into heated discussions and a volcanic situation was checked before it erupted. Considerable wisdom and tolerance marked many of his utterances and occasionally there was a tremendous sense of a figure, Olympian beside the pigmies around him, who quietened the waters with the wand of reason. Unfortunately, this side of Freud's character was heavily qualified by another. When someone put forward a proposition which seriously disturbed his own views, he first found it hard to accept and then became uneasy at this threat to the scientific temple he had so painfully built with his own hands. Thus his tolerance was qualified by insecurity, his breadth of vision by a special form of Jewish patriarchy and, in the event, his own words proved partly true – he was not fitted for the role of leader.

As the members increased, meetings and papers multiplied and discussion intensified, the Society split into two factions, one dominated by the figure of Jung in Zurich and the other by Adler in Vienna. As the Viennese group, including Stekel and Tausk, became jealous of the erudite newcomer Jung, with his powerful personality and obvious appeal to Freud, the Viennese closed their ranks and drew together "in common complaint against Freud".

By 1910 Freud was very worried by the "bickerings and recriminations", once a background murmur, but now plainly evident to everyone involved. The diplomatic side of his nature suddenly saw that something must be done to placate the rebellious Viennese and he decided to give the editorship of the newly founded *Zentralblatt für Psychoanalyse* jointly to Adler and Stekel.

By 8 November 1910 he was writing to Ferenczi: "The tactlessness and unpleasant behaviour of Adler and Stekel make it very difficult to get along together... Jung also, now that he is President, might put aside his sensitivity about earlier incidents." By 23 November he wrote to Ferenczi: "I am having an atrocious time with Adler and Stekel. I have been hoping it would come to a clean separation but it drags on."

Ferenczi replied that perhaps the situation was even more highly charged than Freud suspected because it recalled the whole Fliess episode and Freud might be living over again the Fliess desertion of ten years before. It is some measure of Freud's capacity to be objective that he unhesitatingly agreed. Fliess' Christian name was, of course, Wilhelm and Freud now wrote to Ferenczi: "I had quite got over the Fliess affair. Adler is a little Fliess come to life again. And his appendage Stekel is at least called Wilhelm."

The second International Psycho-Analytical Congress took place at Nuremberg on 30 March 1910 and Freud was one of the very first to arrive on the scene.

His mood can be judged from a letter he wrote to Abraham on 24 February 1910: "I no longer get any pleasure from the Viennese. I have a heavy cross to bear with the older generation, Stekel, Adler, Sadger. They will soon be feeling that I am an obstacle and will treat me as such..." Several interesting scientific papers were read, among them one by Freud called *The Future of Psycho-Analysis*. It was not until discussion about the organization of analysis in a world society arose that the trouble began. Freud had initiated the idea "of bringing together analysts in a closer bond", and Ferenczi, a man of great personal charm, was nominated by Freud to put the proposition to the Congress. He seems to have gone out of his way to indicate that the Viennese analysts were of a decidedly inferior order to those of Zürich and concluded that the future administration should be left in the hands of the men of Zürich. This, in itself, staggered Adler and Stekel, and Adler was said to have intervened and demanded a hearing at once. Ferenczi ploughed relentlessly on and now came an even more startling proposition. "I was surprised", Stekel said, "when Ferenczi (induced by Freud) proposed that Jung should be elected lifetime President of the International Analytical Society...[with] the right (among other things) to examine all papers submitted and to decide which he would publish." This meant, in effect, that no analytical paper would be published without his consent.

Even Jones, who brought the customary gift of academic understatement to a pitch of perfection, had to admit that this last proposition caused "a storm of protest". Jones, in his biography of Freud, lays the blame for what followed on Ferenczi, but Ferenczi merely carried out instructions from Freud, and there were some present at the Congress who believed that Freud had deliberately chosen a "stooge" to present his revolutionary proposition knowing how inflammatory it would be. He remained the power behind the scenes.

Stekel came to his feet to protest against Ferenczi's remarks in the strongest possible terms. "I insisted that our new science would go down if it were not absolutely free... If a lifetime president had to be elected no one but Freud had the right to hold this office."

Stekel's protest steadily mounted and he claims to have spoken for almost half an hour. It was now Adler's turn and he became even more outspoken. At one point Stekel said Adler almost choked on his words in rage. The discussion which followed became so heated and acrimonious that the Chairman suddenly called a halt to the proceedings and the meeting was adjourned until the following day.

Stekel now takes up the story once more, in his autobiography, but it must be remembered in all that follows, that the Freudians regarded Stekel as a most unreliable witness. According to Stekel he now arranged what he describes as a "secret meeting" of his Viennese colleagues, nearly twenty in number, carefully excluding all their rivals from Zurich, and made a rousing, political speech which drew applause from everyone. For years, he said, they, the Viennese, had overcome opposition, defended Freud and fought for his reputation, and now this astonishing little man Ferenczi had the audacity to suggest that the leadership should pass to a newcomer like Jung in Zurich, who knew nothing of the hardships of pioneering. It was outrageous. Were they to be dependent upon the mercy of Zürich, he demanded, and the answer came back unanimously from everyone present – "No!"

"Suddenly the door of the room opened and there was Freud. He was greatly excited and tried to persuade us to accept Ferenczi's motion; he predicted hard times and a strong opposition by official science. He grasped his coat and cried: 'They begrudge me the coat I am wearing: I don't know whether in the future I will earn my daily bread.' Tears were streaming down his cheeks. 'An official psychiatrist and a gentile must be the leader of the movement,' he said."

Stekel added: "He foresaw a growing anti-Semitism."[1]

The scene revealed interesting possibilities. Was Freud deeply distressed because he foresaw the collapse of the psycho-analytic movement, or was he badly thrown because he personally preferred Jung as President and could not face any substitute? His reactions reminded one observer of a frustrated child, and another of a man deeply moved by the threat of disintegration to his life's work. Whatever the true motive, later, the whole theme of anti-Semitism was to play a part in his relations with Jung, and Freud never really escaped, for the rest of his life, from early anti-Semitic bitterness and suspicion.

Stekel's account continued: "We tried to persuade him that his misgivings were exaggerated. There was a long argument, on and on. Finally he proposed a compromise. We should elect a president to serve for two years and every two years there should be a new election. We also agreed that there would be no censorship."[2]

Two divergent accounts are given of what followed. Jones says that Freud announced his retirement as President of the Vienna Society and agreed that Adler should take his place. "He also agreed that partly so as to counterbalance Jung's editorship of the *Jalzrbuck* a new periodical be founded, the monthly *Zentralhlatt für Psychoanalyse* which would be edited jointly by Adler and Stekel."[3]

Stekel's account said: "Freud was surprised when I announced that Adler and I were going to found an independent monthly journal devoted to psycho-analysis. The proposed publication was to be known as *Zentralblatt für Psychoanalyse*." Then came this much more significant phrase: "The fight with Jung was on." Stekel's evidence now becomes somewhat confused. Whether Freud, Stekel, or Adler conceived the idea of the *Zentralblatt* is not clear, but Freud, it seems, next invited a select handful of the Viennese group to a coffee-house meeting of his own.

Over coffee he told them, "I have written to two publishers concerning the journal. Both are willing to accept our offer if I acknowledge that I am the editor." Then came another highly charged phrase: "What kind of guarantee can you give me that this journal will not be directed against me?"

Stekel said that since they were still Freud's pupils it was preposterous to assume that they would write anything against him, but he immediately qualified this with the phrase: "We reserve the right to propound our own ideas."

Freud became suspicious again and suggested that every paper should be submitted to a triumvirate – Freud, Adler and Stekel – before it was published, and that any one of the trio should have the right to veto publication. In effect, of course, this gave Freud considerable control over whatever appeared in the paper, and he presently found occasion to exercise it.

Some months later Stekel wrote a paper entitled *The Obligation of the Name*, which set out to prove, by examples, that the name very often determines the bearer's whole life. Not surprisingly, when he showed this essay to Freud, he felt that it should not be published in the *Zentralblatt*. The essay made fantastically large claims on very flimsy evidence, and revealed Stekel as not only far too easily satisfied with superficial data, but as an ambitious man anxious to burst into print at any cost. Tense argument developed between Freud and Stekel. Freud anticipated that people would sneer at Stekel, which infuriated him.

For over an hour the wrangle went on, until Freud tartly reminded Stekel that he had the right to veto publication, and this threw Stekel into a fresh rage. Finally, Freud did exercise his veto and the first serious rift developed between the two men.

Freud later carried out a post-mortem on the Nuremberg Congress in a letter to Ferenczi: "Evidently my address met with a poor response; I don't know why... Your spirited plea had the misfortune to evoke so much contradiction that they forgot to thank you for the important suggestions you laid before them."

Freud went on to say that they were both "somewhat to blame" for not realizing what an effect their pronouncement would have on the Viennese. This did indeed seem astonishing obtuseness on the part of a man who had unravelled psychological problems of enormous complexity, but Jones always said that Freud was no *Menschenkenner* – judge of individual men. Whether Ferenczi's acid comments about the behaviour and significance of the Viennese were inspired by Freud, or delivered by Ferenczi on the spur of the moment is not clear, but Freud now wrote: "It would have been easy for you to have entirely omitted the critical remarks...then we should have deprived their protest of much of its strength." In the next sentence he more or less admitted complicity: "I believe that my long-pent-up aversion for the Viennese combined with your brother complex to make us short-sighted..." Later in the letter he said that he had almost fallen into the role of the "dissatisfied and unwanted old man", and then came the astonishing admission that he preferred to go before he needed to, "but voluntarily". It seemed incredible that Freud, the originator and founder of the whole psycho-analytic movement, should at this early stage, have feared being deposed by his followers and was prepared to abdicate to save himself the humiliation.

Finally, the letter said he had spent an enjoyable day with Jung in Rothenburg, and he was at the top of his form. "The personal relationships among the Zürich people are much more satisfactory than they are in Vienna where one often has to ask what has become of the ennobling influence of psycho-analysis on its followers."

It looked as though Freud went to the Nuremberg Conference determined to shift the centre of attention to a more distinguished international society led by Jung while he adroitly disengaged himself from what had become the encumbrance of early bohemian followers who had all too clearly revealed serious personal shortcomings.

Among the peripheral figures in the history of psycho-analysis Eugen Bleuler now came briefly to the fore. Eugen Bleuler, Professor of Psychiatry at Zürich, had become deeply interested in Freud's work through his assistant Jung, and correspondence between the two men began in 1907. Following the Nuremberg Conference, the already existing national psycho-analytic societies enrolled as Branch Societies of the International Association, but at this point Bleuler resigned from the Swiss society, ostensibly because he refused to become embroiled with *international* organizations. Jones regarded this explanation as pure rationalization.

From the outset Bleuler had revealed an uncertain attitude towards psycho-analysis, writing papers in support of it one month and criticizing it the next. As the man who introduced the concept of ambivalence into psychiatry – one of course which writers had frequently anticipated in literature – Bleuler became internationally famous, but Freud remarked on one occasion, to

Abraham, "I'm not surprised that he attaches so much importance to ambivalence when I read his papers." Among the psychiatrists at this time, Bleuler was a highly respected figure and Freud seemed anxious to keep his sympathies, in order to preserve a liaison with the world of psychiatry. The trouble between Freud and Bleuler really came to a head through Jung.

A certain rivalry existed between Jung and Bleuler in the Zürich group and this sharpened as it became clear that Freud favoured Jung as his "crown prince". Relations between Jung and Bleuler deteriorated and Freud wrote many letters to Bleuler trying to reconcile them. On 6 November 1910, he addressed a letter to Pfister, a clergyman who had joined the group and become an intimate friend of Freud's. Freud said he had taken considerable trouble over Bleuler, but, "I cannot say I want to hold him to us *at any cost*, since after all Jung is closer to me, but I will willingly sacrifice Bleuler anything provided it would not harm our cause. Unfortunately I have little hope."

Finally, Freud decided that a personal meeting might produce better results and he at last persuaded Bleuler to join him in Munich during the Christmas holidays. What precisely was said has not been recorded, but Bleuler poured out to Freud his troubles with Jung, and for the first time Freud became aware of "difficulties in Jung's personality". When his mind was set on winning someone over, Freud could be a most forcefully persuasive man, and by the time the two men parted, they were on excellent terms again, and Bleuler had agreed to join the International Association. Writing a wonderfully humble and revealing letter to Ferenczi about the episode Freud said: "He is only a poor devil like ourselves and in need of a little love, a fact which seems to be neglected in a certain quarter that matters to him." This was obviously a reference to Jung.

For a time the breach was healed and Jung, in turn, made an effort to be pleasant to Bleuler, but within the year, fresh trouble arose. Once more Bleuler said he could not get on with Jung and again he resigned from the Association. This was the final break.

Meanwhile, back in Vienna, the Society, now eight years old, held a business meeting on 12 October 1910 at which Adler was elected President; Stekel, Vice-President; Steiner, Treasurer; Hitschmann, Librarian, and Rank as Secretary. Despite his protestations that he must go before he felt himself unwanted, Freud now became known as the Scientific President and in effect, all his efforts to efface himself, simply resulted in his retaining office. It was also agreed that the three Presidents should take the chair in strict rotation at the scientific meetings and thus Freud had by no means relinquished his hold on the Society.

Already aware of the feuds and angers which could so easily be stirred among the Viennese group, Freud did not know that this period of uneasy compromise was merely the prelude to far worse frictions, open quarrelling and two major resignations.

NOTES
1. *Autobiography of Wilhelm Stekel*: p. 129.
2. *Ibid.*
3. *Sigmund Freud: Life and Work*: Ernest Jones, Vol. II, p. 77.

Chapter Five

Adler Leaves the Circle

The differences between Adler and Freud really began on 3 June 1908 in Freud's home when Bass, Deutsch, Federn, Hitschmann, Rank, Stekel, and Wittels were present. Adler delivered a paper, Schism in Life and in Neurosis, with that touch of bombast which characterized him whenever he challenged authority. Rank re corded in condensed form the discussion which followed.

> "...Adler has recognized...[he wrote] that the new psychology has to proceed from the instinctual drives. Characters and actions are thus to be defined in terms of the instinctual drives. A symptom is no longer considered to be exclusively a product of the mind, but is also derived from the instinct. It is true that Adler's concept of drive is new in that he assigns an instinct to each organ: this, however, would be legitimate only if drive were defined as an activity. In general, Adler's view does not change much of what we had implicitly assumed. By no means have Adler's assertions been proven."[1]

Like so many statements of its kind this suffers from the obscurity of condensation. Stekel, who at this time still supported Freud, came through more clearly in the Minutes:

> "In Stekel's opinion, Adler's assumptions bring nothing new for practical purposes, nor are they valuable as far as analysis is concerned. Everything is already contained in the Professor's writings. By the term 'defence

neurosis' Freud has indicated that all neuroses are based on the defensive drive [sic]. Freud has also introduced the concept of sublimation... Adler's assertions cannot be proven."

Freud himself, according to the Minutes, now intervened and as usual was considerably more lucid than his disciples: "Professor Freud first observes that he fully concurs with the study of organ inferiority." This disarming way of embracing the views of a would-be rival was characteristic of Freud in those early days, but very soon the qualifications multiplied.

The full meaning of the Professor's position became clear as he quietly took the apparent heresies of Adler and showed them to be nothing more than an old friend – the libido first discovered and named by Freud – masquerading under another name. The Minutes read:

"He agrees with most of Adler's points for a definite reason: what Adler calls aggressive drive is our libido. Adler must be criticized for confounding two things: (i) he lumps together the aggressive drive and sadism (sadism is a specific form of the aggressive drive which involves inflicting pain).

"A drive is that which makes an individual restive (an ungratified need); the instinctual drive contains: a need, the possibility of gaining pleasure, and something active (the libido). The libido however cannot be separated from the possibility of a pleasure gain."

Federn spoke next and, surprisingly, he failed to support Freud. He said that "it was not in accord with Adler's intention to replace the aggressive drive with libido. As Adler put it to the meeting it was the frustration of the various ways of obtaining pleasure which made the child aggressive."

Minute No. 53 continues: "After briefly comparing the contrasting views of Freud and Adler, Federn characterizes his own position on Adler's views: he thinks that Adler was wrong to abandon so rashly the primary significance of the sexual drives."

This came dangerously close to the nub of the fierce argument which was about to develop between Freud and Adler. Towards the end of the meeting Adler summed up, but once again the Minutes are confused:

"Adler, in his concluding words, deals only with the most important views; it is only natural that there are similarities between his and Freud's views. He himself, in the introduction, spoke of his original source... Rank's libido is not identical with his aggressive drive... Rank separates the aggressive drive from the libido... There is no organ drive in Rank's work. Adler advocated the conception of libido in the artist before Rank did, in a paper which Rank has correctly quoted..."

The Minute concludes with the words: "A long debate follows on the identity of or difference between Adler's aggressive drive and our libido."

So the scene was technically set for the multiplying series of differences which led into the final quarrel. Phyllis Bottome opens the chapter "Adler and the Freudian Circle" in her biography of Adler with the words: "In entering on the period of Adler's life which deals with the ten years' ding-dong struggle between him and his life-long antagonist, Sigmund Freud, the author has tried to keep as far as possible to an unbiased point of view in order to show without exaggeration the part which each played in the other's life and work." There follows an account of the "struggle" which from the Freudian point of view is full of bias.

Phyllis Bottome stated that from the very beginning Adler strongly sympathized with Freud's new approach to psychology but did not agree with his pan-sexual interpretation. She believed that Freud's Jewishness made it difficult to reconcile their opposing views and claimed – quite falsely – "that Freud always escaped his fellows whenever possible and did not willingly risk a disadvantage". Adler on the contrary "was full of a sort of open genius, ready to attack or defend himself at a moment's notice. He was a magnificent speaker – never at a loss, not even when questioned in a foreign tongue and without time for preparation...but writing bored him and he often deliberately fogged his meaning..."[2]

There was certainly truth in this last statement. As for the attitude of the two men to their patients, Mrs Bottome firmly believed that Adler treated his patients on a footing of absolute equality:

"There they sat, Adler and his patient – hob-nobbing knee to knee and often smoking like chimneys while they talked, each trying to outwit the other and both agreeing to outwit any thing or anyone else who came up against them."

Mrs Bottome appears to approve of this vulgarization of the role of the analyst. As for Freud, she wrote, "he never unbent with his patients. He was their master and his patient had to be a docile pupil...the dictator influence was always apparent in the Freudian School."

All this, of course, is a travesty of the facts. Adler employed a journalistic camaraderie with his patients and Freud a professional detachment; those who have practised psycho-analysis for years are not in any doubt about which technique produces the best results.

A more interesting picture of Adler's intervention on the scene is given by Wittels in his book Sigmund Freud: "Adler (himself a short and stumpy man) hurled his group of systematized ideas into the intricate network of Freudian mechanisms. I can still picture him at the round table, his eternal Virginia [a long, thin, cigar] between his lips, talking away in the Viennese dialect and perpetually returning to his idea of 'the inferiority of the organs'."

Jones left yet another picture: "Adler had not yet acquired the patronizing benevolence of his later years. He struck me as sulky and pathetically eager for recognition. I remember his writing to me not long afterwards thanking me for quoting him in an article."[3]

Neither Jones nor Jung thought much of the men who had gathered to form the first disciples around the Master, and Jung described them as a "degenerate and Bohemian crowd", an exaggeration no less gross than Mrs Bottome's. They were, after all, practising physicians "and if their cloaks were more flowing and their hats broader than one saw in Zurich, London or Berlin...that was a general Viennese characteristic". Certainly Adler amongst them was a man of very considerable talent and originality, and his battle with Freud now entered a different phase.

Wittels described him as prowling like a cat around a bowl of cream, but unlike the cat a complicated psychological struggle went on inside him. "It was a struggle for the courage to bear testimony when he knew that this could not fail to lead to a breach between himself and Freud. It was no small matter to break with such a man as Freud. One cannot expect to encounter his like again."[4]

Adlerians have consistently tried to show that Adler was never a disciple of Freud but always an independent figure. Ansbacher, their official historian, goes further. He claims that the Wednesday meetings were not convened to discuss Freud's work but were

"in the nature of seminars where members presented papers of their own which were then discussed by the group. The rule was that every member had to participate in the discussion, the order of participation being determined by lot and Freud's comments were not too much longer than those of others. During the fifty-three meetings reported for 1906–1908, Freud actually presented only two papers, whereas Adler presented four."[5]

46

In the spring of 1911 Freud, aware of the growing divergence with Adler, asked him to give "a connected exposition of his ideas". Adler, pleased at the invitation, agreed, and the group decided to grant him three consecutive Wednesday evenings to listen exclusively to his case. Adler himself, according to Wittels, approached these evenings with some optimism, but out walking with Stekel one day just prior to the first meeting, he said to him: "What's the matter with Freud? Is he really willing to compromise with me and to accept my deviations? What's his game?"[6]

Once again, it is possible to quote the actual Minutes of the meetings but they may not be reliable for anything more than a rough résumé of scientific fact. It was not Rank's habit to record the nature of emotional scenes or to include the tension and drama which occasionally built up as the meetings developed. Adler read three papers, one at each meeting, but the last one, on 1 February 1911, called The Masculine Protest as the Central Problem of Neurosis, crystallized his ideas.

The thinking in the paper is complicated and the terms used without sharp definition, but three major points of difference from Freud emerge: (1) That repression is not a motivating force in neurosis; (2) That patients experience inferiority feelings in connection with the inferiority of certain organs; (3) That some patients fear the feminine role and "the masculine protest" arises as a result.

The paper began with the basic thesis that: "The phenomena of repression, as described by Freud, form an important chapter for the neurotic and normal psyche but they likewise contain the very instinctual forces from which neuroses stem." Repression, Adler argued, is said to take place under the pressure of culture but when one asks where does culture itself come from the answer is from repression. Thus, according to Adler, Freud seemed to complete the circle and have it both ways.

In Freud's early theory of sex he spoke of the ego-instinct and Jones gave a clear definition of what Freud meant by that term: "Auto-erotism and object love were contrasted with the non sexual impulses of the personality grouped together under the name of 'ego' impulses."[7] Now Adler offered a different interpretation of the ego instincts. In his view, they were "an attitude against the external world, a wish for esteem, a striving for power, for mastery, for wanting to be superior".

Adler also strongly questioned the validity of Freud's concept of the libido.

"In the incest complex the boy sees that it is manly to be superior and wants intercourse with his mother to raise himself above her and depreciate her. How much libido or whether libido is involved at all, is completely a matter of indifference..."[8]

Adler concluded with a paragraph which reinforced his own concept of the masculine protest:

"One can no longer speak of a complex of libidinal wishes and fantasies; it becomes necessary to understand the Oedipus complex as a partial phenomenon of a larger psychic dynamism, as a phase of the masculine protest – a concept through which more important insights into the character of neurotics become possible."[9]

In effect Adler was asking the meeting to abandon Freud's central and fundamental idea of the Oedipus complex in favour of his own masculine protest. Freud now addressed the circle and at once suggested that Adler's paper suffered from the simple shortcoming of obscurity. Freud put it in other words: "First of all Adler's works are difficult to understand because of his abstract manner..." He went on to complain that old and familiar ideas were dressed up in new guises as if they were intrinsically different; but this was not so.

"Personally I take it ill of the author that he speaks of the same things without designating them by the same names which they already have and without trying to bring his new terms into relation with the old. Thus one has the impression that repression exists in the masculine protest; either the latter coincides with the former or it is the same phenomenon under different viewpoints."[10]

He had already touched on these matters, Freud said, in his own writings. The concept of "flight into illness" seemed to correspond with certain facts isolated by Adler. "Even our old idea of bisexuality is called psychic hermaphroditism by him as if it were something else..."

These phrases had a familiar ring. The disciple had nothing really new to say because the Master had already said it all before. There was some truth in the fact that Freud had touched upon, if not expounded, certain points raised in Adler's paper, but not all of Adler's points by any means were duplicated. Freud now went on to say that there were two traits evident in Adler's work as a whole. First a general anti-sexual trend which included an unpublished paper giving an asexual infantile history, and second, a depreciation of the value of the details of neuroses. "Adler has advocated the unity of the neuroses, which is trivial…what he asserts is actually the sameness of all neuroses. This trend is methodically deplorable and condemns his whole work to sterility…"

In a circle accustomed to cool and careful examination of new ideas, it was unusual to hear outright criticism in these terms, but even stronger words followed. "The whole doctrine has a reactionary and retrograde character… For the most part it deals with biology instead of psychology and instead of the psychology of the unconscious it concerns surface phenomena: i.e. ego psychology." Adler, Freud complained, continuously confused primary and secondary things. He never discovers anything new – "such as we psycho-analysts discover" – but simply reinterprets old ideas. There was undoubtedly some truth in this criticism, but the implication that Freudian psycho-analysts were the only true pioneers once more re-echoed that vanity of which some accused the Master.

Then came the final statement: "One becomes absolutely muddled from Adler's concepts… This shows that a coherent interpretation of neurosis on the basis of Adler's doctrine is simply impossible."

Adler was obviously disturbed by what amounted to an attack. According to Wittels he had agreed to deliver his three papers in the hope of convincing his "teacher" that he, Freud, was wrong but now – as he later told Stekel – this "open hostility" came as a surprise. What he saw as open hostility could be and was read by others as legitimate criticism.

When his turn came to reply, Adler appeared far less cool than Freud, and towards the end he simply repeated his point:

"My findings show that whatever one sees as sexual, behind it are much more important connections, namely the masculine protest disguised under sexuality. Concerning the objection that the masculine protest coincides with repression, I have tried to show today that repression is only a small segment of the effects of masculine protest."

The meeting was thereon closed. The next meeting took place on 8 February, and a comparatively unknown member of the circle, Rosenstein, rose to complain that Adler had really over stepped the bounds of the wildest imaginings when he suggested that the whole cultural history of mankind, including its art and literature, was really the by-product of the masculine protest. Hitschmann in turn criticized Adler for denying the strength of sexual factors in the neuroses. Others now intervened to defend Adler, pointing out that "the masculine protest did not deny sexuality but served only to guide sexual forces in a certain direction".[11] Stekel later spoke in favour of Adler: his concepts "are a deepening and extension of the facts already discovered by us and they are in no contradiction with them. They are simply further constructions on the Freudian foundation." Freud at once disagreed with this:

"When Stekel maintains he finds no contradiction between these ideas and Freudian theory, I want to point to the fact that two of the [main] participants do find a contradiction, namely Adler and Freud."

According to Wittels, the climax came on the fourth evening when general discussion began:

"The Freudian adepts made a mass attack on Adler, an attack almost unexampled for its ferocity even in the fiercely contested field of psycho-analytical controversy... Stekel told me that the onslaught produced on his mind the impression of being a concerted one. Freud had a sheaf of notes before him and with gloomy mien seemed prepared to annihilate his adversary." [12]

As for Phyllis Bottome she went further:

"There is no doubt that Freud had gradually become increasingly jealous of his brilliant younger colleague, and allowed, if he did not instigate, the 'heresy hunt' that followed." [13]

The most casual reading of the Minutes reduces these accounts to lurid farce, but even the Minutes record Steiner as saying that "there was considerable emotion being stirred up in the discussion". He then complained that "Adler has tried to bring us, who gathered together to investigate the vicissitudes of libido, nearer to surface psychology to such a degree that we might have to rename our society into whose programme and framework Adler's ideas do not fit at all."

Stekel, who was present at this meeting, claims that Steiner framed the statement in such a way that it sounded like a motion for the resignation of Adler. Even the restrained Rank was driven to record in the Minutes that Adler shrugged off Steiner's general objections with the remark: "If I were in Steiner's place I would not have had the courage to talk like that."

Perhaps understandably, with Freud's intellect constantly electrifying the air, every other member of the circle became obsessed with the need to discover something new himself and one after another they laid claim to a part or the whole of different hypotheses which sometimes disappeared into the realms of fantasy.

For the moment, Stekel broke into the tense atmosphere of that fourth evening. It was ridiculous, he said, to believe that any deviation from Freud constituted an act of rebellion. Such an attitude would not be in keeping with the idea of the freedom of science: far better if they could find the common denominator in the opposing theories. It was useless. Both sides remained intransigent. Adler left the meeting in a state of bitter resentment and shortly afterwards resigned as President of the Society. His resentment continued to boil up in him, from time to time, for the rest of his life. When a friend was having dinner with him many years later in the Gramercy Park Hotel, New York, the friend recalled his quarrel with Freud and tactlessly implied that he had been one of Freud's disciples. "He became very angry, flushed and talked loudly enough so that other people's attention was attracted. He said that this was a lie and a swindle for which he blamed Freud entirely, whom he then called names like swindler, sly schemer, as nearly as I can recall."[14]

What became known as Adler's Individual Psychology swept away the concepts of repression, infantile sexuality and the unconscious with the result that very little of Freud's psycho-analytical theories were left intact. Adler approached the problem of neuroses from the viewpoint of the ego and Jones complained that in this theory "even sexual intercourse itself was not impelled by sexual desire so much as by pure aggressiveness". It was only possible to reconcile Adler's theories with Freud's if one described them as a "misinterpreted picture of the secondary defences against the repressed and unconscious impulses", which is precisely the way Freud chose to read it. Theoretically a break was inevitable. Personally... Stekel now asked himself the difficult question: "Why did I not leave with Adler?" Adler was his closest ally in the group and no less than eight other members left the meeting with Adler. Why not Stekel? He gave a very frank answer in his autobiography. "I was partly dependent on Freud", he said, "for my practice and, in addition, I wanted to wait and see how matters would develop." Another motive, unstressed at the time, was his devotion to their technical journal, which he still edited with Freud.

Shortly after Adler's resignation, Stekel encountered Freud again one day and according to Stekel, Freud defended his attitude towards Adler. He said that Adler "wasn't a normal man" and added: "His jealousy and ambition are morbid." These sound like the comments of an embittered layman, not those of the high priest of psycho-analytic perception.

Adler remained with the Society as an ordinary member until 24 May, but when Freud suggested that it might be advisable if he resigned as an editor of the Zentralblatt, according to Jones, Adler not merely resented the idea, he took the whole quarrel out of private hands and consulted his lawyers. They then put forward conditions for his resignation which Freud described as "displaying ridiculous pretensions of a quite unacceptable nature". Phyllis

Bottome gives a different version of the final stages of the break. She claims that Freud "begged Adler to reconsider this last decision and asked him to a private dinner so that they might try to find a common field to remain upon together".[15]

Mrs Bottome quotes a very revealing phrase from Adler: "Why", Adler demanded, "should I always do my work under your shadow?"[16] Was it the petulant outburst of a pupil angered by his master and desperately trying to establish his own independence, or was it a genuine protest against Freud's insistence on conformity?

Once again, much of Mrs Bottome's account seems doubtful. It is more likely, as Ernest Jones believed, that Ludwig Jekels worked on Freud and at last persuaded him to try one last attempt at reconciliation with Adler, only to have it degenerate "into such petty reproaches on Adler's side that it had no issue". There remains the evidence of Dr Paul Klemperer who gave Jones a detailed account of those early Adlerian days which he did not publish in his biography of Freud. Immediately after his break with Freud, Adler set about forming a new and rival society. Its first meeting in 1911 took place on the first floor of the Arkaden Café in Vienna and was attended, very much against Freud's wishes, by Paul Klemperer and Hanns Sachs. The main question discussed – Can any member of Freud's old society join the new one and remain a member of both? – led Hanns Sachs into a learned disquisition which denied the possibility, and Dr Klemperer supported him. There were six people present at the meeting, but no one else supported Sachs and Klemperer and after the vote they quietly disappeared into the night. According to Klemperer, Freud never forgave him for his single appearance at Adler's rival meeting.

Many years afterwards he was walking along the Walterplatz in Bozen accompanying a Miss Eisenberg, whose father knew Freud well, when suddenly they encountered Freud and Ferenczi walking in the opposite direction. Freud greeted Miss Eisenberg warmly and completely ignored the presence of Klemperer.

It is interesting from Klemperer's evidence to see what happened to Adler's new society in later years. Klemperer returned to Vienna in 1919 and met Adler who at once said: "It's wonderful to see you again – you must come to our meetings – yes, they still go on – and are better than ever."

Klemperer duly accepted his invitation but came away feeling very depressed. He might have stepped back into the Society exactly as it was nine years before, he said, because they were still mulling over the same ideas with endless elaborations.[18]

Klemperer gave a vivid account of Adler's break with Freud. He did not spare his words. He described Freud's "two-hour critique" of Adler as a tyrannical attack, and said that Freud finally asked everyone present to express his opinion of Adler and his work. It was, Klemperer said, as if he had arranged a trial of Adler. Any chance of compromise vanished because of Freud's intolerance.

In a letter to Dr Pfister dated 26 February 1911 Freud himself half-confirmed what Klemperer said. Adler had "created for himself a world system without love and I am in the process of *carrying out on him the revenge* of the offended goddess of the libido". The italics are mine.

NOTES
1. *Minutes of the Vienna Psycho-Analytic Society:* Vol. I, pp. 406–7.
2. *Alfred Adler:* Phyllis Bottome, p. 58.
3. *Free Associations:* Ernest Jones, p. 169.
4. *Sigmund Freud:* Fritz Wittels, p. 347.
5. *Journal of Individual Psychology:* Vol. 18, pp. 325–35, November 1962.
6. *The Autobiography of Wilhelm Stekel:* p. 141.
7. *Papers on Psycho-Analysis:* Ernest Jones, 3rd ed., p. 47.
8. *Imago:* March 1951, p. 232.
9. *Ibid.,* pp. 232–3.
10. *Imago:* March 1951, p. 233.
11. *Imago:* "On the Disagreement between Freud and Adler", Vol. 8, 1951 p. 235.
12. *Sigmund Freud:* Fritz Wittels, p. 151.
13. *Alfred Adler:* Phyllis Bottome, p. 65.
14. *Journal of Individual Psychology:* Vol. 18, pp. 125–35, November 1962. Note, A H Maslow.
15. *Alfred Adler:* Phyllis Bottome, p. 65.
16. *Ibid.,* p. 66.
17. Personal communication to Jones by Ludwig Jekels.
18. This was not borne out by Jung in later years. In Vol. IV of his *Collected Works* (*Freud and Psycho-Analysis,* p. 87) he said: "Only after the preparation of these lectures in the spring of 1912 did Alfred Adler's book *Über den nervosen Charakter* [The Nervous Constitution] become known to me in the summer of that year. I recognize that he and I have reached similar conclusions on various points but here is not the place to discuss the matter more thoroughly."

Chapter Six

The Struggle with Stekel

Stekel claimed that after the final break with Adler, Freud tried to favour him in every possible way as if having lost Adler, he did not want a repetition of his resignation with Stekel. He is supposed to have said to Stekel: "I think Adler's new ideas are worthless. One of your discoveries in the field of dream symbols has more value than all these far-fetched philosophical hypotheses." What Stekel regarded as the crowning attempt at reconciliation was the gift of "a valuable ashtray" and an accompanying letter which said: "I don't know what could ever separate us." [1]

None the less feuds now spread and behind the scene one member of the group talked about another in a manner characteristic of any cluster of like-minded men, professionally ambitious in an excitingly new field. The evidence is fragile. Much of it comes from casual statements of group members, or is reported second hand, verbally. Jung was supposed to have told Freud that he regarded Stekel as "a nuisance to psycho-analysis", and Freud defended Stekel against the charge. On another occasion Adler told Stekel that Jung was such a victim of his conventional upbringing that he could never face the more abandoned implications of Freud's sexual etiology. He then turned and attacked Freud.

Clearly, as Jones admits, a great deal of gossip, backbiting and malicious talk went on, but it should be stressed that there, was nothing unusual in this. The implication that the psycho-analytic pioneers were in some way viciously abnormal is overwhelmed by the far worse and more malicious feuds which characterized political, artistic and literary groups of the day. This was quite normal behaviour.

Stekel, still a grumbling member of the group, now went to some pains to demonstrate to Freud, through a number of patients, what he regarded as theories of his own. Some of his claims have a very odd ring today. Three patients in particular were involved, one a man of 27, cashier to a bank, who had never loved a woman and suffered from a form of agoraphobia. This man's mother contracted choleoystitis but when the doctor said she must go for a trip to Carlsbad, the son said he could not possibly afford it and was thrown into a state of great distress. Shortly afterwards, whenever he came to the square which led to the bank on his way to work in the mornings, he experienced intense anxiety, his whole body trembled and he had to find a roundabout way to his destination. Even when someone accompanied him, he still could not face crossing the square.

Stekel said: "In my practice I had contended with several cases of agoraphobia. Like a lightning flash it came to my mind: You must discover a psychic cause for this strange illness."

What Stekel conveyed as a revelatory flash should, after Freud's training, have been commonplace practice, but the whole of his claims at this point in his career have the air of someone straining to achieve originality even at the cost of logical confusion. He found, of course, that the young man unconsciously wished to rob the bank to pay for his mother's treatment and the repression of this impulse from his conscious mind set up such a disturbance in his personality that he could not cross the square.

The second case was more dramatic. Called, one morning, to an urgent consultation, he found a young, voluptuous-looking woman holding the hands of a slightly built man and at once the man turned to Stekel and said almost hysterically: "Doctor – you see how unhappy I am. I have to be at the office at nine o'clock and my wife keeps me as a prisoner, because if I leave her she has a fit of panic."

His wife's condition had developed a year before when, suddenly and inexplicably, she found herself unable to go out of the house unaccompanied. Later, she insisted that only her husband could adequately protect her if she was to face the hazards of the outside world and she refused to leave the house without him. "And now", the husband added, "I am the only one who can protect her against this panic."

A remarkable fact quickly emerged under the simplest interrogation. Although they had been married seven years, the wife was still a virgin. Stekel said: "Again my intuition helped me. She is protecting herself against temptation! When her cravings for satisfaction increase it is only her husband who can defend her against the danger of yielding to them."

Stekel next discovered what might have seemed a strong possibility to anyone trained in Freud's school; that her husband was impotent. He concludes his brief account of the cure with the curt comment: "The only treatment that can help her is to cure her husband of impotence. This I did."[2]

Magnificently simple, but it would have been far more interesting to know how he cured the husband's impotence than how he discovered the root cause of the trouble. Finally came this startling statement: "I claim it as a merit to have first recognized that this whole branch of neurosis was psychically determined and that nothing but psycho-therapy would relieve or cure it."

Remembering that Freud had induced psychic factors in sexual troubles from the outset – his whole technique was based upon it – the assertion of originality seems ludicrous, but that was not all. Stekel wrote: "I was proud to explain to Freud the psychic mechanism underlying these cases." An astonished Freud replied:

"But such cases are not 'anxiety neuroses'. They are without exception cases of hysteria."

When Stekel disclosed that he wanted to include these cases in his new book, Nervous Anxiety, Freud said: "I'll give you a royal present: we shall call all cases where the anxiety has a psychological root anxiety hysteria, while cases where anxiety can be traced to injuries of the sex life will be called 'anxiety neurosis'." Until the second edition of Stekel's book, Freud seems to have exercised some influence over what it contained, but in the second edition Stekel "renounced [this] control and corrected some of his errors".

Remembering the Fliess episode, it is interesting to read Stekel's account of what followed: "Freud later adopted some of my discoveries without mentioning my name. Even the fact that in my first edition I had defined anxiety as the reaction of the life instinct against the upsurge of the death instinct was not mentioned in his later books, and many people believe that the death instinct is Freud's discovery."[3]

This running battle of priorities was to produce many more exchanges as time went on, but something far more serious was presently called in question in the Viennese circle – Stekel's integrity. At one unspecified meeting of what had become the Vienna Psycho-Analytical Society, Victor Tausk attacked Stekel and charged him with personally inventing many of the cases he brought forward to support his hypotheses. While he was still speaking, Stekel wrote a note on a scrap of paper and pushed it across to Freud: "If you will not rebuke these personal attacks this is the last time that I shall be a member of this circle."[4] When, at last, Freud himself spoke, he did not rebuke Tausk, but with elaborate politeness suggested that perhaps all members might avoid personal remarks. Temporarily, Tausk was quietened, but the rumour of Stekel's imaginary cases spread and developed. Jones states categorically that Stekel did invent cases. He says that whatever topic was under discussion Stekel had an unfortunate habit of opening his remarks with: "Only this morning I saw a case of this kind." In fact, Jones added: "Stekel's Wednesday patient became a proverbial joke."

All these charges need to be seen in the perspective of another witness. Dr Alan Maberly, who knew Stekel well, says that such accusations were unfair. Stekel, in his view, was a man of integrity but had the unfortunate habit of exaggerating actual cases until they threatened to become absurd. There was no question of fradulent invention.[5]

Another Stekel characteristic which displeased Freud and introduced comic-opera elements into some of their discussions was Stekel's habit, when pressed for evidence, of saying: "I am here to discover things; other people can prove them if they want to." Ironically, on one occasion, he even suggested buying a number of guinea-pigs which would be available free of charge to anyone who insisted that his assertions must be proved. From then on, false evidence in the circle came to be known as Stekel's guinea-pigs.

However, Tausk, too, came in for severe criticism from Freud. On one occasion Freud referred to him as a "wild beast", but this did not prevent Freud from asking him to supervise the book-reviewing in the *Zentralblatt*, which immediately outraged Stekel. According to Jones, Stekel now had an inflated opinion of himself and "his success in the field of symbolism made him feel that he had surpassed Freud. He was fond of expressing this estimate of himself half-modestly by saying that a dwarf on the shoulder of a giant could see farther than the giant himself."[6] Freud, in turn, when he heard this remark, commented, "That may be true but a louse on the head of an astronomer does not."[7] It was a pretty savage rejoinder but Jones, as usual, took it in his stride.

Stekel now said he would not tolerate any interference from Tausk and insisted that no word of Tausk's should be permitted to appear in the *Zentralblatt* while it was under his editorship. Freud tried to persuade him that this attitude was ridiculous and insisted, in turn, that the *Zentralblatt* represented the official organ of the International Association, the pages of which should be open to any member. Freud now found himself a victim of his own ruling that any one of the three editors could exercise the right of veto, and decided to take strong action to remove Stekel from the *Zentralblatt*. He wrote to the publisher, Bergmann, suggesting a change of editorship, but Stekel also wrote presenting his case and the bewildered publisher decided to escape from the claims of both, by maintaining the *status quo* for another year and then ceasing to publish the periodical. Jones asked Freud "why he did not exercise his right as Director to appoint another editor", implying that Freud still had supreme power over the *Zentralblatt*, and the picture which emerged was different from that originally stated by Jones. If either of the other two editors could be replaced at any time by any nominee Freud cared to put forward, then the power of veto became meaningless. Freud said he avoided this direct approach because Stekel had so much influence with the publisher, but he did not hesitate to go behind the scene and circularize everyone, asking members to withdraw their names from the *Zentralblatt*. Simultaneously, he persuaded Jung to call a meeting of the Presidents of the Branch Societies and the officers of the International Association. They duly met and without exception agreed to support Freud which meant that Stekel had been frozen out of the Association and left to cope with the *Zentralblatt* single-handed. By this means Freud evaded direct confrontation with Stekel, escaped, as Jones remarked, an open fight, and even more effectively left Stekel splendidly isolated, editing a periodical with which respectable Freudians no longer wanted to be associated. However, Stekel successfully kept the *Zentralblatt* going for another year or so. Meanwhile, a second periodical, the *Internationale Zeitschrift für Psychoanalyse* was launched to take its place, with the Freudian imprimatur, under the editorship of Jones, Rank and Ferenczi.

Stekel's account of the final quarrel said: "I reminded Freud of our agreement and said that I had the right of veto but he remained adamant. I gave up my membership in the group. At this time I was president."

Stekel went to see Freud for the last time shortly afterwards and the encounter must have been highly embarrassing to bath men. Freud once again said that he had been forced to protect Stekel against "the insinuations" of Jung which rang oddly in the ears of a man who had just been manoeuvred out of Freudian existence.

"Dear Master," Stekel said, "I am afraid that in a short time you will see you have sacrificed your most faithful collaborator for an ungrateful one. Jung will not remain a Freudian for long." "Let's hope you are mistaken," Freud said, sighing.[8]

When Wittels wrote his biography of Freud he gave an erratic and journalistic account of the break with Adler and Stekel, and Freud wrote a letter to Wittels, part of which was printed as a preface and part suppressed because Adler and Stekel were still alive. The suppressed passages said that although Wittels had done him justice where Adler was concerned, he did not know that Freud exercised a similar tolerance and patience with Stekel. Freud had rejected many criticisms made against Stekel, despite his impossible habits, but one final episode between them had become rather ugly, and even Freud's patience had broken under the strain. Another charge remained unchallenged in Wittels' biography: that he, Freud, habitually denied other people's ideas. The truth was that he denied whatever he had not thoroughly assimilated and evalued.

One of the most revealing passages in Wittels' biography carried general significance for the much more important if not traumatic break with Jung. It revealed a characteristic which Freud acknowledged as well known to him. He often found himself "forced to take a detour on [his] way". As he put it, "I know not what to do with the thoughts of others, when they are called to me at an inopportune time." Taken against the bitter background of recent quarrels and the inflammatory situation which developed with Jung, this seemed a masterpiece of understatement.

Lou Andreas-Salomé was one of the few women who ever succeeded in becoming an accepted part of the inner circle of early psycho-analysts. An attractive, highly intelligent and very sensual woman, she was a person of distinction in her own right as a novelist and essayist, and she could claim friends and lovers from Nietzsche, the philosopher, to Rilke, the poet. If the outside world had known her private life, her name would have been hurled in the face of psycho-analysis as an example of the type of woman produced by its doctrines but fortunately, at that time, no one beyond the Vienna circle realized that Lou Andreas-Salomé led a life of sexual polyandry. She, personally, did not regard herself as a loose woman and would have recoiled from the charge of promiscuity with horror but she not merely had a series of lovers: she indulged more than one lover simultaneously.

Not for Lou Andreas-Salomé the drudgery of the domestic round and the ties of motherhood; not for her the well-adjusted conformist woman, the ideal of latter-day American psycho-analysis. A strong-willed, highly sexed person with a tremendous flow of talk and an actively enquiring mind, she was quite capable of shocking a lover when she announced that the most profound ecstasy occurred for her when she felt "the male seed ejaculating into her womb". Of course, much of her behaviour may have been based on her marriage to Friedrich Andreas which was never consummated. Certainly, for an emancipated woman, she inordinately delayed the loss of her virginity. But once released, she challenged ironbound conventions which were far more powerful than anything we know today, and caused a considerable stir when she appeared on the psycho-analytic scene.

Born in St Petersburg in 1861 she was the sixth child of a former general in the Imperial Russian Army, and when she first met Freud had reached her forties. As her biographer H F Peters has written:

"Lou entered upon the fifth decade of her life with the radiance and vitality of a twenty-year-old girl. The discrepancy between her age and her incredibly youthful appearance was so great that her less fortunate contemporaries thought Lou must be in possession of some magic formula of youth. Her husband's mysterious occupation with Oriental folk medicine left ample room for all sorts of speculation. To Lou herself the fountain of youth was love. Love in all its manifestations..."[9]

She was indeed a gifted woman whose physical beauty glowed with a bubbling zest for life. Such a woman might easily have become a lightweight cocotte fluttering from one male flower to the next, but she revealed herself as a deeply thinking woman ruthlessly determined to follow her own beliefs. "The natural love life," she wrote, "in all its manifestations and perhaps most of all in its highest forms, is based on the principle of infidelity." She drew a distinction between the quiet content of conjugal happiness and the divine madness of sexual love. In later life, one of her lovers said of her: "There was something terrifying about her embrace, elemental, archaic", but her biographer added: "Precisely because she conceived of love as an elemental force, she was equally opposed to the false modesty preached by her Victorian contemporaries and to the casual amours practised by many emancipated women."

Such was the person who travelled to the Weimar Congress and there met Freud.[10] She "vehemently expressed a desire to study psycho-analysis", and her intensity amused Freud, but amusement quickly gave way to respect as he realized that here was a woman of no small intellect who "understood him perfectly".

On 27 September 1912 she wrote to Freud:

"Ever since I was permitted to attend the Weimar Congress last autumn, the study of psycho-analysis has had a constant hold on me. The deeper I get into it, the more it grips me. My wish to spend a few months in Vienna is now about to be fulfilled. Would you permit me to attend your classes and be admitted to the Wednesday evening meetings?"

Freud briefly replied on 1 October, saying, "If you come to Vienna we shall all endeavour to make available to you the little there is in psycho-analysis that can be demonstrated and shared."

In her diary from that date on she makes asides which continuously illumine small corners of the frictions and quarrels in the Wednesday group:

28 October 1912.

"First visit to Alfred Adler. Until late at night. He is charming and very intelligent. Only a couple of things bothered me. First that he spoke of the prevailing controversies in far too personal a manner. Second that he looks like a button."[11]

2 November 1912.

"...The present fights have the fascinating effect that Freud set forth his views about the dissensions on different occasions. This time expressly about Jung... He showed a subtle and ingenious bit of malice in his attempt to make the term 'complex' superfluous, pointing out how it had insinuated itself into the terminology out of convenience, without having grown up on psycho-analytic soil, just as Dionysus was artificially exalted from being an exotic god to become the son of Zeus."[12]

By 4 November 1912, when Adler had broken away and started his own group, Freud wrote a revealing letter to Lou Andreas Salomé. "Since you have informed me of your plan to attend Adler's enemy group, I am taking the liberty, unasked, to say a few words to you by way of orientation in this disagreeable state of affairs." He had been forced, he went on, to insist that those who attended one group could not belong to the other, and even guests were invited to choose between the Adlerians and the Freudians. In Lou's case, Freud said, he did not desire to enforce such a limitation, but "I only request of you..." that you "make no mention there of your role here, and vice versa".

On 7 November 1912 Lou wrote in her diary: "When I arrived at Adler's today, he was in the midst of a telephone conversation with Stekel, all of which I heard [on Stekel's impending 'secession' from Freud]. Conversing with Adler I was much enlightened by the history of his development as a student of Marx primarily interested in economics and philosophic speculation."[13]

By now she had become an important part of the circle to Freud and when, on one occasion, she missed a lecture he promptly wrote to her saying: "I have acquired the bad habit of directing my lecture to a particular person in the audience and yesterday I stared as if spellbound at the vacant chair reserved for you."

There were many differences – of a completely amicable kind – between them. Lou Andreas-Salomé's optimistic view of the world contrasted sharply with Freud's pessimism. On one occasion he told her how he had stumbled on Nietzsche's "Prayer to Life" and thought it atrocious. How a philosopher could write such grandiloquent nonsense was completely beyond him:

> Millennia to be to think, to live!
> Hold me in both your arms with might and main.
> If you have no more happiness to give:
> Give me your pain.

"No – no", Freud said. "I could not go along with that. A good head cold would cure me of all such wishes."[14]

Lou Andreas-Salomé came as a happy contrast to most of the men in Freud's circle whom she thought terribly ambitious and too easily hurt. She had a developed sense of humour and according to Peters was devoid of any vanity concerning her own person or her literary achievements. Freud found it a relief to have a woman amongst them who refused to be drawn into their frictions and quarrels and preserved a gaiety which proved a useful solvent at awkward moments. This breadth of vision and toleration certainly did not extend to her love life. Already the mistress of Bjerre, when he introduced her to Freud in Weimar, Bjerre was quickly replaced by a number of others, some drawn from Freud's own circle, like Dr Victor Tausk. She sensed something primal in this tall, handsome man of 35 who was sixteen years her junior, and she ruthlessly set about winning him. On one occasion Tausk invited Ellen Delp, an actress friend of Lou's, to a private reading in his rooms of the Gretchen scene in *Faust*. On the appointed day, Lou went to her friend Ellen with a message – which was pure malicious invention – saying that he, Tausk, had asked to be excused. Tausk, unaware of this, patiently waited for Ellen and later demanded to know why she had not come. No record remains of the scene which must have ensued between Ellen and Lou Andreas-Salomé. Once roused and on the scent of a particularly desired prey, she became unscrupulous and relentless. Certainly with Tausk dramatic methods were required. He drew women magnetically and yet, like so many men of his kind, remained an unhappy man.

A Croatian by birth, Tausk had studied law and risen spectacularly to become a judge but some mysterious disturbance in his life, personal rather than professional, forced him to give up law, whereupon, in contradiction to his austerely disciplined mind, he took to journalism. By now unhappily married, with two children, he suffered from constant anxiety, psychological and financial, one feeding upon the other, and at last took up the study of medicine. Approaching his finals he joined Freud's Wednesday circle and met

Lou Andreas-Salomé. Tausk, an almost slavish devotee of Freud's, became one of his main discussion leaders, and Lou Andreas-Salomé never missed a session led by him. The relationship between them quickly intensified, and for the moment Lou continued to attend both Freud and Adler's meetings. On 21 November 1912, she recorded in her diary:

"Stekel appeared in the group and was frequently quoted in the papers. Although I sat at an adjacent table with Ellen this time, he came over and interrogated me about Freud: we became rather embroiled. As I could not make a scene about it, being Adler's guest, Ellen and I left during the intermission. But Stekel came too. He had to deny that he had adhered to the Adlerian views we had just heard, and this on the street and with all manner of witnesses." [15]

Although still a member of Freud's circle, Stekel was obviously breaking the ban on simultaneously attending Adler's. Meanwhile, Lou's relationship with Tausk steadily deepened, as Freud continued to emphasize the need for solidarity. Of all men, Tausk was most unconditionally devoted to Freud, and his papers never lacked reverence for the Master, but when, on 27 November, he gave a lecture on the inhibitions of artists, Freud took a very severe line in reply. In her diary for 22 November, Lou recorded Freud's words: "With the persistent calumny of our whole movement on the part of official science, we should not dare to move so boldly into new territory, leaving the rear so exposed, and confirmation of earlier discoveries need to be made again and again."

By now Adler had become highly suspicious of his erstwhile ally Stekel, and Lou Andreas-Salomé records how funny she found it to hear Adler complaining of Stekel's disloyalty: "But he also complained of mine, and justly. We met and talked for two hours while racing all over town."

The precise relationship between Tausk and Freud is difficult to establish, but some contradictory element constantly drove Freud to be severe with one of his most genuinely devoted disciples. Lou made this significant comment on 12–13 February 1913:

"There is no doubt about it that Freud acts with complete conviction when he proceeds so sharply against Tausk… It is also clear that any independence around Freud, especially when it is marked by aggression and display of temperament, worries him and wounds him quite automatically in his noble egoism as investigator, forcing him to premature discussion…" [16]

If the relationship between Dr Tausk and Freud had contradictory characteristics, that between Freud and Lou Andreas Salomé was full of mystery. As her biographer H F Peters remarks, it "grew in intensity" as the years passed, and there is one deliberate omission in the diary which I have been unable to clarify. It seems very unlikely that Freud became another of Lou's "sensual victims", but the response between them went deep. Both were persons with intellectual convictions which clashed at many points, and it is remarkable that their friendship ran on for years without any major quarrels.

Jones and many other highly placed members of the psycho-analytic world tend to dismiss the appearance of Lou Andreas Salomé in the circle as a comparatively minor event, but she brought to bear the intuitive insight of the artist on problems which slogging scientific methods sometimes reduced to narrow orthodoxy. Boldly, for a newcomer and a woman, she began to resist what she believed to be Freud's view − that human nature and civilization were inherently antagonistic. She was sceptical of the claim that psycho-analysis could be considered a science, and later she strongly resisted the description of the unconscious as a repository of archaic, infantile and primitive material. It was also, she pointed out, a source of primary and creative fire. She tended to distort Freud's view of human nature and the unconscious and claimed that in most of Freud's writings "civilized man appears as a sadly domesticated savage". The passage continues:

"His sublimation by the aid of his repressed savagery assumes an essentially negative quality... Hence the end of all culture appears as a constant attenuation of the instincts, a frightening transfiguration. In actuality however, health really means their mutual adjustment, neurosis their mutual discord... For culture does not only confront the ego; it also expresses its own individually elaborated development."

Lou Andreas-Salomé finally abandoned Adler's circle and threw in her lot with Freud, but by now her relationship with Dr Tausk had come to dominate all others. Tausk, in turn, was madly in love with her, and found it difficult to accept her emancipated view of her role as mistress. A long conversation about unfaithfulness led him to describe those women who established close intellectual relationships with many men as indulging "sublimated polyandry". She strongly objected. Women, she said, do not necessarily leave one man for the next: they have a need to "return to themselves". A past-master at rationalization she said: "A woman is like a tree longing for the lightning that splits it, and yet also like a tree that wants to grow."

It was Lou Andreas-Salomé who finally broke out of the relationship with Tausk, to his great distress. He was heartbroken. He threw himself desperately into medical work as an anaesthetic to his anguish, and she, once again, began to turn her attentions to another man.

Freud's whole view of Tausk, which, until he became involved with Andreas-Salomé, had been a very dubious one, underwent a change as a result of this relationship. Freud now felt that there "must be more to Tausk than he thought, and he admitted privately that, but for Lou, he would have dropped Tausk because he considered him a threat to the future of psycho-analysis".[19] So there it was again. Yet another member of the circle had come under suspicion from the Master.

Professor Stanley A Leavy in his introduction to Lou Andreas Salomé's *Freud Journal* asks the final question: "Is she to be thought of as one of our teachers, if a minor one, or only as one of our hypothetical patients?" She did, in fact, practise as a psycho-analyst, but her claims to being a teacher rest more on her intellectual independence which enabled her to question Freud's technical concepts from a fresh and arresting viewpoint. She was not a technical teacher of any developed skill, but she qualified some of the more extreme Freudian dogma by a glorious and optimistic commonsense. As for being a hypothetical patient, that question might legitimately be asked about most of us.

NOTES
1. *Autobiography of Wilhelm Stekel*: p. 142.
2. *Autobiography of Wilhelm Stekel*: p. 137.
3. *Autobiography of Wilhelm Stekel*: p. 138.
4. *Ibid.*, p. 142.
5. Verbal evidence from Dr Maberly.
6. *Sigmund Freud: Life and Work*: Ernest Jones, Vol. II, p. 154.
7. *Ibid.*
8. *Autobiography of Wilhelm Stekel*: p. 143.
9. *My Sister, My Spoufe*: H F Peters, p. 17.
10. 1913.
11. *The Freud Journal of Lou Andreas-Salomé*, p. 34.
12. *Ibid.*, pp. 38–9.
13. *The Freud Journal of Lou Andreas-Salomé*, p. 42.
14. *My Sister, My Spouse*: H F Peters, p. 277.
15. *The Freud Journal of Lou Andreas-Salomé*, p. 53.
16. *Ibid.*, p. 97.
17. *My Sister, My Spouse*: H F Peters, pp. 280–1.

Chapter Seven

Jung, Abraham and Freud

In every sense of the word Jung was a bigger person than Stekel, Adler, Tausk or Lou Andreas-Salomé. His intellectual range far outstripped theirs, his knowledge of psycho-analysis was more detailed, he wrote with much greater style and distinction and his powerful insights cohered into a philosophic whole.

It would be a mistake, none the less, to imagine him as a completely rational, integrated man who did not suffer the neurotic qualifications which distinguished most members of the Freudian group. Like Freud, there were periods in his life when he underwent experiences which in anyone else would have been considered deeply neurotic. A number of psychosomatic illnesses troubled him in early years. Even as a schoolboy he felt the split between the individual who could not grasp algebra and was far from sure of himself and another person who became in fantasy an old man living in the eighteenth century.

Frequently, when he was due to return after the school holidays, fainting fits overtook him and one prolonged spell of six months away from school made his parents despair of his ever being able to earn his own living. "I saw clearly", he later wrote, "that I myself had arranged this whole disgraceful situation."[1] As a man of 55 discussing his childhood with a close friend, he admitted to schizoid characteristics with compulsive tendencies.[2]

Later, fantasies of a most intense kind became a real world to him, and he was much troubled by Voices, one of which, the voice of a woman patient, "a talented psychopath who had a strong transference to me", became a living figure in his mind. Once more his attitude towards this voice would, if he encountered it in a patient, have marked that patient down as deeply neurotic. "I reflected", he wrote, "that the woman within me, did not have the speech centres I had. And so I suggested that she use mine. She did so and came through with a long statement." This was explained away as part of his technique for dealing with the unconscious. Personify the powers within you, talk to them, and they will be stripped of their dangerous autonomy and brought into a proper relationship with consciousness. It does not destroy the fact that closely similar involuntary conversations take place within the fantasy world of neurotics. Jung admitted that he underwent schizophrenic experiences in middle life. His most intense periods of adult "disturbance" were roughly coincidental with some of the worst moments of his struggles with Freud.

His occult experiences also had some very odd characteristics. On one occasion the doorbell rang without any sign of human agency and – according to Jung – a throng of spirits took possession of his home. "I was sitting near the doorbell and not only heard it, but saw it moving. We all simply stared at one another. The atmosphere was thick, believe me!..."[3]

Jung firmly believed that the whole house was "crammed full of spirits". Even that description did not satisfy him. "They were packed deep right up to the front door and the air was so thick it was scarcely possible to breathe." He found himself quivering with questions: "For God's sake what in the world is this?" – and immediately an answer came from the spirits: "We have come back from Jerusalem where we found not what we sought."[4]

These experiences could all be rationalized as those of a man more deeply aware of unconscious processes than is given to the common run of men. Encountered in the consulting-room of any Freudian analyst, on the other hand, they would be regarded as fascinating pathological material. In Jung's own words: "It was only towards the end of the First World War that I gradually began to emerge from the darkness."[5]

Thus, on his own evidence, when he first encountered Freud at the age of 32 he was still not a fully mature, integrated personality.

At this meeting, Freud and Jung found each other attractive personalities and Freud was particularly excited by Jung's free-ranging imagination capable of formulating daring hypotheses on the slightest provocation. For the following two years, Jung's admiration for Freud grew and according to Ernest Jones he regarded "his encounter with Freud...as the high point of his life". Two months after their first meeting, Jung told Freud that "whoever had acquired a knowledge of psycho-analysis had eaten of the tree of Paradise and attained vision".[6]

Jung's commanding presence and immense vitality, his flow of language and soldierly bearing, combined to produce a formidable person and Freud at once saw in him the qualities of a leader. Some two months after their first encounter on 24 May 1907, Jung sent Freud copies of two letters attacking psycho-analysis, and Freud replied on 26 May:

"Every time we are laughed at anew I am more than ever convinced that we are in the possession of something great…" As if they must remain life-long friends Freud added: "In the obituary you are to write for me one day, don't forget to bear witness that all the opposition has not succeeded in diverting me from my purpose."

Towards the end of the same year, Ernest Jones, who was to become inextricably involved in Freud's relationship with Jung, wrote to Jung saying that he would be visiting Zürich shortly and hoped to meet him. Jung replied briefly on 23 November 1907. A A Brill and Peterson from New York were already working with Jung at the Burghölzli (the Zürich mental hospital) on what was known as Veraguth's psychogalvanic theory, and within a few hours of Jones' arrival, Brill began explaining its technicalities to him. Much of the information was already familiar to Jones and, reading this on Jones' face, Jung interrupted Brill: "We didn't invite Dr Jones here to teach him but to consult him."[7]

This was given by Jones, in his biography of Freud, as an example of the great charm Jung could exercise whenever he chose. Full of enthusiasm, Jung had already created a small Freud group at Zürich, and among its members were Franz Riklin, Alphonse Maeder and Professor Bleuler, chief of the Burghölzli, a man later to become another cause of friction. The group met at the Burghölzli, and while he was in Zürich, Jones attended one gathering at which a guest member, the famous neurologist von Monakow spoke. Jones gave me an account of this meeting. "It was interesting in the light of what followed to hear Jung defending psycho-analysis and risking Monakow's scorn, although it was difficult to know Monakow's precise reaction – he kept his face pretty masked during the proceedings."

Certainly, in these early days, Jung found himself in the position of a defender of the faith who suffered several personal attacks rather than recant in the face of conventional pressures. No one doubted the horror in certain Swiss circles when sex – which many considered an unfortunate prerequisite of reproduction – was put forward by fully qualified doctors as the hidden cause not only of mental disturbance but of much human behaviour in general. This was supping with the devil indeed. No worse demon could have come out of an intellectual witches' coven.

We find Freud's second letter to Jung dealing with just this situation: "...Don't despair; probably what you wrote was only a figure of speech. It is immaterial whether or not one is understood by official representatives at the moment." Jung presently delivered a daring lecture at Amsterdam, in which he defended some of the main tenets of psycho-analysis, and two weeks later Freud wrote again from the Hotel Annenheim und Seehof on the Ossiacher Lake Annenheim:

Dear Colleague,
Here I sit thinking of you in Amsterdam shortly before or just after your inflammable lecture...and it strikes me almost as an act of cowardice that I should meanwhile be looking for mushrooms in the woods...

It was better for Jung to challenge the opposition, Freud said, because his personality generated warmth and response where Freud's too often struck an alien note. Freud went on to say that he greatly desired to be with Jung at this time if only to savour the experience of no longer being isolated. He had known years in the wilderness, years when even his closest friends could not understand or sympathize with what he was trying to do; there had been times when sudden doubts disturbed even his convictions until at last, with his own mind reassured, he waited for a voice from the outside world to answer his: "and that voice was yours".

It read like the prophet unheard in his own country suddenly finding reaffirmation in an alien land and if later, Jung's claim to detect religious undertones in Freud's words seems strained, there was no mistaking a biblical sonority in the language Freud now used. The letters which passed between them in these early days were revealing in another sense. Each man admitted to having marked neurotic characteristics.

Freud wrote to Jung: "What you call the hysterical side of your character, the desire to create an impression and to influence people – the very qualities that make you a teacher and a pioneer – will come into its own."

And in a second letter (2 September 1907) this very interesting analysis of his own character was given by Freud: "If you, a healthy person, consider yourself a hysterical type then I must claim for myself the class 'obsessive', each member of which lives in a world shut off from the rest."

The seeds of the explosions which followed can be seen in some detail in these letters. Freud, at one stage, spoke of Jung imparting his personal leaven to "the fermenting brew of my ideas" and said that this would remove any differences between them.

"The fermenting brew of *my ideas.*" (The italics are mine.) Jung was not expected to have any ideas of his own but to add the leaven to Freud's.

That Freud, almost from the outset, saw Jung as the Crown Prince of the psycho-analytic movement, the man who must one day inherit the mantle of the Master, is very clear from letters he wrote to Jung, Ferenczi, Jones and others. It is also evident that, from the start, a certain ambivalence characterized the relationship between them. On 16 April 1909, Freud pointed out, in a letter to Jung, an odd coincidence. On the self-same evening that Freud formally adopted him as his eldest son, anointing him as his "successor and crown prince – in *partibus infidelium*", Jung divested Freud of his "paternal dignity". Freud did not explain how this was done but commented: "this divesting seems to have given you as much pleasure as investing your person gave me…"

It was a significant statement. Spelt out, it seemed to mean that the eldest son already took pleasure in divesting the Father of one of his most important fatherly attributes.

There followed, in the correspondence, a long analysis of a number of poltergeist experiences which illustrated very vividly the different approach of the two men. Jung was already very preoccupied with precognition and the occult, and Freud recoiled from such alleged phenomena which he regarded as irreconcilable with reason.

Jung put Freud's position in much stronger terms: "Because of his materialistic prejudice he rejected this entire complex of questions as nonsensical and did so in terms of so shallow a positivism that I had difficulty in checking the sharp retort on the tip of my tongue."

When Jung visited Freud in Vienna in 1909 a remarkable episode occurred which sharpened the debate between them and revealed Jung as so predisposed to read profound meaning into accidental noises that his reactions became slightly farcical. The two men were busy arguing about occult phenomena in what Freud called his "second room", when Jung suddenly felt "as if my diaphragm were made of iron and were becoming red hot – a glowing vault".[8]

Immediately afterwards came "a loud report" from a bookcase which made them jump up in alarm "fearing the thing was going to topple over on us".[9]

Overlooking the extreme facility with which occult forces had come to his aid, Jung said to Freud: "There, that is an example of a so-called catalytic exteriorization phenomenon."

What a burden of jargon to describe a simple contraction of ancient timbers producing noises no less alarming than when old floorboards shrink and give off a report like a pistol.

Freud scoffed at Jung in other words:

"Oh come," he exclaimed, "that is sheer nonsense."

"It is not," Jung replied. "You are mistaken, Herr Professor. And to prove my point I now predict that in a moment there will be another loud report." [10]

The second detonation duly followed from the bookcase. When ancient timbers shrink they frequently repeat cracks and groans which need no metaphysical explanation, but Jung remained convinced that he was right and jubilantly claimed that "hidden forces" were at work. More important, from the point of view of this book, were his comments much later in life:

"Freud only stared aghast at me... I do not know what was in his mind or what his look meant. In any case *this incident aroused his mistrust of me and I had the feeling that I had done something against him.*" [11] (My italics.)

It must have come as a considerable shock to a man like Freud, trained in rational inquisition and the austere discipline of science, to find that his chosen Crown Prince, newly endowed with the right of succession, was capable of interpreting simple phenomena in terms not far removed from those of witchcraft. Even Jung's red-hot diaphragm was open to the simplest explanation. Many a man has had a fire in his belly from argument and the experience may have amounted to nothing more than acute stomach tension from repressing anger. Such was Freud's devotion to Jung at this stage however, or perhaps his need of a suitable successor, that he re-examined all his presuppositions and after Jung had left Vienna wrote a letter dated 16 April 1909 which said: "At first I was inclined to ascribe some meaning to it if the noise we heard so frequently when you were here were never heard again after your departure. But since then it has happened over and over again..."

Something else had become clear, Freud said, to rob the experience of all significance for him. "My credulity or at least my readiness to believe vanished along with the spell of your personal presence."

Occasionally, Jung was said to possess what the sociologists refer to as a charismatic personality, and while he was there, in the room, passionately expounding his beliefs, he carried Freud along with him, but once he had gone...

"The furniture stands before me spiritless and dead, like nature silent and godless before the poet after the passing of the gods of Greece."

The remainder of Freud's beautifully written letter was occupied with explaining a similar delusion which he had once cherished about numbers. Clearly derivative from his experiences with Fliess, Freud had decided that he would probably die between the ages of 61 and 62, but when he came to analyse the origin of this prediction he quickly explained mystical conviction in rational terms. Endlessly the figures 61 and 62 had dogged his life. On a trip to Greece he noticed that vehicle after vehicle included the numbers and his hotel room turned out to be 31, "which, with fatalistic licence, I regarded as, after all, half of 61–62". No. 31 then took the place of 62, recurring with alarming frequency, and for years "31 remained faithful to me with a 2 all too readily associated with it".

No longer under the spell of Fliess or Jung, Freud did not invoke some mystical process to explain these coincidences but rigorously analysed his life in relation to numbers, searching for a key. Two experiences now combined to give him the solution. In 1899, when he wrote *The Interpretation of Dreams*, he was 43 years old, and some years later the authorities changed his telephone number to 14362. "What should be more obvious than that the other figures in my telephone number were intended to signify the end of my life – hence 61 or 62."

At first sight what seemed to be a strained explanation suddenly revealed another far more convincing strand. The superstition that he would die at the age of 61 or 62 turned out to be "equivalent to the conviction that with the book on dreams I had completed my life work…and could die in peace". The last and clinching detail quickly fell into place when he recalled that the superstitious anticipation of death, dated from the very year Fliess had launched his first big attack upon him.

Jung received what he regarded as these rationalizations with a smile. By sheer ingenuity, human reason could reduce all experiences to logical terms, but there remained the question – why did superstitious beliefs arise and could logical explanations of something springing from different roots ever be quite satisfactory to those aware of other dimensions?

In the background, fresh difficulties had arisen between Jung and another brilliant member of the Zurich circle which quickly reached Freud's ears. Karl Abraham was born in Bremen on 3 May 1877, the younger of two sons of a Jewish teacher. Trained as a doctor he developed a deep interest in psychiatry and was appointed to the staff at the Burghölzli under Professor Bleuler. Within a year, a sense of frustration in the Burghölzli drove him to resign and simultaneously he met Freud and moved to Berlin.

A triangular correspondence developed between Jung, Freud and Abraham in the summer of 1908, which steadily became more acrimonious. Jones used some of the letters in his biography of Freud but not, by any means, all. The trouble first arose when Freud expressed the opinion, in personal talks with Jung and Abraham, that dementia praecox (or what we would now call schizophrenia) differed from any other neurosis merely in having a much earlier point of fixation. Jung could not accept this. He insisted that the disease "was an organic condition of the brain produced by a hypothetical 'psycho-toxin". Abraham agreed with Freud and, according to Jones, said "that what was called 'dementia' in this disease was due, not to any destruction of the intellectual capacities, but to a massive blocking of the feeling process". Abraham already disliked what he regarded as the mystical tendencies of several members of the Zürich staff, among them, in particular, Jung.

Matters came to a head at the first Congress – held in Salzburg in 1908. Austrian delegates far outnumbered any other nation at this first historic meeting, with only A A Brill representing America and Jones and Wilfred Trotter, England. Delivering his paper, Abraham completely failed to mention Jung and Bleuler's work on dementia praecox, which not unexpectedly annoyed Jung. After the Congress Abraham wrote to Freud who replied on 3 May 1908:

"...I recollect that your paper led to some conflict between you and Jung... Now I consider some competition between you unavoidable and within certain limits quite harmless." [12] Freud unhesitatingly believed that Jung was in the wrong, due to his "oscillation", but he would not like, he said, any really bad feeling to come between them, and he hoped that Jung might find his way back to views (Freud's views) which Abraham still expressed.

Already the signs of the quarrel which was to explode volcanically were clear, but so were Freud's attempts to reconcile the preliminary antagonists. Since Abraham had revealed himself as a faithful disciple, it would have seemed reasonable that Freud should write to Jung and ask him to keep the peace. Instead he now pleaded with Abraham:

"Thus you will actually be doing me a great personal favour if you inform him [Jung] in advance of what you are going to write and ask him to discuss with you the objection that he then made." It would be an act of courtesy, Freud continued, which could simultaneously serve two, if not three, ends. Dissension would be nipped in the bud and some small demonstration made that they themselves had drawn "practical benefit" from the practice of psycho-analysis. As for the third end, it was a simple and highly personal one: it would give Freud great pleasure. Clearly Jung's ascendancy in the group was now so firmly established that other members were expected to compromise with and not antagonize him. "Do not make too heavy going of the small self-sacrifice demanded," Freud said to Abraham, when, in fact, he was asking Abraham to consult the wishes of Jung before he committed his thoughts to paper. Heavily camouflaged as "an act of courtesy" it could be read in quite different terms and, absurdly, it was Freud's devoted and undeviating disciple Abraham who had to make concessions; not the Crown Prince Jung.

Abraham proved, in the end, to be more far-seeing and perceptive than Freud and now he wrote a letter to Freud which presaged coming events with alarming clarity. The manuscript of the paper which Abraham read on dementia praecox at Salzburg contained, as he said, an acknowledgment to Bleuler and Jung which would have satisfied them, but on a sudden impulse he did not read it out. "I deceived myself momentarily with a cover motive, that of saving time, while the true reason lay in my animosity against Bleuler and Jung." His animosity, in turn, resulted from a paper given by Bleuler in Berlin which omitted any reference to Freud.

Busy psycho-analysing his own motives, Abraham revealed considerable breadth of mind and tolerance when he wrote to Freud saying that now he had come to look upon the matter calmly, he had to thank the Professor for his intervention, "and at the same time for the confidence [he] placed in [him]". He hoped that the action he had taken would have the desired effect.

He had, in fact, written a letter to Jung, and then put it aside for fear the attempted *rapprochement* contained a hidden attack. He scrapped the letter when he came to re-read it, and then wrote a new and, he hoped, better letter.

A month went by and still there was no reply to his second letter. By July Freud wrote again to Abraham: "I greatly deplore your quarrel... I am afraid that, with the exception of what you did recently for my sake, there is a lack of desire for a satisfactory harmony on both sides."[13] He must, he added, for the sake of the cause, find some means of reconciliation.

This was loading the evidence very much in favour of Jung. Abraham had made conciliatory overtures to Jung and he had ignored them, yet here was Freud complaining of Abraham's "lack of desire for harmony". When Abraham again made a brief reference to the Zürich situation, it disturbed Freud afresh. Abraham was at some pains to explain his "tactlessness" in a letter dated 16 July, which steadily mounted, as if carried away by its own momentum, until it read like a wholesale condemnation of the Zürich group.

"My brief reference to Zürich in my last letter did not refer to my personal disagreement with Jung but to the general attitude at present adopted in Zürich."

If Abraham regarded Jung's failure to reply to his letter as inconsiderate, he was still only too anxious to re-establish good relations with him. However, he felt that the matter went much deeper. "I believe all the gentlemen from Vienna had the impression at Salzburg that not much more could be expected from Zürich." He did not, he said, desire to disturb Freud with the details but certain facts which had been brought to his attention were inescapable. "...the sudden fading out of the Freudian evenings [in Zürich], so well attended until April, is striking." Moreover, Jung seemed to be reverting to his old love of spiritualistic enquiry, Abraham said. As for Bleuler, Abraham regarded him as "a mass of reaction formations" whose "external simplicity and often exaggerated modesty cover strong, grandiose tendencies". Riklin too, another member of the Zürich group, became in Abraham's letter "Jung's creature", and Eitingon was unsuitable for "active collaboration".[14] Maeder alone remained a tower of strength. Clearly, by now, Abraham did not think much of the Zürich set, and was prepared to be much bolder in expressing his doubts and hostilities to Freud.

Freud replied on 20 July saying that he was thinking of going to Zürich where he intended to try and clear up the feud himself. "I think a great deal more favourably about Jung, but not about Bleuler. On the whole it is easier for us Jews as we lack the mystical element."

By 23 July, he reinforced that message with a long letter which acknowledged Abraham's paper on dementia praecox, and said that it was marred for him because it brought his quarrel with Jung into the open again. Freud found himself in a difficult position. He now revealed clearly, for the first time, that he had originally thrown out the dementia praecox idea to both men "and had no intention other than that each should take it up and work on it independently". Now he complained, with somewhat tortured logic, that Abraham by adopting it, was forcing Jung into opposition. Again Freud made no reference to the real kernel of the trouble: Jung had rejected the formulation of the idea as presented to him by Freud and insisted on his own interpretation.

"When I go to Zürich...at the end of September," Freud wrote to Abraham, "I shall try to make good what can be made good. Please do not misunderstand me. I have nothing to reproach you with." This seemed to further confuse Freud's idea of the source of the trouble, and another suggestion, thrown out in the letter, added fresh complications. Freud nursed a suspicion, he said, that the suppressed anti-Semitism of the Swiss "that spares me, is deflected in reinforced form upon you". He added that as Jews they must be prepared to "develop a bit of masochism", or they would never hit it off.

This shrewd thrust led in the end into a labyrinth which will presently be examined in detail, but it is worth bearing in mind that a cloud of anti-Semitism did befog a number of issues and if Jung could not be said to be actively anti-Semitic, he was later to face a charge of Nazi fellow-travelling.

Abraham replied to Freud's letter on 31 July with a detailed account of how Bleuler, in his paper, had avoided mentioning anything about psycho-analysis, and Jung had split hairs over toxins. He criticized Meier (who held the chair at Konigsberg) and described him as "a complete nonentity". As for Jung, "we talked at cross-purposes". Once again, he added that "there was universal surprise at the behaviour of the Zürich contingent". In his view, "everyone saw it as a secession". He summed up the situation in these words: "I used [your] idea and Jung deliberately suppressed it. I cannot help seeing it that way. Later events confirm it." Someone who knew nothing of his frictions with Jung had told him: "At the Burghölzli Freud seems to be an idea that has been superseded."[15]

Why – Abraham said – why should people not involved in the quarrel say this so bluntly? "And how could all the tact in the world on my part have helped?" In any case, he had written the diplomatic letter required by Freud, and what was Jung's reply? Silence. He would be very pleased, none the less, if Freud's mission to Zürich proved successful. Clearly the situation now troubled Freud deeply. There was only one certain way of clearing up the confusion – by confronting Jung in person.

In September Freud duly travelled to Zürich and spent several days talking far into the night with Jung, exploring, in the first place, his relationship with Abraham. He explained to Jung – Jones thought very unwisely – Abraham's difficulties and suspicions, and Jung expressed regret at what had happened. Freud brought to bear all his formidable powers of perception and inquisition to discover whether Jung had, in fact, become a hopeless renegade, or just a momentary deviant on a special issue, and Jung countered this with an account of Bleuler's defection from their basic tenets which had led Jung to resign his job as his assistant. Finally, he claimed that he "had got over his oscillations and was fully committed to his [Freud's] work".[16]

Returning once more to Vienna, a much happier man, Freud wrote at length to Abraham reporting the details of the rapprochement. "Nothing will come of Bleuler," he said. "His defection is imminent, and his relations with Jung are strained to breaking point." As for Jung, it was his belief that half their troubles arose from the fact that someone had put false ideas into Abraham's head about Jung's personality.

The sexual basis of Freud's teachings had, by now, caused a considerable stir in the Swiss and German press, technical and non-technical. In the technical journals, Dr Dubois of Berne made an attack on psycho-analysis – "Zur Psychopathologie der Angstzustände" – and Dr Eberhart, a Swiss doctor, told a gathering of general practitioners:

"In these new ideas we are not dealing with anything which can be scientifically tested – we are dealing with thoughts – and where exactly anything so unsubstantial as thought arises has many explanations but that anyone should believe these thoughts all to be 'dirty thoughts' to do with sexual matters can mean only one thing – that those who put forward these propositions have an unhealthy preoccupation with sex bordering on indecency."

The famous neurologist Oppenheim now published a paper supporting Dubois' attack in which he said that it was an urgent duty to fight these psycho-analytic theories since they were spreading rapidly. Oppenheim's wife was said to suffer from bouts of hysteria and it became clear to friends of Freud, who also knew the Oppenheim family, that her husband could not countenance any sexual explanation of her condition. Wulff, who sympathized with Freud, tried to publish a paper in the *Berliner Iclinische Wochenschrift* replying vigorously to Oppenheim but the editor rejected it.

It has been said that Switzerland is sexually one of the most puritan countries in the world. Certainly, in the days when Jung struggled to assimilate and teach the daring theories of Freud, any blunt mention of sexual activity in polite social circles was not merely taboo but a dangerous invitation to social ostracism. Searching for explanations of extreme hysteria, crippling complexes and compulsive anxiety, Swiss doctors recoiled from the idea that they had anything to do with sex. Homosexuality was a criminal condition, impotence an unfortunate derangement of the sexual organs, cunnilingus and fellatio unpleasant perversions of "natural" love-making. Women still wore skirts to the ground, some men married women in total ignorance of their anatomy, fathers were regarded as infallible, and elaborate evasions of any direct confrontation with sexuality were widely practised in even the most educated homes. As for the newspapers, no open discussion of sexuality ever occurred.

Against such a background, to suggest that children underwent sexual experiences, or that decently brought-up young women could become hysterical from sexual frustration, was bad enough; but to elevate sexuality into a philosophy which explained not merely mental disturbance but the hidden motives which drove the psyche down some of its most alarming and inspiring paths, was intellectually irresponsible and indecent. Swiss society and the Swiss press put this point of view vigorously at many different levels and in varying forms.

Jung's position, as a responsible psychiatrist at the Burghölzli, became hazardous when he sought, like Havelock Ellis, and many another late-nineteenth-century pioneer, to break into the conspiracy of silence about sex and it was not surprising that he quickly revealed a shifting ambivalence. Swiss society reacted no less strongly against Jung than Viennese society against Freud, and some sections let it be known that they would not tolerate such behaviour. The staff of the Burghölzli at first tried to reconcile their differences, but tension mounted as attitudes hardened until Jung suddenly resigned as Bleuler's assistant, and the remaining doctors and psychiatrists closed their ranks once more.[18]

Freud wrote to Jung on 25 January 1909 saying that after the first honeymoon encounter with psycho-analysis there follows "a bitter period during which psycho-analysis and its founder always get cursed". He knew this had happened with Jung. His letter revealed that Bleuler had in fact deprived Jung of his job,[19] but Freud said he wasn't at all sorry. "You are destined to be a teacher anyway; sooner or later you will have more than enough of medicine; whereas into psycho-analytical practice one has to be forced."

Meanwhile, Abraham was fighting fresh battles in the *Berliner Gesellschaft für Psychiatrie und Nervenkrankheiten*. Oppenheim spoke once more at a key meeting, and again recoiled in distaste from the subject of Abraham's address – "Intermarriage between Relatives and Neurosis". Abraham wrote to Freud: "I avoided mentioning several important points (for instance the connection with homosexuality) because these would have aroused opposition, but stood very firm on all my references to sexuality." As for Freud's name, he seldom mentioned it because it acted "like a red rag to a bull".

After Abraham had delivered his paper, Oppenheim opened his address with a number of concessions, but when he came to infantile sexuality – no – there he took "a most determined and resolute stand". Theodor Ziehen, Professor of Psychiatry in Berlin (Charité), spoke next, and he baldly and bluntly stated that Freud's theories were based on the wildest assumptions which did not stand examination.

A recently converted Christian followed Ziehen, and he arrogantly denounced Abraham's theories in moral terms which Abraham thought more suitable to the public platform than science. "I had, *inter alia*, mentioned Conrad Ferdinand Meyer (as has Sadger) as an example of love for the mother. That was unheard of. German ideals were at stake. Sexuality was now even attributed to German fairy-tales, etc."

Finally, one member asked the Association to express its disapproval of the new Freudian madness which sought to reduce mother love to yet another sexual encounter, and the converted Christian expressed his relief that Oppenheim and Ziehen had made such a determined stand against these new idiocies. When Abraham delivered his summing-up, he modestly persisted in finding sexual elements in mother love, but selected Ziehen for a counter-attack because there was no mistaking the deliberate rudeness of Ziehen's address.

It was after this dramatic meeting that Abraham sent Jung his paper "Intermarriage between Relatives and Neurosis" for publication in the *Jahrbuch* and now fresh troubles developed between them. On 18 December 1908, Abraham wrote to Freud complaining bitterly about a letter he had received from Jung. "Only now, after the *Jahrbuch* has gone to press, does he tell me that he has postponed publishing my reviews which he has had for over two months." Jung had, apparently, explained the change on the grounds that for propaganda purposes he wanted to make the first issue a very varied one, and Abraham had leapt to the worst possible conclusion: "I can scarcely be wrong in assuming that at the last moment he substituted a paper of his own for my reviews." This was the over-sensitive assumption of a man who by now approached a paranoid state, but it was rare, at this stage, for the various protagonists to apply the laws of psycho-analysis to their own personalities. Abraham went on to say that he had written to Jung in a calm and factual manner which was hardly borne out by his letter to Freud. In the circumstances, he had suggested to Jung that he should withdraw the reviews on German and Austrian literature but "urged him to print the reviews of [Freud's] now". "I assure you", he concluded, "that I would have preferred not to permit the publication of all three manuscripts so as to show Jung that his arbitrary behaviour must have its limits."[20]

Not unexpectedly, Freud was shaken by this renewal of hostility which seemed to him, with considerable reason, quite un necessary. He wrote on 26 December: "I am really very sorry that you are at loggerheads with Jung. At Zürich I tackled him vigorously and found him amenable, and only recently he wrote to me saying he was glad he had established good relations with you."

On this occasion, Freud continued, he could not agree that Abraham was in the right. Jung had merely exercised his powers as an editor without any deliberate prejudice or hostility towards Abraham. On the other hand, this exclusion of Abraham's reviews coming fast on the heels of their last quarrel, might easily have been a conscious or unconscious desire on Jung's part to put this troublesome man Abraham in his proper place in the queue waiting for publication. Freud, who usually refused to accept obvious explanations, was far too ready to simplify Jung's motives. In the event, Freud proved hopelessly wrong about Jung, but now claimed to be absolutely right. Abraham's predictions of Jung's behaviour, he said, had turned out to be false. "You see from this how important it is to me that in these affairs in which each of you forms an opinion of the other, both of you should turn out to be wrong and I to be right."

Abraham took this with good grace. He did not fight back but simply said that he was in no way offended by Freud's criticisms.

Ferenczi's name now began to appear in Freud's correspondence and I have been fortunate enough to talk to Dr Michael Balint, a very close friend of Ferenczi's, about his relationship with Freud which, in the beginning, had some of the elements of a love relationship. Sandor Ferenczi was a man of tremendous enthusiasms whose speculative flights produced brilliant hypotheses. From the outset Freud and Ferenczi enormously enjoyed each other's company. When Ferenczi went to stay with Freud or joined his family on holiday he was accepted as one of them. Ferenczi's name will recur throughout these pages with a different emphasis from that which Jones gave it in his biography.

For the moment, as another preliminary skirmish with Jung subsided and peace among his followers was temporarily restored, Freud gave his attention to a major rearrangement of his domestic life. His sister, Frau Rosa Graf, had a flat opposite his and when she decided to leave it, he moved in with his family, destroying in the process a mass of documents and letters, including some from Jung, Abraham and Ferenczi.

NOTES
1. *Memories, Dreams, Reflections*: C G Jung, p. 43.
2. Information from the friend who asks to remain anonymous.
3. *Memories, Dreams, Reflections*: C G Jung, p. 183.
4. Ibid.
5. *Memories; Dreams, Reflections*: C G Jung, p. 186.
6. *Sigmund Freud: Life and Work*: Ernest Jones, Vol. II, p. 37.
7. *Sigmund Freud: Life and Work*: Ernest Jones, Vol. II, p. 43.
8. *Memories; Dreams, Reflections*: C G Jung, p. 152.
9. *Memories; Dreams, Reflections*: C G Jung, p. 152.
10. Ibid.
11. Ibid.
12. *Letters of Sigmund Freud and Karl Abraham*: edited Hilda C Abraham and Ernst L Freud, p. 34.
13. *Letters of Sigmund Freud and Karl Abraham*: edited Hilda C Abraham and Ernst L Freud, p. 43.
14. Ibid., p. 45.
15. *Letters of Sigmund Freud and Karl Abraham*: edited Hilda C Abraham and Ernst L Freud, p. 48.
16. *Sigmund Freud: Life and Work*: Ernest Jones, Vol. II, p. 55.
17. *Berliner klinische Wockenschrift*: XLVI, 1293, 12 July 1909.
18. Professor Manfred Bleuler, son of Professor Bleuler, wrote to me: "He left the clinic because he wanted to go into private practice." 30 November 1965.
19. Jung said he resigned. Professor Manfred Bleuler also stated categorically in a letter to me that there was no question of his father depriving Jung of his job.
20. *Letters of Sigmund Freud and Karl Abraham*: edited Hilda C Abraham and Ernst L Freud, p. 61.

Chapter Eight

The Visit to America

The spread of Freud's international fame became clearly evident in December 1908 when Stanley Hall, then President of Clark University, Worcester, Massachusetts, invited him to visit America and give a course of lectures. At first sight the magnitude of this new development seemed self-evident, but Freud's initial excitement was quickly qualified by a mysterious reluctance. At the outset sheer considerations of money made him unenthusiastic. He did not regard himself as rich enough to lose three weeks' earnings from his practice in Vienna, and when he discussed the matter with his wife she was equally reluctant to see him setting out on a vast undertaking to cross the Atlantic and lecture in a foreign tongue, without fees.

A month later, Stanley Hall wrote again to say that the celebration of the founding of the University, which was the excuse for his invitation to Freud, had been postponed until September, and he was now able to offer Freud a fee of 3,000 marks. Freud wavered for a few more days and then accepted. Immediately he wrote to Ferenczi suggesting that he should accompany him.

Freud's curious mental block about America continued when he found himself unable to read any of the multitude of books which Ferenczi proceeded to buy in the hope of unravelling the mystery of that strange remote continent and its avid people. Ernest Jones discussed Freud's reluctance with me and said that – extraordinarily – the man now so confident in Vienna, the thinker who had complete faith in his reinterpretation of the human psyche, seemed intimidated by the thought of America and deliberately belittled the importance of his visit, the better to face up to it.

Towards the end of March, Jung travelled with his wife to Vienna and visited Freud. Little is known of what took place between them beyond a paragraph in Freud's letter to Abraham which passed from a quick mention of their visit to an attack on someone quite different in outlook and personality. Albert Moll had written a book (*The Sexual Life of Children*) in which Freud said there were several passages capable of justifying a libel action. Not unexpectedly, when Moll called to see him, presumably while Jung was still there, trouble quickly arose. Freud wrote to Abraham on 27 April: "It came to hard words and he left suddenly with a great deal of rapidly secreted venom."

Four months later, Freud learnt that Stanley Hall had suddenly issued a similar invitation to Jung, to visit America, and now his view of the whole trip changed. He wrote to Oskar Pfister on 13 June: "You, too, must have been impressed by the great news that Jung is coming with me to Worcester. It changes my whole feeling about the trip and makes it important..."

All three, Freud, Jung and Ferenczi, arranged to sail together from Bremen on the *George Washington* on 21 August and now occurred an incident which clearly revealed the astonishing intensity both of Freud's passionate nature and his relationship with Jung.

Two very different accounts of this episode are available. When Jones wrote the first one, in his biography of Freud, he did not have at his disposal Jung's personal testimony given to Aniela Jaffé in his eightieth year.

According to Jung, the three men met in Bremen, where Freud was host at a luncheon party, and Jung turned the conversation to the so-called peat-bog corpses in certain districts of northern Germany. These were said to be the bodies of prehistoric men who either drowned in the marshes or were buried there. The bog water contained humic acid which simultaneously tanned the skin of any corpse to a mummified toughness while eating away the bones and preserving the hair. Jung was fascinated by the legend and talked on interminably about it until Freud burst out several times: "Why are you so concerned with these corpses?"

In Jung's own words Freud "was inordinately vexed by the whole thing and during one such conversation...he suddenly fainted".[1] According to Jung, when he came round again, Freud said that he was "convinced all this chatter about corpses meant I had a death wish towards him. I was more than surprised by this interpretation. I was alarmed by the intensity of his fantasies – so strong that obviously they could cause him to faint."

Many years later, E A Bennet discussed this episode with Jung and according to Bennet he said: "I had branded myself in becoming identified with Freud. Why should I want him to die? I had come to learn. He was not standing in my way; he was in Vienna, I was in Zürich."[2]

Jones, in turn, gave a different interpretation. Freud, he says, was in high spirits at the luncheon, *doubtless elated at winning Jung round again.*[3] Jung made no reference to the fact that "Freud had won a little victory over Jung". This victory, according to Jones, consisted in breaking Jung's fanatical anti-alcohol tradition and persuading him to drink wine during the luncheon party. Bleuler, Jung's professor until recently, shared his repugnance for alcohol and Jung's breakaway set up fresh friction between them.

For the moment Ferenczi was more disturbed than Jung by the fainting fit and wondered, with remarkable prescience, whether it would happen again. Freud himself later psycho-analysed the occurrence, turning his own techniques on himself with considerable honesty, but the explanation – like some other clever pieces of psycho-analytic interpretation – seemed unnecessarily complicated. As a boy, he had often wished his baby brother Julius dead, and when at the age of one year and seven months the boy did die, it left a terrible sense of guilt with Freud. Jones commented: "It would therefore seem that Freud was himself a mild case of the type he described as those wrecked by success, in this case the success of defeating an opponent – the earliest example of which was his successful death wish against his little brother Julius."

If Freud himself had cherished in Bremen a death wish against Jung, Jones' case would have carried greater force, but according to the available evidence, Freud believed that it was Jung who had a death wish against Freud. The guilt therefore should have been Jung's. Why, then, should Freud, a normally quite healthy man, react in such a dramatic fashion as to faint? He had just survived a period when Jung's defection seemed a dangerous possibility, and to reinforce their reconciliation he had just won another minor victory over Jung by persuading him to drink at lunch. Was it a violent shock, contradicting the implications of these two victories, to find that Jung, instead of cherishing their new relationship, really wished him dead? Did he mean – as indeed proved true in the long run – that the whole of their *rapprochement* was false and not to be relied upon? When he realized that all his struggles, all the hours of argument to win Jung back into the psycho-analytic fold had only produced a theatrical victory, did Freud find the shock too much for him and faint?

Using another piece of Freudian anthropological interpretation, did Jung wish for the death of the Father in order to replace him and thus reach right back to those highly charged disturbances with Fliess and the whole question of originality? Whenever his authority was challenged Freud reacted strongly, but when originality threatened – as with Jung – to undermine the validity of his life's work, he naturally reacted in a more dramatic way – who would not?

Hence his collapse had much to do with the threat to his life's work, even if it was intensified and brought to the fainting pitch by infantile fixations.

On the morning following the fainting fit the three men boarded the *George Washington* and Freud settled down to keep a diary of the trip. He quickly found that writing long letters to his wife took up most of his spare time and the diary stopped abruptly after two days. Relations between all three men were relaxed and amiable. There is no record of their actual conversations but Jones asserted that "they had discussions and pleasant laughter all day long" – an unusually generalized statement for him.

The weather held good until they ran into one of those thick midsummer mists which sometimes bedevil ships on the Atlantic and Jung was gripped by the primeval majesty of the ship slipping blindfold through the daylight darkness like some cautious prehistoric monster wallowing "towards its objective with regular deep-throated cries from its foghorns".[4] He spoke to Freud about the sense of slipping back into the primeval past, and Freud confessed some sympathy with the feeling when his cabin window revealed a dank wall of mist, and every sound in the ship seemed muffled and subdued to what he called "The mating cry of the foghorns".[4] A tiny incident occurred on the first day which gave Freud considerable pleasure. To his astonishment he found his cabin steward reading *The Psychopathology of Everyday Life*, and "it gave him the first idea that he might be famous".

Far more important, during the voyage, the three men spent no small part of their time analysing one another's dreams. According to Jones, Freud's dreams were mostly concerned with the future of his family and his work. When Jung plunged in to analyse one of these, he told Freud that a great deal more could be induced from it if Freud would supply him with some additional details from his private life: "Freud's response to these words was a curious look – a look of the utmost suspicion. Then he said: 'But I cannot risk my authority!'" Jung added: "At that moment he lost it altogether. The sentence burned itself into my memory."[5] Jung felt that the phrase foreshadowed the end of their relationship because "Freud was placing personal authority above truth". This, of course, did not necessarily follow from what Freud had said. There were two other possible meanings. Freud might have felt that the revelation of some inner weakness of his own would endanger the respect in which his disciples held him, and at this stage he did not wish to undermine his precarious authority. Alternatively, he was so determined to keep his authority over the psycho-analytic movement in what he regarded as the interests of its survival, that he refused to run unnecessary risks. Neither interpretation invoked "placing personal authority above the truth". It could be seen as a piece of diplomacy. Revealing the whole truth might at this stage have been a tactical mistake. However, later in life both Jung and Freud tended to give extravagant interpretations of each other's behaviour.

As for Jung's dreams, he claimed that Freud could make nothing of them, or if he did attempt an interpretation, broke down before he achieved anything satisfactory. None the less, one dream of historic importance occurred. It was the dream which led him to formulate the concept of the collective unconscious "and thus formed a kind of prelude to my book, *Wandlungen und Symbole der Libido*".

The dream – retold to Freud – took him into a strange house with two storeys which, despite its unfamiliarity, was his own house. Beginning at the top floor he moved down to the ground floor and there found that this part of the house was older, with medieval furnishings, floors of red brick and furniture out of the fifteenth century. Fumbling in the darkness he moved from floor to floor, thinking that he must explore the whole house. "I came upon a heavy door and opened it. Beyond it I discovered a stone stairway that led down into a cellar. Descending again I found myself in a beautifully vaulted room which looked exceedingly ancient."[6]

Layers of brick among the stone blocks told him that this must date from Roman times, and now his interest became intense and he began scrutinizing the stone slabs of the floor until, as if guided by an unseen hand, he found an iron ring in one of the slabs. Heaving at the ring, the stone slab shifted and now his excitement knew no bounds as he saw stretching away into an even more Stygian darkness, a flight of stone steps. Feeling his way down in the darkness he entered a low cave cut in the solid rock, and there in the thick dust on the floor were scattered bones and broken pottery from a very primitive culture, with, focusing his attention beyond anything else, two human skulls, half-disintegrated. The dream came to an abrupt end, and suddenly he awoke.

Freud listened fascinated to the recital of this dream and fastened on the two skulls as the key to the whole experience. Gesturing with his hands as though one of them held a skull, he pressed Jung to find a wish connected with it.[7] What did Jung think about the skulls and whose skulls were they? In short the death wish was dominating Freud's thinking and Jung "felt a violent resistance to any such interpretation". He had his own view of what the dream meant but in those early days he still did not trust his own judgment and "wanted to hear Freud's opinion". Anxious to placate Freud, eager to learn from him and not wanting to reopen dangerous differences, Jung kept his counsel. When he thought of blurting out the truth he felt sure that he would encounter "in comprehension and vehement resistance". He did not "feel up to quarrelling", and feared that he "might lose his friendship" if he insisted on his own point of view. Presently, he settled on an extraordinary expedient which he rationalized to some extent in his talks with Aniela Jaffé. He wanted, he said, "to see what [Freud's] reaction would be if [he] deceived him by saying some thing that suited his theories". Thus he told Freud a deliberate lie. He suggested that the two skulls belonged to his wife and his sister-in-law in order to fit the theory, adding to Aniela Jaffé: "After all I had to name someone whose death was worth the wishing."[8]

Extraordinarily, Jung seems to have overlooked the fact that the selection of a fake person in order to deceive someone else might easily involve the same psycho-pathology as the selection of a genuine person. The attempt to fictionalize might itself be more revealing than telling the truth. In other words, what were Jung's relationship with his wife and sister-in-law at this point? Unfortunately I have not been able to fill the gap. If Jung entered an unconscious conspiracy to conceal the true meaning of the skulls in his dream it was nothing beside the hushed silence with which Jungians draw a veil over the private life of their god.

Jung, of course, had his own explanation of the dream, a master piece of simplicity which any poet accustomed to invoke symbols would reject as too obvious to be true at any other than the superficial level. He solemnly explained to Aniela Jaffé that: "The ground floor stood for the first level of consciousness... In the cave I discovered remains of a primitive culture, that is, the world of the primitive man within myself." So there it was: the great message of the unconscious within oneself; spelt out by the demons of the dream.

Shortly before Jung's dream occurred he had been analysing the premises on which Freudian psychology was founded and what, if any, were its relations to general historical fact. The dream, he said, now gave him the answers. "It obviously pointed to the foundations of cultural history – a history of successive layers of consciousness...it postulated something of an altogether impersonal nature underlying the psyche."

His first inkling of a "collective a priori deep beneath the normal psyche" came from this dream and later he formulated from it his famous archetypes. Of course, it is easy to fall a victim to images in which "above" and "beneath" are meaningful, but these comparisons with caves and seas falsify, in scientific terms, the whole concept of the human mind which does not obey the laws or symbols of imaginative literature.

E A Bennet has recorded a conversation said to have taken place between Freud and Jung as their ship approached that forest of steel and concrete with the beckoning figure of the Statue of Liberty which is New York City. Gazing at the skyline with some excitement Freud said: "Won't they get a surprise when they hear what we have to say to them!"

Of course, what Freud meant was that the revelation of the permeation of sex into so many forms of neurosis and human behaviour would certainly shock and distress "pure-minded" American intellectuals. It had nothing to do with personal ambition. Yet according to Bennet, Jung answered the remark: "How ambitious you are."[9]

Again quoting Bennet: "Me?" said Freud. "I'm the most humble of men and the only man who isn't ambitious."

Jung replied: "That's a big thing – to be the only one."

The whole speech sounds very uncharacteristic of Freud, but it could be read as an omen of things to come. Whatever interpretation the two men put on this conversation – and its details are recollected by Bennet from Jung's account of the episode – the bustling, raw reality of New York presently overwhelmed all other considerations.

They arrived on Sunday evening, 27 September, and A A Brill was waiting on the quay to receive them but US immigration laws prevented him from going aboard. He sent a Dr Onuf – whose remarkable name was surrounded by obscurity – to greet them, Dr Onuf having some unspecified "diplomatic immunity". The inevitable cluster of reporters busied themselves with celebrities but Freud received scant attention and the next morning's paper cryptically referred to the arrival of "Professor Freund of Vienna" in a single line.

Brill quickly took charge of the party, and they were given a lightning tour of New York which carried them first to Central Park West and then into the crazy contrast of the Chinese quarter and Harlem. The following day, Freud satisfied his deepest desire and buried himself delightedly in the Grecian antiquities of the Metropolitan Museum. A tour of Columbia University followed and now the party was joined by Ernest Jones who had undertaken to give his own lecture on the "Analysis of Dreams". They all ate dinner on Hammerstein's roof garden, and then the American sense of "fun" insisted on their going to see one of those early films, in which one comic chase followed another. Jones recorded: "Ferenczi in his boyish way was very excited at it but Freud was only quietly amused."

Jung left a vivid picture of these early American days in a letter to his wife from Clark University, Worcester.

"…I have to tell you about the trip. Last Saturday, there was dreary weather in New York. All three of us were afflicted with diarrhoea and had pretty bad stomach aches... In spite of feeling physically miserable and in spite of not eating anything, I went to the paleontological collection..."

Later he met Jones and all four men took the elevated from 42nd Street to the piers and there they boarded an old-fashioned steamer with beautiful white decks.

Jung went on to describe how they were given separate cabins and the ship moved out around the point of Manhattan with its tremendous skyscrapers, to proceed up the East River under the Manhattan and Brooklyn Bridges, feeling its way through a maze of ferryboats, tugs and cargo vessels until they reached Long Island. They still felt depressingly ill: "It was damp and chilly, we had bellyaches and diarrhoea and were suffering from hunger besides, so we crawled into bed".

It was an ignominious beginning to what had promised to be a triumphal intellectual expedition, but very soon they arrived at Worcester and now the picture began to change. Jung found the scenery enchanting with "low hills, a great deal of forest, swamp, small lakes, innumerable huge erratic rocks, tiny villages with wooden houses, painted red, green or grey...tucked away under large beautiful trees".

They stayed at the Standish Hotel, on the American plan with board, and at six o'clock in the evening had their first meeting with Professor Stanley Hall, a man close on 70, refined, distinguished and endowed with a wife who cooked wonderful meals. She was, according to Jung, "plump, jolly, good-natured and extremely ugly".

Professor Hall lived in a big, comfortable house, alive with books, and had clearly taken careful note of Freud's chief indulgence because the three men encountered boxes of cigars wherever they went, even down to the toilet. Two pitch-black Negroes in dinner jackets, "the extreme of grotesque solemnity", acted as servants, Jung wrote, and there were "carpets everywhere". All the doors were open, even down to the bathroom door, with people going in and out all the time.

It was significant that in the lectures which followed Jung alone among the visitors gave two complete talks on his own work, mentioning Freud in the third lecture only. Jones and Ferenczi kept strictly within Freudian precincts and paid tribute to the Master throughout. Ferenczi was introduced under the title of Neurologist and Court Medical Expert in Budapest. Freud opened his first lecture with an elaborate burst of – was it modesty?

"Granted that it is a merit to have created psycho-analysis it is not my merit. I was a student busy with the passing of my last examinations when another physician of Vienna, Dr Josef Breuer, made the first application of this method to the case of an hysterical girl..."

On 8 September, Jung wrote to his wife that Freud had delivered his lecture the previous day and received great applause. "We are gaining ground here and our following is growing slowly but surely... I was greatly surprised since I had prepared myself for opposition."

The following day he was due to deliver his own first lecture, but all dread had vanished because the audience seemed friendly and the Americans gave every appearance of being open-minded. Jung now wrote to his wife that the European trio were the men of the hour and added: "I can feel that my libido is gulping it in with vast enjoyment."

Jones makes no reference, in his account of the American trip, to the generous way in which Jung responded to the overwhelming response given to Freud: "Freud is in his seventh heaven," he wrote, "and I am glad with all my heart to see him so." However, Jung's letters to his wife were not then available and Jones may not have known what Jung felt. Certainly, at this stage the *rapprochement* with Freud seemed complete and Jung spoke of "our following", expressing great pleasure in Freud's happiness.

Ferenczi also played a part in Freud's success. As Freud later admitted he often asked Ferenczi in the mornings what he should lecture about in the afternoons. "Thereupon he gave me a sketch of what half an hour later I improvised in my lectures." [10]

Freud made many new friends in America including J W Putnam and William James. He described his meeting with James in his *Autobiographical Study*, [11] and said he would never forget one little scene which occurred while they were walking together. "He stopped suddenly, handed me a bag he was carrying and asked me to walk on, saying that he would catch me up as soon as he had got through an attack of angina pectoris."

James died of the disease within a year, and Freud commented: "I have always wished that I might be as fearless as he was in the face of approaching death." [12]

Freud certainly found a liberation and respect in America which were denied him in Europe. He felt himself "despised" – his own word – in Europe, but in America "the foremost men" received him "as equal". Clearly he did not understand his own emerging greatness at this time and regarded it as a privilege that he should be received on equal terms by men whose names would be forgotten while his survived. The whole experience came as a surprise to him.

However sympathetic Stanley Hall may have been, his understanding both of psycho-analysis and Freud's special brand of humour was limited. Convinced that the new Messiah of the human psyche could lay on his hands and cure an acquaintance of his, he introduced the man to Freud, who quickly established that a severe case of agoraphobia was caused by an overwhelming desire for support from a stern, patriarchal father. When Hall, pleased with the diagnosis, said, "What can we do about it?" Freud jocularly replied: "Kill his father!" Astonished and alarmed Hall protested against any such idea and Freud had to explain that it was a joke.

More important, from the point of view of this book, was a small brush with Jones which very much later had serious reverberations. It seemed impossible that anyone could question the faithful attitude of Jones to Freud, but in these early Worcester days he had not yet committed himself completely and Freud quickly formed an exaggerated idea of his independence. "He feared, quite unwarrantably," Jones wrote, "that I might not become a close adherent."

Clearly, Jones must have been an attractive person to Freud, who went to considerable lengths to reaffirm their relationship, and when Jones had to rush back to Toronto it was Freud who personally saw him off at the station. Before the train left he repeated his strong desire that they should "keep together". His final words were: "You will find it worth while." Any ambiguity in this last statement might have been intentional. Psycho-analysis was certainly a worthwhile subject and in the long run brought fame to Jones as well as Freud, but Freud, during these last days in America, was sensitive not only to possible disloyalties, but also to his growing age. When Jung, Freud and Ferenczi went to see the Niagara Falls, in the Cave of the Winds, the guide asked the other visitors to stand back and "Let the old fellow go first", and this upset Freud who later remarked: "After all fifty-three was no great age."

One other episode needs emphasizing in view of what followed. Before he left, Jones had a brief talk with Jung, and was startled to hear him say that he "found it unnecessary to go into details of unsavoury topics with his patients". It was disagreeable when one met them at dinner socially. Such matters should be hinted at and the patients would understand without plain language being used. Jones commented: "It seemed to me very different from the uncompromising way in which we had been dealing with very serious matters." Astonishingly, in view of his close collaboration with Freud at this point, Jung himself gave the American visit as the date of his first dissension from Freud's work.

Throughout the remainder of the American trip a number of small complaints which Freud might have classified as psychosomatic in anyone else, troubled him. When they spent four days in the Adirondack Mountains near Lake Placid, living in "Putnam's camp" which consisted of "a collection of huts in a wilderness", he experienced a mild attack of what seemed to be appendicitis. Somewhere in that wilderness one night, the empty spaces also witnessed the remarkable phenomenon of Jung roaring out German songs in his powerful voice while Freud made inadequate attempts to accompany him.

As their visit drew to a close, Clark University awarded both men honorary doctorates and Jung described the scene to his wife: "Last night there was a tremendous amount of ceremony and fancy dress with all sorts of red and black gowns and gold tasselled square caps…"

They were all tired by now, and Jung was "looking forward enormously to getting back to sea again". The Americans had fulfilled their reputation for high-powered entertainment and every minute of the day seemed crammed with activity sometimes so frenetic that Jung felt his "head spinning". In a revealing passage Jung confessed to his wife that "I have, thank God, completely regained my capacity for enjoyment so that I can look forward to everything with zest."

Inevitably his reaction to American culture was mixed. In America, he wrote, "an ideal potential of life has become a reality…but it is all frightfully costly" and "makes one ponder social evolution deeply". Already the great experiment carried "the germ of the end in itself".

On 18 September, Jung told his wife that they had seen enough of America and "tomorrow morning we are off to New York – on 21 September we sail…" They embarked on the *Kaiser Wilhelm der Grosse* and quickly ran into heavy gales which Freud survived without any threat of seasickness, his sole concession to the vast rolling of the ship being an early bed on two particularly rough evenings. Once more Jung evoked the scene vividly in yet another letter to his wife: "Most of the day I stood up front, under the bridge on a protected and elevated spot, and admired the magnificent spectacle as the mountainous waves rolled up and poured a whirling cloud of foam over the ship."

Whatever other troubles disturbed the two great analysts it certainly wasn't seasickness: "In all the cabins round about, unspeakable groans betrayed the secrets of the menu. I slept like a top…"

The ship reached Bremen at noon on 29 September, the crossing having taken eight complete days. All three men were glad to be back on European soil. Despite the tremendous reception in America and the undoubted success of the lectures, Freud returned with a bad impression of the United States. Analysing his reactions it becomes clear that this was based more on prejudice than fact. He claimed that American cooking had left his stomach permanently disturbed and was seriously put out by the lack of public lavatories in America which made his prostatic trouble more acute. "They escort you along miles of corridors", he complained to Jones, "and ultimately you are taken to the very basement where a marble palace awaits you only just in time." Language difficulties also troubled him. Once in the company of Jung, one American turned to another and asked him to repeat something he had said, whereupon Freud commented to Jung in German: "These people cannot even understand each other!" What would normally pass as a series of small prejudices built up in Freud's case to a final extravagance when talking to Jones one day: "America is a mistake; a gigantic mistake, it is true, but none the less a mistake."[13] As Jones remarked, the man endowed with a brilliantly complicated intelligence, whose insights into human nature seldom took anything at its face value, was prepared to judge certain people in black-and-white terms quite alien to the subtlety of his professional techniques. Perhaps his inadequacy with the language gave him a feeling of inferiority, and Freud did not like to feel inferior. Jung, too, had his qualifications about America but was much more sympathetic and returned later to give another course of lectures.

Following the American trip, Jones had a disagreement with Freud about the American psychiatrist Morton Prince who has since become famous for his study of the girl with "multiple personality". Prince had rejected an abstract of Brill's because he felt that its forthright language would offend his lay audience and build up unnecessary resistance in America. Freud became very angry when he heard this, and even went so far as to say that Jones should break off relations with such a hypocrite. Jones insisted that Prince was not a hypocrite but a thoroughgoing gentleman whose fears about Brill's abstract were only too well founded. According to Jones, Prince had one major failing which, in Freud's eyes, was unpardonable: "he was rather stupid". Once again it seemed extraordinary that such a brilliant intelligence as Freud's should regard stupidity as unpardonable, but a very familiar and quite different fear underlay surface appearances. It was Freud's fear of the rejection of his sexual theories. Whenever any one tactfully tried to modify his professional language Freud grew angry because this made unnecessary concessions to the enemy. He wrote to Pfister on 6 June 1910: "Your analysis suffers from the hereditary weakness of virtue. It is the work of an over-decent man who feels himself obliged to be discreet." Discretion, he went on, is incompatible with the proper presentation of psycho-analytic detail. There followed these revealing lines: "One has to become a bad fellow, transcend the rules, sacrifice oneself betray and behave like the artist who buys paints with his wife's household money..."

In 1910, Jung visited Freud in Vienna once more, and now Freud's concern over any possible apostasy sharpened. He said to Jung one day: "My dear Jung, promise me never to abandon the sexual theory. That is the most essential thing of all. You see, we must make a dogma of it, an unshakeable bulwark."[14]

Taken aback, Jung said, "A bulwark – against what?" Freud replied "Against the black tide of mud..."; he hesitated and added: "of occultism."

The words "dogma" and "bulwark" alarmed Jung in this statement. Dogma, according to Jung's view, was an undisputable confession of faith which had for its main aim the suppression of doubts once and for all. This seemed far removed from science or scientific judgment and he could only associate the words with "a personal power drive". Of course, by this definition, the Roman Catholic Church became a "personal power drive", but Jung, a fundamentally religious man, did not discuss such implications.

The conversation with Freud struck a chill to Jung's heart. He suddenly felt that all their differences and reconciliations were meaningless beside the arbitrary nature of Freud's demands. "What Freud seemed to mean by 'occultism' was virtually everything that philosophy and religion, including the rising contemporary science of parapsychology had learnt about the psyche." As Jung saw it, a scientific truth was a hypothesis which might be superseded by another hypothesis and was certainly not "an article of faith for all time."

Of course, Jung's inescapable religiosity matched Freud's secular dogmatism and Jung, in later years, claimed – how infuriated Freud would have been – that Freud's statements revealed "the eruption of unconscious religious factors".

Jung spelt out his objections: "Freud, who had always made much of his irreligiosity had now constructed a dogma; or rather in place of a jealous God whom he had lost, he had substituted another compelling image, that of sexuality." Certainly it was another image but not another god; a dogmatism but not a divine dogmatism. In fact divinity and metaphysics were totally opposed to Freud's way of thinking, and anathema to him personally.

The demands of a father-figure who insists that you accept his view as the only correct one, can obviously concern matters which have nothing to do with religion. Such was the case with Freud. Thus he would have recoiled in horror, and rightly so, from Jung's attempt to invest his propositions with religious meaning: "At bottom, however, the numinosity, that is the psychological qualities of the two rationally incommensurable opposites – Yahweh and sexuality – remained the same." This was, of course, nonsense to Freud and came close to inverting Jung's accusations. Jung's dogma was, in turn, trying to swallow Freud's dogma. Throughout several astonishing pages of Memories, Dreams, Reflections, Jung develops a series of mystical attacks on Freud which use an ill-defined farrago of terms totally alien to the vocabulary of Freud. Like many attempts to name and describe religious or mystical experience, they fall back on portentous words like numinosum which merely put a blurred label on experiences insusceptible of clear definition, and hence of clear understanding.

Jung acknowledges that his conversation with Freud in Vienna added to his confusion. Certainly, the thoughts which he records, following the meeting, were anything but lucid. Having given his view that Yahweh and sexuality remained the same, he went on to say: "But what difference does it make ultimately to the stronger agency if it is called now by one name and now by another?... The problem still remains how to overcome or escape our anxiety, bad conscience, guilt, compulsion, unconsciousness and instinctuality. If we cannot do this from the bright idealistic side then perhaps we shall have better luck by approaching the problem from the dark, biological side." However, far more personal matters were revealed to Jung by thoughts "darting" – in his own words – "like flames through his mind". One characteristic he insisted on was Freud's bitterness. "It had struck me at our first encounter, but it remained inexplicable to me until I was able to see it in connection with his attitude towards sexuality. Although, for Freud, sexuality was undoubtedly a numinosum, his terminology and theory seemed to define it exclusively as a biological function." Jung went further. Freud taught, he said, that "sexuality included spirituality and had an intrinsic meaning". Unfortunately, Jung commented, "his terminology seemed too narrow to express this idea". Freud, of course, would have said that his terminology was scientific and not mystical, sharper and not narrower than Jung's. But Jung, possessed by his own vision and no less blind to anyone else's, pressed on: "He gave me the impression that at bottom he was working against his own goal and against himself." This extraordinary intellectual somersault once more twisted all Freud's motives towards the goals that he, Jung, regarded as the right ones. Jung continued: "There is, after all, no harsher bitterness than that of a person who is his own worst enemy. In his own words, he felt himself menaced by a 'black tide of mud' – he who more than anyone else had tried to let down his buckets into those black depths."

Struggling to justify this charge, Jung continued: "Freud never asked himself why he was compelled to talk continually of sex, why this idea had taken possession of him." Untrue, of course. Freud knew quite well why sexuality obsessed him.

Many of Jung's charges become superfluous if one remembers Freud's proposition that the unconscious could condition our behaviour in a highly irrational manner. The substitution of irrational for mystical gave Freud the extra dimension without which Jung claimed he "could never be reconciled to himself".

One tremendously important reaction occurred as a result of Jung's re-examination of Freud, Nietzsche and Adler. He embarked on an investigation, lasting thirty years, of the black tide of mud which, translated into his own language, meant "the conscious and unconscious historical assumptions underlying our contemporary psychology". From this he formulated some of his more important theories.

The dream of the house with skulls concealed in the basement persisted long after Jung's return from America, and as a result he began a feverish bout of mythological reading. One book in particular fired his imagination: Friedrich Cruizer's *Symbolik und Mythologie der Alten Völker*. It led him to consume scores of similar books, until he found his mind seething with the kind of perplexities which he had known once before at the Burghölzli, when he first probed into the mysteries of psychotic states. He became so deeply lost in this new work that he had the illusion of disappearing into a madhouse where gods, goddesses, centaurs and nymphs came to him as patients for treatment and analysis. It was during these frenzied encounters with such figures that he discovered the "close relationship between ancient mythology and the psychology of primitives". Next followed the reading of Miss Miller's fantasies in the *Archives de Psychologie* and the sudden realization of a relationship between myth and fantasy. Slowly, from this ferment of reading and thought, from the crystallization of disorderly ideas brought about by Miss Miller's fantasies and the constant search for underlying meanings, emerged his great book *Psychology of the Unconscious*.

Deeply lost in work, to the exclusion of many friends and even some patients, he had a powerfully recurring dream about Freud which "presaged the forthcoming break". Significantly, the dream took place on the Swiss–Austrian border and involved an elderly man dressed as an Imperial Austrian customs officer.

Incidental figures in the dream informed Jung that the customs official had really died years ago and that this was only his ghost. One man added: "He is one of those who still couldn't die properly."

It quickly became apparent to Jung that this was a dream about Freud who, in the role of a Customs official, waited at the border between the conscious and unconscious to censor his ideas.

Jung wrote: "At that time Freud had lost much of his authority for me. But he still meant to me a superior personality upon whom I projected the Father and at the time of the dream this projection was still far from eliminated."[15] He regarded Freud as a wiser man with much greater experience and believed that he should simply listen to what he had to say "and learn from him".[16]

The key characteristics of the dream, could in fact, contradict any such veneration. First, the Customs official was really a ghost and second he had refused to die properly. If Freud's principle of the death wish meant anything at all, it could not have expressed itself more clearly. Jung refused to accept this interpretation. "I could find no part of myself that normally might have had such a wish, for I wanted at all costs to be able to work with Freud."

It is fascinating to see how the masters of psycho-analysis require complete subservience to the holy tablets in other people but frequently resist their self-application. Creator of the collective unconscious, devotee of the personal unconscious and a man given to exploring hidden motives within the profoundest dungeons of the mind, Jung now accepted surface interpretations of the most superficial kind and released a cloud of woolly definitions to explain away what, in everyday language, could be reduced to simpler terms. Clearly, with Freud out of the way, he would become the Holy Master himself – in later years that was the term he used to describe Freud. Freud also represented a formidable intellectual challenge far more serious than anything offered by any of his disciples. The reasons for the death wish were clear, but Jung wrote: "The dream could be regarded as a corrective, as a compensation or antidote for my conscious high opinion and admiration." [17]

A second dream followed which Jung related to the first. Now he was walking in a modern Italian city, with a fierce sun beating down on the narrow streets, but the city had ambivalent characteristics drawn from the Swiss town of Basle and an Italian city like Bergamo. In the heat of a midsummer day, a stream of people dressed in the modern manner, came pouring towards him, but suddenly there appeared among them a remarkable apparition – a medieval knight in crusading dress. Even more remarkable, the knight passed through the modern streets full of contemporary men and women but no one drew back to comment on this extraordinary anachronism. "It was as though he were completely invisible to everyone but me," Jung wrote. Bewildered by the contradiction, he desperately desired to ask someone what it meant, but before he could formulate the question a voice spoke in his head: "Yes, this is a regular apparition. The knight always passes by here between twelve and one o'clock, and has been doing so for a very long time (for centuries I gathered) and everyone knows about it." [18]

Jung regarded the first dream as quite prosaic and the second as "numinous in the extreme". Interpreting the second dream, Jung related the knight's medieval trappings to the twelfth century, a period when alchemy developed and the quest for the Holy Grail began, both matters of the highest importance to Jung from the age of 15. Similarly, when he identified his world with that of a medieval knight's he remained logically sound. He had always imagined that a great secret lay hidden behind the stories of the Holy Grail, and the knights of the Grail and their quest were equivalent to his own search for "something still unknown which might confer meaning upon the banality of life".

If this introduced an old-world chivalry into his search, that was not unexpected because Jung never fell short of aspiring to gracious objectives, but when the interpretation stopped at this point, it failed to complete the triple allegory – Freud – Jung – Knight. It was easy to see Freud also as a crusader who brought an entirely new message to mankind but the common herd did not even notice his presence in their midst. Not merely the common herd, but doctors and psychiatrists made it necessary for Freud to fight a crusade which, indeed, he was most bravely accomplishing.

No single dream has one interpretation, but when Jung claimed that these two dreams were in effect one, then interpretation of the first should have extended into the second. Instead, perhaps once more anticipating the break, he excluded Freud from his interpretations of the second dream.

As early as February 1909, Jung's nervousness about Freud's concentration on sexual etiology became clear. On the 25th he wrote to Jones: "We should do well not to burst out with the theory of sexuality in the foreground... Both with students and with patients I get on further by not making the theme of sexuality prominent." Reflecting on the ethical aspects of sexuality he had come to the conclusion, he said, that "in publicly announcing certain things one would saw off the branch on which civilization rests." Since this converted doubts into organized resistance it was remarkable that Jones and Freud did not at once realize the direction which Jung must eventually take.

NOTES

1. *Memories, Dreams, Reflections*: C G Jung, p. 352.
2. *C G Jung*: E A Bennet, p. 44.
3. *The Life and Work of Sigmund Freud*: Ernest Jones, Vol. II, p. 165.
4. Verbal evidence from Ernest Jones.
5. *Memories, Dreams, Reflections*: C G Jung, p. 354.
6. *Memories, Dreams, Reflections*: C G Jung, p. 155.
7. Verbal evidence from Ernest Jones.
8. *Memories, Dreams, Reflections*: C G Jung, p. 156.
9. *C G Jung*: E A Bennet, p. 41.
10. *International Journal of Psycho-Analysis*: Freud's Obituary on Ferenczi, 14 (3), pp. 297–9.
11. *An Autobiographical Study*: Sigmund Freud, p. 95.
12. *Ibid.*

13. *Sigmund Freud: Life and Work*: Ernest Jones, Vol. II, p. 67.
14. *Memories, Dreams, Reflections*: C G Jung, p. 147.
15. *Memories, Dreams, Reflections*: C G Jung, p. 159.
16. Ibid.
17. *Memories, Dreams, Reflections*: C G Jung, p. 160.
18. Ibid.

Chapter Nine

Disagreements with Jung

It is important to remember that in the labyrinth which now engulfed the leading figures of psycho-analysis, Freud – according to some of his own disciples – had one driving purpose. He wanted to reorganize the psycho-analytic movement with a new centre in the heart of Europe under a leader who did not generate the confused love and hate which had grown up around his own person. Above all, he wanted to create conditions which would preserve the purity of psycho-analytic practice as he saw it, for the future. This meant accepting a minimum number of basic concepts, without agreement on which men could not, he felt, work together.

In the long run Jung's archetypes, collective unconscious and individuation all differed from Freud's doctrines. Jung's modifications of sexual etiology and of very early conditioning were followed by differences about the interpretation of the word libido. There were also divergencies about "prospective tendencies", the "need for psycho-synthesis", and the Oedipal complex.

For the moment, these issues had not led to the final clash and in March 1910 Jung hurried off to America to lecture once more. When he repeated the visit in 1911, Freud became worried about the recurring absences of the "Crown Prince". They were now coming to the crucial stage of their relationship between the years 1911 and 1913 and Freud wrote to Puister: "Jung is in America... I am trembling about his return. What will happen if my Zürichers desert me?" Shortly afterwards he wrote to Pfister again asking him to stand loyally by Jung: "I want him to acquire an authority that will later qualify him for leadership of the whole movement." One of the roles of this leadership he later revealed was to "instruct and admonish", a duty which, he admitted, "he himself had carried out until then".[1]

Fresh trouble presently broke out with Bleuler and he wrote once more to Pfister saying that Bleuler's charges against what he called "an intolerant sect" were easy to refute. "The intolerance is really not on our side."

Abraham wrote to Freud on 24 October 1910, stating that he had been in continuous correspondence with Bleuler and "things are as you say". Bleuler's arguments were vague and full of imponderables. "I have agreed to go to Zürich over Christmas if he will give me a chance to compose matters." Bleuler himself had expressed a wish to discuss the matter personally and Abraham "had, of course, no intention of sacrificing the society".[2]

Late in 1912 the clouds began to darken. The pressures of puritan social sanctions were driving the Swiss analysts into a corner and the popular press now denounced the iniquitous ideas which were pouring into Switzerland from Vienna. Only three Swiss analysts held out against the mounting tide of public opinion but several followed an ambiguous course which made a qualified loyalty possible. Jung was writing in *Wissen und Leben*:[3]

> "The sexual indelicacies which unfortunately occupy a necessarily large place in many psycho-analytic writings are not to be blamed on psycho-analysis itself. Our very exacting and responsible medical work merely brings these unlovely fantasies to light, but the blame for the existence of these some times repulsive and evil things must surely lie with the mendaciousness of our sexual morality."

Other difficulties were of more immediate concern to Freud. It distressed him that the man he had hoped would play the role of International President, acting as a central focus for all psycho-analytic activities, supervising the administrative work of congresses and inspiring fresh psycho-analytic research, was too absorbed in his own researches to carry out these duties adequately. Freud was no judge of persons and he had mistakenly expected from Jung administrative capacities which were alien to the creative research worker. He was, in short, as Jones remarks, entirely unsuited to the job of President. Obsessional concentration on detached research made him an erratic correspondent and Freud became disturbed when replies to his letters were not immediately forthcoming. Freud had something of a neurosis about letters. Any delay in receiving a reply would worry him and his imagination sometimes invoked a series of unnecessary troubles and disasters. Now, with

Jung, he experienced what he had known with Fliess. Jung's answers to his letters became very uncertain.

Something far more serious now supervened. Jung had been working for some time on his great book *Psychology of the Unconscious*, and as he approached the chapter called "The Sacrifice", he knew, in advance, that its publication would cost him his friendship with Freud.

Quite unknown to Freud, Ferenczi, Jones or any member of the inner circle, Jung now underwent a great personal struggle with himself. The conflict reached a pitch where he could no longer convey a word to paper — which explained his failure to reply to Freud's letters — and for two whole months such was his state of torment, that he could not touch his pen. "Should I keep my thoughts to myself or should I risk the loss of so important a friendship?" In the end he decided to take the risk. As he wrote the chapter, Jung knew that Freud would find it impossible to accept his interpretation of the concept of incest.

Perhaps because he feared Freud's reaction to the publication of his book, or because he had finally made up his mind to break with Freud, Jung failed to meet him at Kreuzlingen when Freud went to visit a sick friend there, and found himself close to Jung. A dangerous operation which threatened Binswanger's life had drawn Freud away from Vienna and an overwhelming mass of work, to visit Binswanger and he had written to Jung saying that he would be in Kreuzlingen for forty-eight hours. Jung might have felt that if Freud was not prepared to extend his journey by the small distance required to reach Zürich from Kreuzlingen then he was equally unwilling to travel to Kreuzlingen, but the onus to make the journey did seem to rest on him. Freud duly arrived in Kreuzlingen and stayed from Saturday midday to Monday, but there was no sign of Jung.

The word Kreuzlingen took on a special meaning for the two men. According to Jones, "Jung made sarcastic remarks in letters to Freud about 'understanding his gesture of Kreuzlingen'." Certainly Freud's mode of address in his letters slowly under went a change until "Lieber Freund" became "Lieber Herr Doktor".

In May 1911 Jung revealed to Freud that he could not accept a strictly sexual interpretation of the word libido and now regarded it as almost synonymous with general psychic energy. Both discussed their respective definitions in the correspondence which followed. Surprisingly Frau Jung herself entered the correspondence and warned Freud that he would not sympathize with what her husband was about to say in print.

Jung's famous paper, *Symbols of the Libido*, first appeared in two parts in the *Jahrbuch der Psychoanalyse* for 1911.[4] Jones read a proof of the second part and wrote to Freud outlining the essay. This drove Freud to send for a copy of the Jahrbuch and immediately he had read the paper he wrote to Jones pinpointing the precise page where Jung had, in his view, gone astray – page 174. However, much later,[5] Freud himself wrote a paper *On Narcissism: An Introduction*, which struck some of his followers as unexpected and gave a new resolution to the whole issue.

Jung now came right out into the open and told Freud that incest wishes were symbols of other tendencies and could not be taken literally. As he later wrote:

"To me incest signified a personal complication only in the rarest cases. Usually incest has a highly religious aspect for which reason the incest theme plays a decisive part in almost all cosmogonies and in numerous myths. But Freud clung to the literal interpretation of it and could not grasp the spiritual significance of incest as a symbol."[6]

Correspondence then broke down for five weeks. On 13 June, Freud made an attempt to save the situation, and wrote saying that there was no need for theoretical differences to disturb their personal relations.

In August, Abraham, writing to Freud, was still hopeful. "I have heard quite a lot about Zürich in the last few weeks... My own prognosis is not too unfavourable." Jung's attitude reminded Abraham of Adler's but "since we are dealing with a person without a paraphrenic tendency, it may all change again, just as it did four years ago". According to Abraham's letter, Jung was still uncertain which precise path to follow.

Freud replied to Abraham saying that his prophecy about Jung in an earlier letter – "to which he had at the time refused to listen" – was coming true, but he had no desire to precipitate a break.

Jung once more crossed the Atlantic to lecture to the Americans and now, on his return, he wrote a long letter to Freud in which he claimed that by omitting sexual themes he had made psycho-analysis much more acceptable to many American intellectuals. Freud brusquely replied that it needed no great brilliance to carry out such a feat. Indeed why not go further? Why not leave out more and win even more false sympathy?

James Putnam wrote to Ernest Jones from Boston on 24 October 1912 giving an account of his encounters with Jung in America:

"...I made two attempts to meet Dr Jung in New York and the last one was in so far successful that I heard his address, though unfortunately missing the first part of it; and I had a few words with him afterwards...

What Dr Jung said in effect was that while he still held to the importance of the psycho-analytic technique he had come to rate the infantile fixations as of far less importance than formerly as an etiological factor and indeed as I understood him, as an almost neglible factor in most cases – though I hardly think he could really maintain this if he were pushed for a positive opinion. At any rate, the point on which he seems now inclined to lay emphasis is the difficulty of meeting new problems and environmental conditions which arise at the time of the actual onset of the neurosis. It seems to me that we all recognize the importance of these influences and I cannot as yet feel that anything is won through minimizing the significance of the other factor..."[7]

Relations between Freud and Jung now seemed to go from bad to worse, but as late as September 1912, Freud said that if their earlier personal feelings could be restored there was no real danger of a break. A meeting which followed in Munich in November seemed superficially to reconcile them. It was a meeting called by Jung himself to transfer the editorship of the *Zentralblatt* to Stekel while a new *Zeitschzrift* was founded to take its place. Jones records a small confusion over the arrangements whereby he almost failed to arrive in time. He was staying in Florence for a month and Jung not only sent the notification of the meeting to his home in Wales, but actually gave Jones the wrong date substituting – was the unconscious at work? – 25 November for 24 November. It is conceivable that Jung did not want Jones to be present because Jones was clearly an unquestioning disciple of Freud's. When Jones told Freud what had happened, Freud remarked with his usual wit: "A gentleman should not do such things even unconsciously." Jones did, in fact, turn up on the correct day, but only because he discovered the date by accident from Vienna.

The meeting began at nine o'clock in the morning when Jung proposed that the change-over of journals be accepted without further discussion, but Freud insisted on giving an account of the difficulties he had encountered with Stekel. Everyone sympathized with Freud, his proposals were accepted, and the meeting ended just after eleven o'clock.

Later, Freud and Jung set off on a long walk together, and now, the mystery of the Kreuzlingen gesture became clearer. Jung first complained with some bitterness that he had not received Freud's letter about his visit until Monday, the day on which Freud returned to Vienna. Freud was astonished. Both letters he protested – one to Binswanger and one to Jung – had been posted simultaneously on the preceding Thursday. He agreed that if his letter to Jung did not arrive until Monday, then he had every excuse for not meeting him, and his own behaviour had been questionable. And then Jung suddenly recalled that he had in fact been away for two days at that weekend which explained why he had not received the letter until Monday.

According to Jones, Freud "let off steam" and "did not spare him a good fatherly lecture". Jones added, Jung accepted all the criticisms and promised to reform.[8]

Luncheon followed, and Freud was in high spirits, believing that once more all their troubles were over, and the Crown Prince had abandoned any idea of abdication. From what followed, it is clear that whatever his conscious mind believed, unconsciously Freud remained very anxious and unconvinced. Towards the end of the luncheon he suddenly turned to the two Swiss analysts, Jung and Riklin, and asked them why, in recent articles explaining psycho-analysis, they had not mentioned his name. As the unquestioned originator of the whole psycho-analytic movement, Freud certainly had grounds for complaint. Jung rationalized the omission by oblique flattery. It was too well known that Freud had founded psycho-analysis, he said. There was no need any longer to mention his name in historical recapitulations. This, of course, sounded very disingenuous to Freud, who suddenly wondered, all over again, whether his attempts at *rapprochement* with Jung were doomed to failure.

A dramatic reaction followed. He slid to the floor in a dead faint. This was hysterical transference with a vengeance, but none of the distinguished psycho-analysts who recorded the event described it as such.

The very powerful Jung at once picked Freud up in his arms and "carried him to a couch in the lounge". Quickly Freud revived and his first words as he came round were: "How sweet it must be to die." Commonsense interpretation said that he could not face the possibility that Jung was still a traitor and blotted out the thought with unconsciousness. Secondary interpretation said that he had registered Jung's hidden desire to break away from him as a death wish against him and so powerful did it become that momentarily he underwent a kind of death. Beyond these explanations lay many other complexities: one which Freud himself elaborated to Jones: "I cannot forget that...years ago I suffered from very similar though not such intense symptoms in the same room of the Park Hotel." He had first seen Munich when he visited Fliess there and the town "acquired a strong connection with my relations to that man". The time has come to examine in greater depth the evidence which points to a homosexual element in Freud's nature. The evidence cannot be seen in perspective unless we follow the line of development from those early days of Wilhelm Fliess, a man whose presence re echoed throughout many years of Freud's life. It is necessary to leave for the moment the crucial meeting in Munich and dip back deeply into the early history of the late 1900s.

Something very profound maintained Freud's relationship with Fliess at an intense pitch over the course of fifteen years. There was an emotional tie which can be seen in the letters as more powerful than any previous biographer has so far acknowledged. Far back on 7 July 1897 Freud had written to Fliess: "What has been going on inside me I still do not know. Something from the deepest depths of my neurosis has been obstructing any progress and you were somehow involved in it all..."[9]

On 23 March 1900, in a long, moving and beautifully written letter he said that he had been through a "profound inner crisis" and "your suggestion of a meeting at Easter greatly stirred me". He would willingly sacrifice everything he wrote "for the satisfaction of having you near me for three days". "...it is a matter of feeling – of an exceedingly obscure nature."

An extraordinary coincidence followed in 1902. Fliess had fallen ill in the same room of the Park Hotel, Munich, where Freud ten years later met Jung and fainted. During the visit to Fliess, Freud suffered, in the same room, "very similar though not such intense symptoms". Then came this vital statement in a letter to Jones: "*There is some piece of unruly homosexual feeling at the root of the matter.*"[10]

Now it would be easy to conclude that Freud had homosexual elements in his make-up, but were these elements more marked than they are in the "normal" individual? Such feelings certainly played a part in his relationship with Fliess. If this supposition provokes a storm of protest from orthodox Freudians it will put them in the awkward position of regarding as a smear on Freud what they would claim to be "normal" for the rest of mankind. Jones categorically stated: "There is ample evidence that for ten years or so...[Freud] suffered from a very considerable psycho-neurosis". He also claimed that during the years when the neurosis became fierce (1897–1900 the most intense years with Fliess) Freud did his most original work. Thus it is possible that his sublimated homosexual impulse redirected his libido to the highest creative purposes. The neurotic symptoms were "one of the ways in which the unconscious material was indirectly trying to emerge", and without these psychic pressures Freud might have remained a clever but unoriginal professor living out a peaceful academic life in Vienna.

Jones admitted that the unconscious conflict of his relationship with Fliess "must have played an important part in Freud's temporary outbreak of neurosis". He did not point out that the preliminary symptoms of heart trouble in April 1894 were followed in August 1894, when he met Fliess in Nuremberg, by very similar symptoms to the fainting fit which followed with Jung in 1912. Jones admits that "the more passionate side of married life subsided with [Freud] earlier than it does with many men".[11] Jones also states: "Freud was quite peculiarly monogamous. Of few men can it be said that they go through the whole of life without being erotically motivated in any serious fashion by any woman beyond the one and only one."[12] There was, again, a very deep attachment if not fixation on the mother. It emerges first in Freud's letter to Fliess of 15 October 1897: "I was crying my heart out because my mother was nowhere to be found... When I found that my mother was not there... I cried still more."[13] But much more powerfully in Freud's letter of 3 October 1897 he recalled spending a night with his mother, seeing her naked and having sexual wishes about her. In a later letter to Fliess he spoke of his infatuation with his mother. He also records a very vivid dream in which he saw his "beloved mother" carried into a room by two or three people with birds' beaks instead of noses. "This anxiety dream could be traced back to an obscure and evidently sexual craving."[14] All this fits the classic Freudian syndrome as a prerequisite for many homosexuals. In short, the mother fixation seems to come through more powerfully than the father fixation. Even more explicitly, Freud had written to Ferenczi on 6 October 1910 saying that he no longer had any need to uncover his personality completely and that Ferenczi had correctly discovered why: "Since Fliess' case...that need has been extinguished. A part of homosexual cathexis has been withdrawn and made use of to enlarge my ego."

Take all these factors together: a deep devotion to, and sexual interest in, the mother, a failure to respond erotically to any woman except his wife, the cessation of sexual relations between them, a volcanic upheaval in his own nature which came to him as a shock simultaneously with his passionate devotion to Fliess and the remark – there is some piece of unruly homosexual feeling at the root of the matter – and they seem to point in an obvious direction. Did Freud suddenly discover in middle age a repressed homosexuality in himself which broke through into consciousness and revealed a serious neurosis? If there was a powerful homosexual pull towards Fliess it would explain his experiences in the Park Hotel, his neurotic heart condition and his final determination to discover the cause of his profound inner crisis by a brave, if not masterly, attempt at self-analysis. Moreover, the issue over which they finally broke was the issue of bisexuality and once again Jones believed that the final quarrel took place in the same room of the Park Hotel. Above all it would give a gigantic new thrust to Freud's growing belief in the hidden sexual secret beneath every neurosis and reaffirm him in the true nature of his life's work if a latent homosexual impulse had suddenly revealed itself in his own person.

Yet another factor becomes explicable. How Freud managed to sustain reverence for, and utter devotion to, a man whose theories not merely undermined the validity of his own, but belonged to the world of novelty rather than science certainly needs explanation. According to Fliess the onset of neurotic symptoms, their development, change and even cessation were all determined by the crucial dates revealed in his periodic laws and this "revelation" disintegrates the etiological character of Freud's interpretation. Jones remarked that "neither could have had much real understanding of the other's work, all they demanded was mutual admiration of it". The professional relationship then was a camouflage for the personal relationship and the personal relationship never fully expressed itself. Freud, above all men, had supremely the capacity for sublimation.

Although I have not myself directly read the full correspondence between Freud and Jung,[15] I have had the advantage of discussing those letters I have not read with Ernest Jones and with one other person who has seen every letter. Both agreed that the subject of homosexuality is discussed in the unpublished correspondence. In the midst of many uncertainties one point at least is clear. Whatever degree of homosexual attraction may have occurred between these three men, none was what the law calls a *practising* homosexual.

It remains to say that if these interpretations seem valid within Freud's own theories, some modern psycho-analysts have carried their investigations of homosexuality into more complex places. Freud held that paranoia and fear of being pushed into a weak position by men, were characteristics of homosexuality, which seems to fit my interpretation and his behaviour, but as Dr Charles Rycroft has stated: "Contemporary analysts tend to reverse the relationship and regard homosexuality as a defensive technique for dealing with paranoid fears by submission." He also points out that Freud's statement about his homosexual cathexis "is not admissible evidence in support of the thesis since it is a theoretical inference not a statement of psychological fact arrived at by introspection".

Certainly Freud had an unresolved conflict about men which "led him to reject his father...seek support and approbation from younger men", and desire to establish them as authorities. Thus he did not accept the presidency of the International Psycho-Analytical Association even though he could naturally claim it, but instead nominated successive disciples. This conflict can, in his own terms, be characterized as having homosexual elements but Dr Rycroft qualifies this:

"As Rado pointed out many years ago the notion of 'latent homosexuality' is misleading since it implies that persons who display the pathology so designated are really homosexual. But persons with 'latent' homosexual problems do not, if analysed, become manifest homosexuals; they become less frightened of men, less dependent and more heterosexual. Clinically, even overt homosexuality regularly turns out to be a defensive manoeuvre not an instinctual activity." [16]

NOTES

1. On the History of the Psycho-Analytic Movement: Sigmund Freud (Collected Works, Standard Edition, Vol. 14, pp. 42–43).
2. Letters of Sigmund Freud and Karl Abraham: edited Hilda C Abraham and Ernst L Freud, p. 95.
3. Translated from Zur Psychoanalyse Wissen und Leben (Zürich; former title of the Neue Schweizer Rundschau), V (1912), pp. 711–14.
4. C G Jung, Wandlungen und Symbole der Libido, Erster Teil, Jahrbuch der Psychoanalyse, 1911, III, 120–227 Zweiter Teil, 1912, IV.
5. 1914.
6. Memories, Dreams, Reflections: C G Jung, p. 162.
7. I am grateful to Dr Marian C Putnam for permission to quote from her father's letter.
8. Sigmund Freud: Life and Work: Ernest Jones, Vol. II, p. 165.
9. The Origins of Psycho-Analysis: Sigmund Freud, p. 337.
10. My italics. Freud to Jones, 8 December 1912.
11. Sigmund Freud: Life and Work: Ernest Jones, Vol. II, p. 431.
12. Ibid., p. 469.
13. The Origins of Psycho-Analysis: Sigmund Freud, p. 222.
14. The Interpretation of Dreams: Sigmund Freud, Vol. II, pp. 583–4.
15. Both the Freud and Jung Archives have agreed to suspend publication for thirty years.
16. Letter to the author, 19 January 1966.

Chapter Ten

The Break with Jung

When the five men dispersed from the Munich meeting again, they were superficially reconciled to Freud's leadership and Ferenczi remained optimistic about the future. Jung reassured Freud as they parted and wrote a letter from Zurich which Jones said was a humble letter "expressing again his great contrition and desire to reform".[1] It has been said that in certain moods, Freud could, when he chose, convert his personality into a charismatic presence which people found magnetic, and either this magnetism worked its way with Jung once more, or Jung had indeed changed his mind.

The *rapprochement* did not last. Once removed from the magnetic presence, Jung's doubts, resistance and finally hostility, broke through once more. Freud pointed out to Jung that his view of the incest complex had certain resemblances with that of Adler, and Jung wrote a strong rebuttal saying that the charge was a bitter pill for him to have to swallow. A fascinating slip occurred in one angry passage of the letter. Jung wrote: "not even Adler's companions think that I belong to your group", instead of writing, "their group". This seemed to let the cat fully out of the bag. Jung's unconscious had certainly defected from the Holy Writ, if his conscious self still refused to admit it. Jung professed to take an objective view in all this, and Freud could not resist asking him for an opinion of his slip of the pen. "By return of post there came an explosive and very offensive reply on the subject of Freud's 'neurosis'."[2]

Freud told Ernest Jones that he "felt humiliated at being addressed in such a manner", and wondered what to say in reply. Finally he wrote a letter but did not post it. The letter, dated 22 December 1912, has since come to light. Among other things it said: "I regret that my reference to your slip of the pen has irritated you so much and I feel that your reaction is out of proportion to the occasion." He would not presume to judge, Freud said, Jung's reproach that he, Freud, abused psycho-analysis in order to keep his pupils "in infantile dependency", or that he alone was responsible for "their infantile behaviour towards" him, because personal judgments were very difficult and subject to sad errors. He would only say that in Vienna, they charged him with the precise opposite, namely that he concerned himself "too little with the analysis of his pupils". Both with Stekel and Adler, he had avoided for many years any references to the analysis of their own persons. The letter ended "With cordial greetings".

Three months later Freud wrote to Abraham on 27 March saying that Jung was once more in America working more for himself than psycho-analysis. "I have greatly retreated from him and have no more friendly thoughts for him. His bad theories do not compensate me for his disagreeable character."

His mood fluctuated widely in the following weeks. On 13 May he wrote arrogantly to Ferenczi: "We possess the truth; I am as sure of it as fifteen years ago."

Even as late as 1 June 1913 he wrote to Abraham: "Jung is crazy but I have no desire for a separation and should like to let him wreck himself first." By 31 July, he said to Abraham that he had received a letter from Jung, "complaining about misunderstandings and making some supercilious remarks that I find difficult to follow." Remembering the everlasting misunderstandings he only regretted that the Zürichers had "lost the gift of making themselves intelligible".

Far into the year, both Freud and Jung were still trying to prevent personal differences from interfering with professional relations and leading to a final break. Freud optimistically believed that formal co-operation was possible even within the bickering which had now become commonplace and wrecked their personal ties. Both men approached the last Congress of the International Psycho-Analytical Association at Munich, on 7 September 1913, "in the expectation that there would be no open break".

From America, England, Germany, Austria and Hungary, eighty-seven members and guests of the still rapidly growing psycho-analytic movement converged on the Bayerischer Hof on 7 September. They quickly fell into different groups with different sympathies and many small private "meetings" were held to examine the latest developments in the schism which now threatened to break right out into the open. Ferenczi, Freud and Jones were seen together frequently and Ferenczi was said to have coined the witty remark which has since re-echoed down the corridors of psycho-analysis: "The Jung no longer believe in Freud."

According to Ernest Jones "the scientific level of the papers was mediocre" – but he graciously allowed two close Freudians, Abraham and Ferenczi, the distinction of delivering "two interesting ones". Still the careful devotee, he recorded that one Swiss paper, overwhelmed with statistics, became so prolonged and tedious that Freud remarked: "All sorts of criticism have been brought against psycho-analysis but this is the first time anyone could have called it boring."[3]

Since Ernest Jones wrote his biography the private journal of Lou Andreas-Salomé has become available and it throws new light on the Munich Congress. Under the date 7–8 September, she wrote:

"At the Congress the Zürich members sat at their own table opposite Freud's. Their behaviour towards Freud can be characterized in a word: it is not so much that Jung diverges from Freud, as that he does it in such a way as if he had taken it on himself to rescue Freud and his cause by these divergences. If Freud takes up the lance to defend himself it is misconstrued to mean that he cannot show scientific tolerance, is dogmatic and so forth. One glance at the two of them tells which is the more dogmatic, the more in love with power. Two years ago Jung's booming laughter gave voice to a kind of robust gaiety and exuberant vitality, but now his earnestness is composed of pure aggression, ambition and intellectual brutality."[4]

She had never felt so close to Freud, she wrote, and she realized that it was only with the greatest difficulty that Freud restrained himself under the conflicting pressures. She and Tausk sat beside Freud, but Freud was still holding Tausk off, although he realized that he represented a wonderful ally in a situation of this kind.

Jones, another eyewitness of the proceedings, merely records that Jung now conducted "the meetings in such a fashion that it was felt some gesture of protest should be made". Lou Andreas Salomé spelt out the difficulty. "…at last all political manoeuvring was at an end after a winter when it reigned supreme; one could, one ought, one had the right to thunder. And Tausk knew how. He had to leave again on the second morning after he had done his task. But Jung had improperly shortened the time of our paper." Freud himself later explained that in his view Jung needlessly restricted the time given to individual speakers and allowed discussion to overwhelm the papers.[5]

Between meetings, considerable lobbying went on behind the scenes, but no one knows how belligerently Jung's supporters worked on his behalf or how far Freud's friends went in stiffening the morale of the faithful.

In the presidential election which followed, Jung accepted re-election with 52 votes against 22. Moreover this was not the result of a free vote. Abraham had suggested that those who disapproved should abstain from voting. Jones abstained and afterwards Jung came up to him and said, "I thought you were a Christian." According to Jones, Jung meant by this that he was not a Jew, but colloquial English allows the more common interpretation that he was not a generous, tolerant person. Jones, quite rightly, wondered how far Jung's anti-Semitism conditioned this remark and his whole attitude to Freud, and it will be necessary later to enquire in detail, whether Jung was in fact anti-Semitic.

In the midst of many uncertainties, the last International Conference drew to an uneasy close and Freud immediately went off to his beloved Rome, where his sister-in-law, Minna Bernays, joined him. It was interesting that his sister-in-law not his wife went to Bologna to meet him. Helen Puner has already referred to "Freud's extraordinary married life", but she was so wrong about the presence not merely of passion in his early love for Martha, but a poetic, romantic love since revealed in a series of beautiful love letters, that her account of Freud's "double" family life needs sceptical examination. The arrangement whereby he lived under the same roof with his wife and his wife's sister, relegating to Martha the endless domestic duties and finding intellectual companionship with Minna, certainly seemed odd. According to Helen Puner, "outwardly the marriage was as orthodoxly correct as Freud's morals. Inwardly, as Freud unconsciously revealed, it lacked lustre and joy. It was as if Freud's capacity for love, naturally great, were encased in a block of ice."[6] Helen Puner read into a dream of Freud's considerable distaste for his wife which may have had no basis in fact. In the dream a woman he later identified as his wife had a "pale puffy face and false teeth". Freud admitted that he had treated his wife very ungallantly in the dream, and what husband, at some time, has not had an ugly dream about his wife?

The family pattern, none the less, did to some extent, reinforce the possibility of homosexual inclinations. "It was as if Freud's capacity for love...were encased in a block of ice." It also revealed an authoritarian pattern characteristic of a Jewish family. As Helen Puner said: "the atmosphere of rigid Jewish ethics which he fought so furiously, he succeeded in re-creating in his own household", and to her, the extension of an authoritarian father became clear in his psycho-analytic circle.

The women of the household created a perfect domestic background where everything ran with clockwork precision and the children were expected to conform to the prescribed pattern. Helen Puner repeats a story which was circulating among a group of disciples: "When one of the children had been away from the house for a time and was met by another, it was said the child who had been at home was quick to pass on the latest development in the household. 'Father now drinks his tea', the story made the child say, 'from the green cup instead of from the blue one.' "[7]

Helen Puner comments: "As the children grew, their awe for him grew. But it grew neither as fast nor as luxuriantly as his own patriarchal, Mosaic attitude towards them."

Did he extend this attitude towards his professional children in psycho-analytic circles? Was he incapable of allowing the spiritual sons of psycho-analysis "any greater degree of self-determination or freedom than he could the children of his flesh"? Helen Puner thought so, and Jung agreed with her but traced it back to different origins. Jones flatly denied that Jung's interpretation of his troubles with Freud was valid, and poured scorn on Helen Puner's picture of Freud's family life.

The last few months of 1913, brought the whole question of the secession of Jung to a new head. Jung wrote to Ferenczi asking him why he had not supported him as president at the congress, and Ferenczi gave this reply: "It was only the absolutely improper way in which you as Chairman of the Congress dealt with the suggestions we put forward, the quite one-sided and partial comments you made on all the papers read, and also the personal behaviour on the part of your group, that caused us to protest by voting with blank cards."[8]

Before Jung received this letter, he had already written a final note to Freud saying that he had "heard from Maeder that Freud doubted his 'bona fides'."[9] After the reception of such news no further collaboration with Freud was possible, he said, and he forthwith resigned his editorship of the *Jahrbuch*.[10]

On 2 November, Freud passed on the news to Abraham. Jung, he said, had given up the editorship "with a display of injured innocence". What he really wanted, he said, was to get rid of the editorial board and then take over sole control of the journal himself. The board, Freud said, unanimously believed that they should not abandon their rights or their position. He was quite prepared to continue the *Jahrbuch* if Abraham would edit it.

His letter, a very straightforward, business-like letter, outlined two questions, the second of fundamental importance: "We think the time has come to think of a severance of old ties with Zürich and thus to dissolve the International Psycho-Analytic Association."

What followed revealed that Freud not Jung took the initiative in forcing Jung out of the Freudian School. The best way of bringing about the dissolution, Freud wrote to Abraham, was to send the Central Office a resolution signed by the Budapest, Vienna and Berlin groups, calling for a dissolution. if Jung and the Zurichers rejected the proposal, the three groups could withdraw independently and "promptly form a new organization". It would be a tactical mistake he thought to "begin by resigning", because Jung would remain president. "Similarly, in the event of our resignation, the new organization would have to elect me as President to put an end to the falsifications of the Zürichers."

This introduced a political element into the quarrel and carried echoes of party manoeuvring to oust from power a distasteful deviationist. Freud added that they were in touch with Jones about the possibility of support for their plan from America. "Please keep the matter secret for the time being," he concluded.

Abraham read this letter with some anxiety and confusion. In his desire to re-form their ranks as quickly as possible, Freud over looked a number of delicate constitutional difficulties which Abraham was quick to point out to him on 4 November 1913: "On going through [the rules] I notice that the President is elected for a term of two years. We could not, therefore, elect a different President in the autumn of 1914." Abraham questioned the wisdom of adopting a new policy at this time, since the proposal made by the three groups could "too easily come to nothing", and they "would then be forced to secede" themselves, which would bring their wrath down on their own heads. He could not, he added, be certain that Berlin would follow Freud as a group because only nine of the eighteen members were in Berlin, and one at least, Stockmayer – a man who had settled in Berlin recently – remained very close to Jung. "Berlin", he added, "may become very important in future and it would be a pity if political differences were to occur in our circle just now." [11]

Freud replied on 6 November discussing tactics in detail, and trying to find some means of making Jung take the initiative in the dissolution. He now clearly saw that under the terms of their contract they could not prevent the Zürich members from insisting on their right to continue publishing "all [their] rubbish in the *Korrespondenzblatt*". On the other hand, a clause occurred in the rules which said that the society was conceived for the purpose of cultivating Freudian psycho-analysis and if he, Freud, issued a statement showing the deliberate deviation [12] of the Zurichers, "that would give us a smooth handle to call for its dissolution". If this did not work, in the last resort the risks of secession by the three groups had to be faced even if it meant losing "about a third of their membership".

Because he felt so uncertain which course of action to follow, Freud decided to circulate Abraham's letter to "our friends" and "then you and all the others must consider the most advisable course".

Abraham replied the following day with an unexpectedly powerful attack on Jung. Both the Freudians and the Jungians had been in touch with Deuticke the publisher of the *Jahrbuch*, making independent offers for continuing to edit that journal, and Freud had read into Jung's approach a desire "to gain sole control of it after my withdrawal". This was complicated by the fact that Jung, initially, had told Deuticke that he wanted to give up the *Jahrbuch*. Now Abraham read the worst possible motives into Jung's manoeuvres.

"I consider it unethical for the President of an Association to negotiate with a publisher behind our backs, as Stekel once did... In my opinion the Association cannot tolerate such underhand activity."[13] Suddenly his mood had changed and he was now in favour of taking extreme measures against Jung. Jones made it clear to Freud that he thought Ferenczi's plan for the Vienna, Berlin and Budapest groups to join forces and request Jung to wind up the International Association, was too full of hazards. Ferenczi expected Jones to persuade the British and American Societies to take similar action, but Jung had not yet recognized the British Society, and the Americans, who had seen more of Jung than of any other psycho-analytic leader, were unlikely, with the exception of Brill, to agree. Jung had visited America on two recent occasions and received a warm reception. Like Abraham, Jones saw clearly that "if Jung refused to dissolve we should have to resign and he would be left in possession". When Jones put these doubts to Freud he at once telegraphed: "Letter just received. Excellent. Will have moderating effect and will be sent to our friends at once..."

The advice of Jones and Abraham prevailed. Even the impetuous Ferenczi agreed to abandon his plan and proceed with greater caution. Freud wrote to Abraham giving him this news on 9 November and added: "You know that in these matters I gladly let myself be advised by my friends as since being taken in by Jung my confidence in my political judgments has greatly declined."

The strain of these last months had taken its toll of Freud. He told Abraham that he was struggling with a severe laryngotracheitis which "I cannot account for". Self-diagnosis of psychosomatic symptoms did not come easily in the prolonged struggle with Jung. Early in April, two members of the American group visited Freud and tried to reassure him about the situation in the United States. Jung's influence was small in their own group, they said, but a second group strongly supported him. On 24 April, Freud wrote to Abraham: "You were certainly just as surprised as I was at how meticulously Jung carried out our own intentions; somehow we shall get rid of him and perhaps of the Swiss altogether."

From the letters which followed it looked very much as though the Freudians were about to deliver a series of attacks on Jung's next book. Certainly a number of very critical reviews appeared in the *Zeitsckrift*, but a bigger "bombshell" had been devised by Freud. It was a powerful polemical essay written by Freud himself. On 25 June, after the essay had at last appeared, Freud wrote to Abraham. "So the bombshell has now burst... I think we should allow the victims two or three weeks' time to collect themselves and react."

And then, at last, came news that Jung had already resigned his Presidency and it was unanimously decided that Abraham should become Acting President until the next Congress. In the outer world, international affairs were hurrying implacably towards the nightmare of the First World War, but before hostilities were openly declared Jung announced his withdrawal from the International Association and let it be known that no Swiss analyst from Zürich would attend the next Congress due to meet in Dresden in September.

Freud could not resist his jubilation: "I cannot suppress a cheer," he wrote to Abraham on 18 July. "So we have got rid of them."

Interestingly, the *British Medical Journal* for January 1914 gave an account of the split in which it referred to Jung's "return to a saner view of life".

Freud himself made a last comment which struck an entirely new and ruthless note. "So we are at last rid of them," he wrote to Abraham on 25 July, "the brutal, sanctimonious Jung and his disciples."

Both sides have subsequently claimed malicious damage from the other as a result of the final break-up. Jung said that the Freudians circulated rumours about his possible schizophrenia, and so adept and sustained were these rumours that it caused some damage to his practice and "lost me some of my students".

In the reminiscences he wrote at the age of eighty, he said: "After the break with Freud all my friends and acquaintances dropped away. My book was declared to be rubbish; I was a mystic and that settled the matter. Riklin and Maeder alone stuck by me."[14]

Freud later wrote an account of the break-up in his *History of the Psycho-Analytic Movement*. He had no idea, he said, that he had chosen a man who could neither tolerate nor wield authority, and "whose energies were relentlessly devoted to the furtherance of his own interests".[15] Freudians still maintain that throughout all these struggles Freud did not desire to establish a complete and fixed structure of psycho-analytic dogma, but merely a minimum of agreed concepts without which the working of any team must break down.[16]

Whatever the exact nature of his intention, the ironic counterpoint of human and international affairs now saw fit to make the cessation of strife between Freud and Jung almost coincidental with the declaration of the long-drawn-out, savage and unnecessary First World War.

NOTES
1. *Sigmund Freud: Life and Work*: Ernest Jones, Vol. II, p. 166.
2. *Ibid.*, p. 167.
3. *Sigmund Freud: Life and Work*: Ernest Jones, Vol. II, p. 115.
4. *The Freud Journal of Lou Andreas-Salomé*, p. 168.
5. *On the History of the Psycho-Analytic Movement*: Sigmund Freud (*Collected Works*, Standard Edition, Vol. 14, p. 45).
6. *Freud*: Helen Walker Puner, p. 136.
7. *Freud*: Helen Walker Puner, p. 141.
8. 13 November 1913.
9. *Sigmund Freud: Life and Works*: Ernest Jones, Vol. II, p. 169.
10. 17 October 1913.
11. *Letters of Sigmund Freud and Karl Abraham*, pp. 153–4.
12. Freud did not use the word deviation.
13. *Letters of Sigmund Freud and Karl Abraham*, pp. 153–4.
14. *Memories, Dreams, Reflections*: C G Jung, p. 162.
15. *On the History of the Psycho-Analytic Movement*: Sigmund Freud (*Collected Works*, Standard Edition, Vol. 14, pp. 42–43).
16. *La Révolution Psychanalytique*, Marthe Robert, Vol. I, p. 226.

Chapter Eleven

Was Jung Pro-Nazi or Anti-Semitic?

On 18 April 1946, Carl Gustav Jung wrote to the doyen of the Jungians in London, saying that the story of his anti-Semitism and Nazi sympathies originated with the Holy Father himself. When Jung quarrelled with him he had to find a reason for his incomprehensible behaviour and decided that he must be anti-Semitic.

Was there any truth in this? Did Jung reveal Nazi sympathies during the German occupation? Unravelling the whole complex story and assessing the reliability of witnesses has led into a labyrinth from which certain factors emerge clearly.

Although Switzerland remained unoccupied during the German occupation of Europe, a process of subtle infiltration seems to have penetrated the Psychiatric Clinic of the Burghölzli in Zurich in 1934. In his book, *The Solution of the German Problem*, Wilhelm Röpke claimed that when the famous Professor Kretschmer "found himself unable to continue his function as President of the German Association for Psychotherapy and as editor of the leading periodical, Professor Jung obligingly filled the vacancy left by his honest German colleague and accepted the Nazi invitation to take over his function."

Röpke's account continues: "After the *Gleichschaltung* (bringing into step) of the Association and its periodical, the first number of the Nazified paper (*Zentralblatt für Psychotherapie*, December 1933) was opened by a solemn introduction written by Professor Jung underlining the necessity of distinguishing thenceforward between a Germanic and a Jewish psychology, while in the same number the new *Reichsführer* of the psychotherapists, Professor M H Göring, pledged the members of the new association to Adolf Hitler's fundamental book *Mein Kampf*. In order to make it perfectly clear what the obliging attitude of Professor Jung meant, a few pages later (p. 142) the Reichsfuhrer declared: "Thanks to the fact that Dr C G Jung accepted the presidency...it has been possible to continue the scientific activity of the Association and of its periodical."

We need to turn to the year 1934 to discover the real roots of these charges. Jung had written in the *Zentralblatt für Psychotherapie* for January of 1934:

"The Aryan unconscious has a higher potential than the Jewish; that is the advantage and the disadvantage of a youthfulness not yet fully escaped from barbarism. In my opinion it has been a great mistake of all previous medical psychology to apply Jewish categories which are not even binding for all Jews, indiscriminately to Christians, Germans or Slavs. In so doing, medical psychology has declared the most precious secret of the Germanic peoples – the creatively prophetic depths of soul – to be a childishly banal morass, while for decades my warning voice has been suspected of anti-Semitism. The source of this suspicion is Freud. He did not know the Germanic soul any more than did all his Germanic imitators... Has the mighty apparition of National Socialism which the whole world watches with astonished eyes taught them something better?"

Written one year after Hitler came to power in Germany, this characteristically obscure passage is open to several interpretations. Threading through the contradictions three statements appear. The higher potential of the Aryan unconscious has advantages and disadvantages; there is a difference between Jewish and Aryan psychology; the mighty apparition of National Socialism has something better to teach us.

Taken together these statements do not amount to anti-Semitism. They do involve association with the Nazis. In December of the previous year (1933) Jung had discriminated sharply between Jew and Gentile in the *Zentralblatt für Psychotherapie*: "The factual differences between Germanic and Jewish psychology which have long been known to intelligent people shall no longer be wiped out and that can only be helpful to science." In any normal atmosphere these words were innocuous enough, but seen against the blazing context of Nazi anti-Semitism and the proclaimed intention of Hilter to obliterate the Jews, they could be read as endorsing the philosophic assumptions by which Himmler justified his purges. However, the statement that Germanic and Jewish psychology were different did not ask for any form of Jewish persecution.

On 27 February 1934, the Neue Zürcher Zeitung carried an article on German psychotherapy by Dr Gustav Bally, a Swiss psychiatrist. He wrote:

"Political conditions force scientific and learned societies in Germany to undertake a reorganization which is described in that country as 'co-ordinating them'. This consists essentially in the exclusion of all Jewish members and all those who do not subscribe to the national racial doctrine.

"The General German Society for Psychotherapy had to cease publication of the Zentralblatt für Psychotherapie in February 1933. Almost a year later, the periodical has appeared again [issue December 1933]. Dr C G Jung makes himself known as editor of this co-ordinated periodical. So we find a Swiss citizen editing the official organ of a Society which, according to the statement of one of its leading members, Dr M H Göring [a relative of Hermann Göring], requires of all its actively writing and speaking members that they shall have studied Adolf Hitler's fundamental book Mein Kampf with full scientific thoroughness and shall recognize it as the basis of their activity."

Jung could not ignore this challenge. On 13 March 1934 he replied with the first of two articles:

"I found myself faced with a moral conflict...should I as a prudent neutral withdraw into security on this side of the frontier, live and wash my hands in innocence, or should I – as I was well aware – lay myself open to attack and the unavoidable misunderstanding which no one can escape who, out of a higher necessity, has to come to terms with the political powers that be in Germany? Should I sacrifice the interests of science, of loyalty to my colleagues, of the friendship which binds me to many German physicians, and the living community of German language and intellectual culture, to my egotistic comfort and different political outlook?... So I had no alternative but to lend the weight of my name and of my independent position for the benefit of my friends..."

The last paragraph of Jung's second article said: "I have no hesitation in admitting that it is a highly unfortunate and confusing coincidence that my scientific programme should have been superimposed without my co-operation and against my express wish,[1] on a political manifesto."

Under the eyes of his Nazi "sponsors" these were bold words. He took the risk of causing grave offence whether they had deliberately deceived him or not. One flaw – a very serious flaw – remains in the second possibility. Assuming that Jung had discovered their duplicity, why did he not resign? He was still listed as sole editor of the *Zentralblatt* until the end of 1935 and the January 1936 edition called Carl G Jung and M H Göring co-editors.

From time to time charges of anti-Semitism have flared up against Jung. They have been challenged, rejected and recurred again. It remained a sore point with him all his life. In the letter written to Dr Fordham on 18 April 1946 he made an elaborate answer to a new campaign against him. The attacks were savagely sustained in America, where a man called Albert D Parelhoff wrote letters, reprinted articles and caused scenes at psycho-analytic meetings. Jung's reply to these attacks said that during the Second World War his book *Psychology and Religion* sold five editions in America, and his enemies could find nothing pro-Nazi in that book because he severely criticized the Nazis, but they constantly returned to the year 1934. What were the facts about that year? Threatened with suppression, the German psychotherapists sought for somebody non-Jewish to prove that their work was not exclusively Jewish, and no better figure could be found than the German-speaking Jung with his reputation for independent thinking. There remained quite a number of Jews among the psychotherapists and Jung thought that he could help to protect them by accepting the Presidency of the International Society for Psychotherapy. In his letter to Dr Fordham, Jung claimed to have made daring statements in favour of the Jews, but where these statements appeared is not clear. His activities had to be surreptitious, he said, to avoid creating open hostility with his Nazi "hosts". Jung also claimed, in his letter, that he was on the Nazi Black List, but I have not been able to confirm this. If the Germans had invaded Switzerland, he said, he would have been one of the first to be shot. This is difficult to reconcile with his Presidency of the Society under German sponsorship.

His letter to Dr Fordham seemed to strain in search of redeeming detail and pointed out that he had never had any particular sympathy with Germany, choosing to study as a young man in Paris and not Berlin like so many of his friends. Similarly, living for twenty years on the Alsatian border, he had come to under stand the true nature of the Germans.

The whole story of pro-Nazi-anti-Semitic sentiments was, he went on, absolute nonsense, a cheap attempt to discredit a man who had refused to accept the Freudian Party Line. A counter-charge of an extraordinary character now disfigured the attempted logic of the letter. These unscrupulous Freudians, Jung said, had not even stopped at the mutilation of his photograph in order to represent him as a two-headed monster. In Calcutta University, a photograph of himself had come into his hands, distorted by the addition of pince-nez and an emphasized nose which caricatured the worst kind of Jew.

The feud now re-echoed across the Atlantic. In 1949–50 the *Saturday Review of Literature* and the *American Journal of Psychotherapy* carried a fierce exchange of letters which threw fresh light on charge and counter-charge.[2] Dr Eleanor Bertine, a New York analyst, wrote on 9 July:

"…I would like to say that for about thirty years I have been in fairly close contact with Dr Jung and have talked with him about these matters both orally and by letter. I can state positively from first-hand knowledge that, after the first few years when a dead Germany came alive under Nazism, he has deeply felt the tragedy being heaped up for the whole world by all that totalitarianism implies. His Nazi propaganda activities are simply non-existent."

As for the anti-Semitism in Switzerland: "Another thing that Dr Jung…put through as President was to open the International Society to individual members as well as to national groups. This was for the purpose of giving a scientific home to the Jews, whom Hitler had disqualified from membership in their national group." Dr Bertine did not deal with another charge which arose out of this inclusion of Jews in the International Society. It has been alleged that Professor Göring did not need help from the Gestapo to uncover the whereabouts of Jewish analysts and psychiatrists when the Society's ready-made list was placed in his hands. Clearly Jung never intended to act as a decoy and any suggestion that he deliberately inveigled Jews into the net of the Society as a prey for Goring, is maliciously untrue. His intention was quite the opposite as Dr Esther Harding, a practising Jungian, revealed in another letter:

"I am in possession [she wrote] of a copy of the circular that accompanied the *Zentralblatt für Psychotherapie*. It carried the date 12 January 1934 and is signed by Dr C G Jung. It contains the amendment mentioned by Dr Bertine that enabled members who had been expelled from their national groups, to become independent members of the International Association for Psychotherapy. The Association is described as 'politically and confessionally neutral'."

Confessionally seemed an odd word, and Dr Goring's own proclamation was anything but neutral, but Jung never claimed to be politically

125

sophisticated and he could easily have become the dupe of men astute in tactical deceptions.

Mrs Cary F Baynes, one of Jung's translators, wrote another letter on 15 October 1949 in which she said:

"Dr Wertham, in a recently published book, has discussed, with the insight of a psychiatrist, the psychology of a murderer. No one has assumed that Dr Wertham condones murder. Yet it has been a constant tactic of Jung's calumniators to construe Jung's efforts to interpret the psychological drives underlying National Socialism as an apologia for Nazism."

Dr Wertham replied:

"...It was not I who made the statement that Jung was an 'ardent Nazi collaborationist' (although I know, of course, that it is true). This statement was made by a man who won the highest distinction as an editor and writer, first in Europe, and then in the United States, Franz Schoenberner. He was the renowned editor of the two famous magazines *Jugend* and *Simplicissimus*... He is the author of two books: *Confessions of a European Intellectual* (1946) and *The Inside Story of an Outsider* (1949)... Schoenberner had the opportunity to make a Nazi career in literature at the very same time that Jung made a Nazi career in psychotherapy. But whereas Jung took up the editorship of a Nazi-sponsored journal in collaboration with a relative of Göring, Schoenberner – an *anima candida* if ever there was one – gave up the editorship of his magazine and took upon himself the better fate of an exile..."

Wertham next quoted part of Schoenberner's grossly exaggerated attack on Jung: "He became an ardent Nazi collaborationist, attacking Freud's 'dirty mind' and 'Jewish psychology' in general."

There is absolutely no evidence to show that Jung called Freud's mind dirty, and his coexistence with the Nazi regime had nothing in it which justified the words *ardent collaborationist*.

Another letter followed from Clara Thompson who was Executive Director of the William Alanson White Institute of Psychiatry.

"It is well known that Jung was the editor of a Hitler-sponsored psychiatric publication in Germany. Since he is a Swiss citizen and did not have to live in Germany, he obviously did not have to accept this position under any pressure or threats. It must have been an expression of his own interests. Also the fact that he has sponsored race prejudice in various ways can be documented from his writings."

Can it? I can find no documentation for race prejudice. At the most he was guilty of a dangerous ambiguity when he made distinctions between Jewish and Gentile psychology.

Jung's final letter in what developed into a prolonged and bitter exchange came in 1951. Written in English and addressed to a leading American psychiatrist it said that if he wanted to know the truth he should consult some of Jung's Jewish pupils who were better informed about him than the rumour-mongers.

The fact was that when the International Medical Society for Psychotherapy first came into being, his German colleagues deliberately set out to find a leader who was not German. They were afraid that under a German leader the Nazis would be in a much stronger position to outlaw psychotherapy. Jung accepted the role and immediately permitted alienated Jewish doctors to become members.

When the Nazis appointed Göring, Jung wanted to resign, but many other members of the Society pressed him to stay, believing that it was in their interests for him to do so. A clumsily worded sentence now spoke of pushing psychotherapy away in a remote corner where the Nazis failed to reach it. In 1937, Jung said, he wanted to resign once more, but the Dutch and the English used all their powers to persuade him to stay. For the second time he decided not to desert his colleagues.

In an aside, Jung complained bitterly that he did not have the advantages of a Secret Service to uncover the precise motives of the Nazis and he therefore had to move diplomatically – although he hated it. His Wotan Essay, he claimed, had made him suspect to the Nazis and only a fool could misread it as sympathetic to them.

He flatly denied taking an anti-Semitic view at any time, and said – somewhat ambiguously – that his opinion of the Nazis had not changed. On the other hand, it was absurd to suggest that the Jew and Gentile had the same psychology. Their psychology, like that of the French and the English, was different.

Finally, he thought that some rumour-monger must be feeling very uncomfortable to foment all this trouble in the USA.[3]

The rumour-monger referred to in Dr Jung's letter did not, in fact, feel the least bit discomfited. This anonymous figure was Albert D Parelhoff, a salesman for Lever Bros, the soap manufacturers, in the USA. A man obsessed by his vendetta with Jung, Parelhoff made a habit of attending psychiatric meetings and on 18 January 1954, at the New School for Social Research, he caused a scene while Dr Jolan Jacobi was lecturing. When question time came, Mr Parelhoff at once raised his hand and said:

"Dr Jacobi, you are the author of a book entitled The Psychology of Jung published by Yale University Press. It contains something I have not as yet found in any other book on Jung and his theories. In the bibliography you list Jung's 'Reply to Dr Bally' which was published in the Neue Züricher Zeitung in March 1934. Why do you list as one of Jung's achievements this vicious, anti-Semitic 'Reply to Dr Bally' in which Jung confesses his collaboration with the Nazis?..."

Taken aback, Dr Jacobi stood silent a moment, while boos and hisses broke out. Then she said: "This is not the time to discuss the matter. It would take too long."

Someone shouted: "Who are you? Why don't you get out?"

Dr Jacobi called the meeting to order and said: "I am a Jewess and my husband is a Jew. Does anyone here believe that I would defend Dr Jung if he were anti-Semitic? We thrashed out charges against Dr Jung at my first lecture."

Parelhoff replied: "I didn't know of your lectures until today or I would have attended sooner."

The shouting and heckling now threatened to overwhelm Parelhoff. "Don't try to shout me down", he cried. "Why doesn't Dr Jacobi or anyone else in this audience read publicly the material I have brought?"

The outcry now became an uproar and Dr Jacobi, failing to make herself heard above it, walked swiftly from the platform and demanded to know Parelhoff's name. Once he had given it she said: "So you are the person who is always writing against Jung?"

The scene slowly subsided, order was restored and Parelhoff at last disappeared from the lecture room. Another small episode in the prolonged attempt to prove Jung's "disgraceful conduct" had come to an unseemly end.

What emerges from it all? Was there enough evidence to show that Jung's defection from Freud had elements of anti-Semitism openly avowed or unconsciously engendered? When Freud first selected him as Crown Prince, Freud said that "he seemed ready for my sake to give up certain racial prejudices which he had previously permitted himself".[4] Their long-drawn-out quarrel may have revived such prejudices but it looks very much as though Jung was manoeuvred into leaving the International Society by a powerful group of Freudians. On the other hand, was he guilty of association with the Nazis under doubtful conditions for a period of three years? The answer must be yes.

When Jones came to write his biography of Freud, the irrepressible Parelhoff wrote to him and Jones included a number of passages analysing anti-Semitic charges against Jung. His publishers felt that with Jung still alive statements of this kind might be regarded as libellous and he was asked to remove them, which he did. Meanwhile, preparing the Collected Works of Jung, the editors discussed whether they should include his rebuttal of the charges, in the English translation, and decided against it.

What was Freud's view of Jung's alleged anti-Semitism? Ernest Jones told me that Freud believed a streak of something indistinguishable from it appeared in Jung's character, but Freud himself had some very interesting views on Jews and Gentiles.

I am indebted to Joseph Wortis, who was analysed by Freud, for an account of a long talk he had with Freud about Judaism, the Jewish personality and anti-Semitism. Wortis had been reading Einstein and one day he said to Freud: "Einstein is an interesting and likeable man but his attitude towards the Jewish question is somewhat puzzling to me and I confess I am not easily in sympathy with his or your Jewish nationalism."

Wortis had regarded himself as more American than Jewish and now he asked Freud: "How far ought I to let my allegiance to the Jews bring me?"

"That is not a problem for the Jews", Freud answered, "because the Gentiles make it unnecessary to decide; as long as Jews are not admitted into Gentile circles they have no choice but to band together."

Wortis said he understood the historic necessity of the past; but would it not be a better future if the Jews were assimilated into the Gentile ranks? Freud answered: "The future will show how far that is possible. I, personally, do not see anything wrong in mixed marriages if both parties are suited to each other. I must say", Freud continued, "that the chances for success seem greater in a Jewish marriage: family life is closer and warmer and devotion is much more common." Not individual marriages with certain complementary characteristics, but Jewish marriages had a greater chance of success.

"A Jew ought not to get himself baptized and attempt to turn Christian because it is essentially dishonest and the Christian religion is every bit as bad as the Jewish... Jew and Christian ought to meet on the common ground of irreligion and humanity."[5]

The talk between the two men rambled on, and then, according to Wortis, Freud suddenly produced this statement: "Ruthless egotism is much more common among Gentiles than among Jews and Jewish family life and intellectual life are on a higher plane."

"You seem to think", the astonished Wortis said, "that the Jews are superior people."

Quite unshaken Freud quietly replied: "I think nowadays they are. When one thinks that ten or twelve per cent of the Nobel Prizewinners are Jews and when one thinks of their other great achievements in science and arts, one has every reason to think them superior."[6]

After years of negative persecution in Vienna it was not surprising that Freud should react by exaggerating the powers of his own race. However, the word "race" is so suspect biologically that it is unsophisticated to assume a special Jewish gene from which springs the whole forest of wildly differing personality, character traits and behaviour which we so conveniently label Jewish, and which Freud seemed to invoke when he spoke of their superiority. Genetically, there is a Negro race and membership of it implies that one is "black" but need imply nothing else. There is no special colouring which goes with being Jewish. Each Jew may be as individual as each Gentile, but centuries of abuse and persecution have produced in some a reaction formation which gives them a pseudo-identity.

Freud was speaking casually to Joseph Wortis, and being a man who could passionately react to challenging questions, he might easily overstate, in conversation, a case he would qualify in print. Very much later, in his many talks with Wortis, he said that a spontaneous answer was not to be taken too seriously and was certainly not something on which he would base a scientific paper.

One other crucial fact remains to be recorded. Ernest Jones told me that after what he called "Jung's defection", Freud never fully trusted another Gentile again.

NOTES

1. My italics.
2. *Saturday Review of Literature*, 9 July 1949; *American Journal of Psychotherapy*, Vol. IV, No. I, pp. 130–40, January 1950.
3. Letter dated 17 December 1951.
4. *Collected Works. On the History of Psycho-Analysis*, Vol. 14, p. 43.
5. *Fragments of an Analysis with Freud*: Joseph Wortis, p. 144.
6. *Fragments of an Analysis with Freud*: Joseph Wortis, p. 145.

Chapter Twelve

The Formation of the Committee

As the stresses and tensions subsided following the major break with Jung, the remaining members of Freud's circle looked uneasily at the future and decided that some more disciplined organization of the psycho-analytic movement had now become imperative. The form it took was surprising. In politics a three-line whip frequently becomes obligatory and individual members suffer under disciplinary pressures, but Freud's new "Committee" reached beyond the political sphere into the mystical.

It was Jones who first conceived the idea of an Old Guard surrounding Freud which would dedicate itself to the "high purposes of psycho-analysis". Jones met Ferenczi in Vienna and proposed that "a number of men who had been thoroughly analysed by Freud" should be stationed in different countries. The terms were almost those of the more extreme forms of political organization where agents are first trained and then sent abroad as unquestioning emissaries, but the analogy is not exact. Deviation was made possible under certain carefully controlled conditions. "If anyone wished to depart from any of the fundamental tenets of the psycho-analytical theory...he would promise not to do so publicly before first discussing his views with the rest."

Jones had no idea that while negotiations were still proceeding with Ferenczi and Otto Rank, Ferenczi had already become suspicious of his own and Rank's loyalty. Shortly after their meeting, Ferenczi wrote to Freud on 16 August 1912: "It has seldom been so clear to me as now what a psychological advantage it signifies to be born a Jew...you must keep Jones constantly under your eye and cut off his line of retreat." This came close to anti-Gentilism, but the mercurial Ferenczi was not a man to conform to the flat-footed laws of consistency and two months afterwards he wrote another letter in which he thought Jones, "unflinchingly steadfast".

The idea of an inner council of carefully chosen, trustworthy men quickly fired Freud's imagination and he at once saw something boyishly romantic in a "Secret Committee", but hoped "it could be adapted to meet the necessities of reality".

Since Ernest Jones, in his brilliant biography of Freud, has spelt out this part of the story, there is no need to repeat the details, but Freud's initial letter, accepting the idea, had one surprising feature in a man of his stature. He insisted that the Committee would have to be "*strictly secret*", and the italics were his. As the plan developed into reality its secret-society characteristics multiplied. It was reasonable enough to nominate men like Jones, Ferenczi, Rank, Sachs, Abraham and Max Eitingon for the inner council, but when, on 25. May 1913, Freud issued special insignias to everyone, the Committee acquired the characteristics of a blood brotherhood. Freud presented to each member an antique Greek intaglio which all six mounted in gold rings, and they became the seven rings of the mystic circle, with direct roots in a tradition reaching back to King Arthur and his knights, a world more suited to Jung than Freud.

As we have seen, Ferenczi was by far the most spontaneous and ebullient member of the Committee with a nature full of warmth and enthusiasm for his friends. However, according to Marthe Robert he made childishly extravagant demands on Freud and wanted him to love him completely.[1] A brilliant lecturer, he also had considerable gifts as an analyst but his spontaneous talk made him the living incarnation of one chapter in The Psychopathology of Everyday Life. Slips of the tongue came as naturally to him as breathing and he was known among the Committee as the King of Parapractics.

Photographs of Rank show an overgrown, bespectacled schoolboy, looking as if he were expecting a blow, and this reflected itself in the living man as an ineradicable timidity. If social origins were any justification, he had every reason to be deferential. He came from a much lower strata of society than the others, and had been educated in a technical school which harnessed his intelligence to practical purposes but left other potentials unawakened. An ugly man, with an uncertain manner, his high intelligence enabled him to contribute to psycho-analytic techniques and his willingness to play the psycho-analytic packhorse made him accept tedious secretarial jobs from which most other members of the Committee recoiled. Technically he "had a special analytic flair for interpreting dreams, myths and legends. His great work, *Das Inzest-Motiv in Dichtung und Sage* (1912), which is not read nowadays, is a tribute to his truly vast erudition."[2] Rank had day-to-day contact with Freud for years and became a kind of Super-Secretary to him, but some lack of spontaneous charm which Freud needed in close friends kept them at a professional distance.

Jones regarded Abraham as the most normal member of the Committee, which implied that neuroses troubled the remainder, as indeed they did. Abraham certainly had one quality invaluable in the alarms and excursions which had become part of everyday psycho-analytic politics – an unshakeable calm. A man emotionally self-contained, he had none of Ferenczi's charm and was strongly averse to rash action or snap judgments. Departing momentarily from his usual self-effacement Jones, in his Freud biography, says: "It was he and I, usually agreeing with each other, who supplied the element of judgment in our decisions." None the less, the Abraham letters show Abraham as a faithful appendage to Freud whose bursts of criticism were overwhelmed by a general deference.

Hanns Sachs appeared to be everything that Abraham was not. Primarily a literary man, he had a whole repertoire of Jewish jokes, was witty, urbane, and excellent company. Not unexpectedly, administrative problems bored him and he found political manoeuvring distasteful; but he was completely faithful to Freud, who was prepared to overlook congenital laziness because Sachs brought out all his own brilliant conversational powers.

Max Eitingon differed from Sachs as Sachs differed from Abraham. He was a nondescript little man with a balding head and a weak-looking face who "felt his Jewish origins more acutely than other members of the Committee". There is no record of any persecution he may have suffered, but his face was slightly apprehensive and his psychological make-up reflected this in a complete inability to take a strong line of his own. Freud, to him, was God, and whatever opinion Freud held from week to week, Eitingon slavishly followed. Like many gentle people he had a delightful nature and any softness in his character was reaffirmed by a considerable private income which protected him against the worst shocks of economic reality. Time and again he financially underwrote psycho-analytic projects and his gentleness was matched by his generosity. Intellectually he had little to contribute and did no original work of note, but as a practising psycho-analyst there were those among his patients who "swore by him" and others who were greatly helped by his treatment.

All members of the Committee were freethinkers without religious problems and at different times Freud corresponded extensively with each of them. It is obligatory today for any psycho-analyst to undergo analysis himself but in those pioneer days Jones alone made a sustained attempt to achieve the ideal. He went to Budapest and spent a few months with Ferenczi under taking "two or three hours a day" intensive analysis. It is interesting to reflect that the revered members of the Inner Committee would be frowned on by the profession today as inadequately trained, but Jones conceded that Abraham survived remarkably well without analysis, which, he commented, showed how "original character and temperament are of the highest importance for success".

Despite the ever-widening international repercussions of the psycho-analytic movement, with the exception of Jones, the Committee could not claim any extensive personal experience beyond Austria's boundaries, and there were occasions when provincial limitations left its members nonplussed at the behaviour of the outside world. Some people regard Jones as a mere expositor of the Master's ideas without any very great originality in his own right, but he had travelled widely in Europe and America and become a cosmopolitan intellectual who "dropped in on" more Congresses than any other living analyst. Like Otto Rank, Jones came from a lower social strata than the other members of the Committee. Welsh by descent, he said – probably ironically – that coming, as he did, from an "oppressed race", it was easy for him to identify himself with the Jewish outlook. Certainly, years of contact with Jewish colleagues made him familiar with their idiosyncracies and he had a wide knowledge of Jewish anecdotes, sayings and customs.

Jones' role in the psycho-analytic movement is commonly underestimated and it is worth briefly examining the details of his life to see the extent of his achievement. Born in an obscure village, Rhosfelyn in Wales, his father began life as a clerk in a coal company, and subsequently qualified, by private study, as a colliery engineer. He had two failings which led to difficulties between father and son. He found it impossible to admit that he was in the wrong, and believed in the ascendancy of the adult over the child to the point of total subordination.

Jones' sexual precocity was something to wonder at, and he categorically stated that "the practice of coitus was familiar to me at the ages of six and seven, after which I suspended it and did not resume it till I was twenty-four".[3] At the age of seven, a slightly older boy told him the facts of life in a brutally straightforward manner and expressed a wish to sleep with Jones' mother. Language, in childhood, was blunt and uncomplicated, and a boy with acute stomach-ache rolling on the floor informed him that "It hurts so much I don't think I could fuck a girl if she was under me at this minute."[4]

These were interesting beginnings for a man to become the close friend of Freud and a trusted member of the Inner Committee. Later, he qualified as a doctor and began to specialize in neurology. At first tremendously successful, a series of setbacks led to the situation where he was reduced to "applying...in vain for admission to the staff of various second or third-rate hospitals... A vicious spiral developed. Every failure was registered and added complications to previous failures."[5] Audaciously, Jones next set up in Harley Street, in partnership with a surgeon, Wilfred Trotter, and then at last managed to get himself appointed as assistant physician to the Dreadnought Seamen's Hospital at Greenwich.

Presently, one of the most puzzling phenomena in the neurologists' world – the functional disorders – began to absorb him and he read the works of William James, Frederic Myers, and Milne Brammell, soaking himself in the literature of psychological medicine. He became a contributor to the *Journal of Abnormal Psychology*, and now read the work of Janet in France, and Boris Sidis and Morton Prince in America. One day, Wilfred Trotter mentioned the name Freud to him, and he sought out and read Mitchell Clarke's review of *Studies in Hysteria* in *Brain*, finally stumbling on the Dora analysis in *Monatsschrift far Psychiatric*. It became imperative to Jones to know more about Freud's work. "I sometimes say", he said, "that I learned German from reading Freud's *Traumdeutung* and Heine's *Reisebilder*, and for some time my vocabulary showed amusing traces of its compound restricted origin."[6]

In November 1907, Jones set off to attend a special postgraduate course in psychiatry at Kraeplin's Clinic in Munich and on his way back to England made a detour to visit Jung at Zürich. Jung was already a distinguished psychiatrist and had published his two works, *Studies in Word Association* and *The Psychology of Dementia Praecox*. Correspondence developed between the two men, and in the following February, Jones again visited Jung and suggested organizing the first Psycho-Analytical Congress. In his reminiscences, against all later allegiances, Jones commented: "I remember vainly protesting about his wish to call it a Congress for Freudian Psychology, a term which offended my ideas of objectivity in scientific work." Jung, Brill and Jones then proceeded to Salzburg and in April 1908 the first personal encounter at last took place between Freud and Jones.

By 1914 Ernest Jones had become the key British member of the Inner Committee, and the ring adorning his finger clearly indicated his future path. The Jones I knew was a short, dapper, quick-eyed Welshman who spoke spontaneously in animated spurts. Temperamentally, he had much in common with Freud and Ferenczi, but his capacity for rational discipline brought passionate impulses easily under control.

I remember the almost military precision with which he marched me round his lovely garden at the Plat in Sussex, England, and the sense of a rigorously disciplined life which he conveyed on that beautiful summer day in 1953. A sick man already, he dominated and concealed all symptoms by an erect carriage, a brisk walk and a rigid adherence to time. As we paused at the rose beds, and he explained what havoc some mysterious insects had wrought, he suddenly glanced at his watch: "Just four," he said. "Time for tea." His wife Katharine Jones produced a lavish tea, and we relaxed for half an hour. Then he said: "Well, I'm afraid a patient is waiting," and he came out of his chair with one brisk movement.

I talked to Jones about the early days of the Committee. "Don't be misled," he said, "by the boyish business of the rings. They didn't amount to anything, and at least two members of the Committee were embarrassed to wear them. Indeed, I once caught Eitingon without his ring and when I remarked on it he said, 'I must have left it in the bathroom', but he looked embarrassed for some reason I could only guess at. You must understand that the rituals involved in the Committee were the inevitable reaction towards greater discipline as a result of Jung's defection. The combination of external hostility and internal dissension drove us to somewhat picturesque methods – and – alas – even those in the long run didn't save us."

I asked Jones whether he was resented as the only Gentile among the Jews. "They were all highly sensitive to any sign of anti-Semitism," he replied, "and Freud himself was no exception... He used to look at me sometimes quizzically as if to say – what on earth are you, a Gentile, without German for a mother tongue, doing among us? He had by no means escaped the Jewish persecution heritage and there were times when it worked in reverse. I did not escape the doubt – even suspicion – on one or two occasions – which caused difficulties with others, and on at least one occasion, I thought being a Gentile had something to do with it."

"Was there any real warmth between you," I asked, "such as appeared between Fliess, Ferenczi and Freud?" "No," Jones said, with a wry smile. "But we had a pretty close understanding. In the beginning, too, there were a great many Jewish jokes which I easily understood – I became soaked in the peculiarities of Jewish humour. Freud, as you know, was a very witty man. He once remarked casually to the assembled circle that the day when the Viennese shops advertised, 'Gifts for all stages of the Transference', would be the day when psycho-analysis had really become a part of the social conventions."

"What was the first sign of the disharmony in the Committee?" I asked him.

We were walking in the garden of Plat at the time. Once again it was a warm summer afternoon, and Jones sighed and dug his stick sharply into the earth.

"Why", he said, "do you concentrate so much on our troubles? After all, there were long, long periods when everything ran smoothly. Take the Committee for instance. It worked very well for eleven or twelve years and when you remember what an oddly assorted lot we were, that is a very long stretch of time indeed. Anyway we didn't value harmony as highly as that. Complete harmony so easily leads to inertia."

Jones went on to explain that one of the primary functions of the Committee – to reassure Freud in the midst of the many savage attacks made on him – was accomplished without difficulty. Similarly a unified policy made it much easier to cope with the complicated problems which constantly arose.

Some time later, as we were returning to the house for lunch, Jones said: "Of course, the war years which followed were terrible for everyone but at least we, in England, did not suffer hardships equivalent to a Siberian winter. Freud, as you know, went hungry in these years and literally suffered from frost bite."

He broke off and opened the door for me. "It reminds me", he said, laughing, "of a letter I had from him just before war broke out. It was a perfect example of a significant slip of the pen and you can read into it what you will."

Freud, it seems, had referred back to his troubles with Jung but instead of writing "Jung's gospel" in the letter, he wrote "Jones' gospel". In another letter to Jones dated 25 March 1914 he said: "Now my interesting Versckreiben may have aroused your suspicion. But you remember I did not try to conceal it but even called your attention to it..."

Instead of leaping at the obvious psycho-analytic interpretation, Freud skilfully rationalized the slip. "It is a common trick of my unconscious to supplant a person disliked by a better one." What it really revealed was a "veiled tenderness towards Jones". So now the intricacies of psycho-analytic interpretation permitted Freud to substitute Jones' name for Jung's, not because his concealed hostility to Jones was thus revealed, but because it was "a veiled tenderness towards" Jones. The hidden thought really said: "Why can Jung not be like Jones?" The explanation gathered greater substance when Freud recalled that "after the Munich Congress, I could never utter the name 'Jung', but had to replace it by 'Jones'."[7]

None the less, on a number of occasions, within a few years he was not only suspicious of Jones, but openly complained about his behaviour.

137

The 1914—18 war broke into the psycho-analytic world as into any other, and lack of communications between new frontiers made it difficult to sustain any intimate relationship between members of the Committee.

During the last two years, Hanns Sachs was the only one to remain in Vienna with Freud. Ferenczi and Eitingon were doctors in the Austrian—Hungarian army, Rank went to Cracow and Abraham became a doctor in the German Army of East Prussia. Sachs spent many a long evening alone with Freud in his unheated study, but towards the end he was in no condition to contribute very much because undernourishment and wartime conditions had exacerbated his tuberculosis. He left a vivid picture of the two men sitting in Freud's study, heavily clothed in every possible garment, from overcoats and hats to gloves and mufflers, "suffering from the emptiness of our stomachs and frostbites on bare hands". While Sachs, huddled up, tried to forget the pain in his stomach, Freud, he recorded, continued to talk brilliantly, his intellectual energy only slightly diminished. It revealed a familiar streak in his character: the ability to face up to whatever hardship fate chose to put in his path.

Correspondence between Jones and Freud was, at the outset of the war, unsatisfactory. In the first few months several letters simply vanished in transit, but Jones ventured the opinion in one which survived that Germany would lose the war in the long run, and Freud acidly commented to Ferenczi: "Jones is talking about the war with the narrow-minded outlook of the English." One year after war began Freud wrote to Abraham (3 July 1915): "All my friends and helpers are now in the army and have, so to speak, been taken away from me. Even Rank, who is still in Vienna, has not appeared since his call up..." The situation, he added, was similar to those very early days when he suffered intellectual isolation but carried out a great deal of work. In an attempt to preserve some continuity in their psycho-analytic work Freud now made great efforts to save their periodicals, but in order to sustain the *Zeitschrift* and *Imago* he was forced to "serialize" a projected book in both, and even then the *Jahrhuch*, starved of copy, slowly dwindled to a stop.

By August, Freud still seemed able to get letters through to America and on 13 August, J W Putnam wrote him a long letter which revealed a decided difference in the outlook of America and Vienna.

> "As regards the difference in our attitude [Putnam wrote], I believe that in the end it will not turn out to be so great as it now seems and I hope to be able to make it clear that you believe in a free will and in religion as much as I do or more than I do. It cannot be that we differ radically in the workings of our minds...or in our ability to see the truth..."

A series of long, undulating sentences followed and finally reached this paragraph.

"I am sure you do not believe, either as a scientist, or as a man, that when you make some great sacrifice for the advancement of truth (as you have done so often) or when you do some painful task in obedience to a sense of duty, you do not exert any power of free will or choice, or that you do not rearrange the forces of the world in a way that they never could have rearranged themselves. I feel sure that if anybody should threaten to take away that amount of freedom – be it never so small – which you feel yourself possessed of you would resist the attempt with all your strength and with your life."[8]

Freud replied ironically that his sense of duty to truth had been sadly inhibited by the clumsy intervention of a force called War at the most inconvenient moment when, having closed its ranks, psycho-analysis was ready to move forward again. Perhaps Putnam felt that the Kaiser's free will was at war with Freud's, but he could assure him it wasn't; just a series of clumsy deterministic forces had become confused and the subjection and possible mutilation of a few million people was the inevitable consequence.

Despite wartime difficulties and confusions, for nearly ten years the Committee functioned smoothly and then Ferenczi and Rank became involved in a quarrel with Ernest Jones, and the air grew thick with accusation and counter-accusation all over again. In the biography Jones states that "the first sign of anything going wrong was a gradual mounting of tension between Rank and myself over the business of publication". He does not say that he simultaneously tried to cope with a difficult and all too familiar situation centred on Sandor Ferenczi which concerned a series of priority claims.

An exchange of papers and letters led first to a misunderstanding between Ferenczi and Jones, and then to bitter criticism. The trouble involved certain details of the hypnotic process. Ferenczi seems to have put forward the proposition that in hypnosis one of the most important elements was the auto-suggestive ideas of the patient and that these ideas were libidinal and infantile in origin. Ferenczi said: "*dass meine Erkennung der Auto-Suggestion em Truism ist, kann ich nicht anerkennen. Sie ist nur Truism, seitdem ich sie veröffentlichte.*"[9] (I cannot let it be said that my idea of auto-suggestion is a truism. It has only become a truism since I began writing about it.) Jones retorted that if Ferenczi would only refer to his last letter he would see that what he, Jones, had labelled a truism, was the general proposition that the processes in the person hypnotized were more important than those in the hypnotist's mind. This was very different from the charge Ferenczi now made. Jones could produce a long list of authors who had stressed the importance of what happened to the patient, and to call it a truism was no exaggeration. Moreover, the patient's own thoughts during hypnosis need have had nothing to do with the strict meaning of the term auto-suggestion which Ferenczi mistakenly used. None the less, Ferenczi had made an essential contribution to knowledge by identifying the libidinal and infantile character of the patient's internal ideas. Discussing this quarrel with me, Jones said: "On endless occasions in debate Ferenczi had put forward his theory and I always supported it, although wishing to clarify it. I found it absolutely astounding that when I made a casual reference to the historical derivation of the idea Ferenczi leapt down my throat and accused me of stealing it."

Jones decided to discuss his troubles with other members of the Committee. At first they could not understand what it was all about, but three at least, finally agreed that Ferenczi had become unnecessarily sensitive. No record remains of the view of the other members of the Committee. On Ferenczi's side, it has to be said that Jones could be very impatient of failings in others and he might easily have framed his comments in such a manner as to offend Ferenczi.

The correspondence between them reached a climax in a letter written by Jones on 15 December 1923. It was a long, carefully prepared letter which attempted to bring about a reconciliation between them, but a certain ambivalence must have made it hard for a man like Ferenczi to swallow. Jones' indignation matched Ferenczi's pain. Ferenczi seems to have openly charged Jones before the Committee with misrepresentation if not deliberate theft, and Jones felt that Ferenczi must be called on to explain to the Committee the true nature of their misunderstanding and to admit that these charges were grossly exaggerated. Simultaneously he made it quite clear that he valued Ferenczi's friendship very highly and the letter was charged with regret that things should have come to such a sorry pass between them. However, a warm desire to achieve a reconciliation was qualified by some gratuitous advice about the undesirability of priority disputes. They were regarded in England, Jones said, as an expression of personal vanity and had no place in science. It was most unwise, Jones persisted, to publish the details of any such *Nachtrag* (quarrel). Malicious intent did not exist on either side, but it might be read into the situation by anyone who did not have all the documents and details at their disposal. It was clear, Jones concluded, that he had been careless and Ferenczi mistaken, but why not accept that interpretation and forget the whole matter? After all, he could say from the bottom of his heart that there were few things he would miss so much as Sandor's friendship.

Jones' dispute with Rank had a quite different basis, and drew from Jones an admission of one of his own weaknesses. He had "a rather obsessive insistence on doing things in what [he] conceived to be the best way, with an impatience of sloppiness and a risk of provoking the sensibilities of other people concerned".

Trouble began when they jointly attempted to keep various psycho-analytic publications in print during the immediate post war years and Otto Rank was burdened with a host of menial tasks. Complications arose from a foolhardy desire to take advantage of the devalued Austrian currency which theoretically allowed them to "produce goods in that currency and sell them in a better one". The fact that prices rose sooner or later, despite devaluation, to meet international prices, escaped their attention and as this slowly became an accomplished fact, their work soon became "a race against time".

Rank, in Austria, found himself battling with overwhelming difficulties and when Jones' obsession with doing things the "correct way" drove him to remonstrate, Rank struck back in letters which Jones considered "overbearing and hectoring". Matters steadily worsened until Rank was either overruling or simply ignoring Jones' ideas of how the Press should be run. Jones commented: "What had aroused this harsh, dictatorial and hitherto unseen vein in Rank's nature I could not guess."

In the long and tortured story which followed, it is worth bearing in mind that when anyone openly quarrelled with Jones, he sometimes explained it away as a sudden neurotic outbreak. The same convenient occurrence of mental illness was frequently used to explain the new defections from Freud as they occurred. No one normal ever went into the wilderness because he rationally or sanely differed from Freud. Both men invoked their own most precious weapons to explain the deviations of others who became fiercely hostile or openly renegade. Thus with Rank, Jones said: "It took a couple of years before it became plain that a manic phase of his cyclothymia was gradually intensifying."

Living in a forest thickly populated with hidden psycho-analytic demons it was not unexpected that they should be invoked by living practitioners, but there was something specious in the consistent coincidence of psychological illness with distasteful behaviour. Jones elaborated his diagnosis of Rank's behaviour. "I had known that Rank had suffered much in childhood from a strongly repressed hostility to his brother and that this usually covered a similar attitude towards a father. This was now being unloaded on me." In cold fact, Jones' diagnosis could be sustained with Rank, but with Ferenczi and others it was seriously open to question.

Determined to preserve Freud's peace of mind, Jones went to great trouble to conceal his quarrel with Rank, but Rank was living in Vienna and took every opportunity to pour into Freud's ears a long account of what he regarded as Jones' impossible behaviour. All Jones' attempts to limit the extent of the quarrel failed, and his constant efforts to reassure Freud were received at first with suspicion and later coldness. Freud would not accept his plea that the two men could arrange matters between them selves and gave a sympathetic ear to each fresh complaint levelled by Rank.

According to Jones, a suspicious stalemate persisted for three years during which he "lived with the fear lest Rank's 'brother hostility' regress to the deeper 'father hostility". Whether this did in fact happen, is open to question, but a number of remarkable oversights on the part of Freud, have to be assumed if the account is accepted at its face value.

What were the precise details which led up to the break? Jones found himself working against a powerful anti-German atmosphere in England after the war, and the growing enemies of psycho-analysis vilified all its publications as "typical products of German decadence and general beastliness". Jones naturally desired to avoid any unnecessary emphasis on German origins and simultaneously protested to the English that Freud was more Jewish than German, and to Rank, that they must avoid Germanisms in the Journal. Rank seemed unsympathetic and pointed out that it was impossible to use English type because none could be found in Austria. Jones had not expected to find an English fount anywhere in Austria, but insisted on removing the Germanisms wherever they occurred on the printed page. This involved having the proofs sent from Vienna to London and the posts being still erratic, considerable delay ensued. There seemed every justification for the January number of the first volume appearing late, but when publication was constantly postponed and spring spread into summer, Freud began to worry. Finally, the January number appeared in July and some irritated letters revealed a growing tension between Freud, Rank and Jones. Rank now took matters into his own hands. Without warning Jones, he began correcting the proofs of the International Journal himself in Vienna, thus removing the chief cause of delay, but his poor English produced some unfortunate slips. As Jones said to me:

"It became something of a nightmare. I constantly opened the pages expecting to find another useful weapon for our enemies in England. The last straw that broke the camel's back was to find a Frau prefixing the name of Mrs Riviere. I wrote off at once to Rank explaining that if the proofs were to be read in Vienna we really must have someone there who thoroughly understood English."

A man called Eric Hiller set off for Vienna shortly afterwards and the proofs now began to approximate to the standards Jones required. Anna Freud also played a part in perfecting them.

NOTES
1. *La Révolution Psychoanalytique*: Marthe Robert, Vol. II, p. 82.
2. *Sigmund Freud: Life and Work*: Ernest Jones, Vol. II, p. 181.
3. *Free Associations*: Ernest Jones, p. 31.
4. *Ibid*.
5. *Free Associations*: Ernest Jones, p. 33.
6. *Ibid*.
7. Letter to Jones dated 25 March 1914.
8. I am grateful to Dr Marian C Putnam for permission to quote from her father's letter.
9. December 1923.

Chapter Thirteen

Struggles within the Committee

To see the whole struggle in perspective it is necessary to stress the ever-widening resistance to the "science" of psycho-analysis. Not only its suspicious German character but the dark nature of its investigations troubled the English newspapers, the Church and some medical circles. Charlatans took full advantage of the widespread publicity. Every kind of exploitation for commercial purposes was tried. The English Psycho-Analytical Publishing Company put an advertisement in the Evening Standard which read: "Would you like to earn £1,000 a year as a psycho-analyst? We can show you how to do it. Take eight postal lessons from us at four guineas a course."[1] Quack analysts began to appear all over the country and men who were equipped to read fortunes from cards, but not to master the arduous techniques of analysis, set themselves up as "Viennese-trained specialists". One man claimed: "Turn your neurosis to creative purpose. Are you a potential artist? Success guaranteed because Victor Johnstone has been analysed by Freud." Needless to say Freud had never known a patient named Victor Johnstone. In the United States the fashion caught on in even wilder form. Paralytics were promised dramatic cures by Top Analysts: the Secrets of Analysis were revealed in Six Easy Lessons: photographs of Freud were used to give authority to advertisements for quacks who were quite incapable of understanding, quite apart from applying, his techniques.

The clash between charlatans anxious to make money from a new fashion and intolerant moralists who regarded any intrusion into sexual privacy as iniquitous, became acute. The moralists seized on the worst crimes of the charlatans and saddled serious psycho-analysis with the consequences. As Jones wrote: "When an American 'teacher' was sent to prison and then deported for indecent behaviour with 'patients' that again was an example of our perfidy and The Times declined to publish a letter we sent them disclaiming any connection with him."

In fact, a whole correspondence sprang to life in The Times beginning with a little masterpiece by Archdeacon J Malet Lambert who wrote on 23 September 1922 deploring an alleged move to introduce psycho-analysis into schools. Teachers, he said:

"will at once find themselves confronted with a theory of psychology which traces by far the greater part of the content of the mind, conscious or unconscious, to the sexual impulse.

"They will be required to saturate their minds with pornographic detail set forth with a particularity greater than that required for a medical student. To the most ordinary events of everyday life will be given a connotation incompatible with what we have been accustomed to regard as a clean mind."

Dr Cyril Burt disposed of the charges in a quiet and sensible letter, but The Times leader retaliated:

"Indeed it is no exaggeration to say that no other system of psychology has ever enjoyed so swift or wide a popularity. The reason is somewhat difficult to determine for the essential doctrine of Freud is that the mind of man is swayed by impulses over which his will has little or no control; in other words that we are more nearly related to the creatures of instinct than to the gods. It dethrones the will. The astonishing thing is that so many modern thinkers or perhaps half thinkers do not appear to object to this idea. On the contrary, they welcome it as though the lure of irresponsibility outshone all others in their eyes. This is a state of matters which cannot be regarded as healthy."

Archdeacon Malet Lambert also replied on 12 October.

"I happen to be chairman of a large public library... Not long ago Freud's 'Lectures' as a work of public interest was admitted... It was clear to me that I could not take the responsibility of admitting it for miscellaneous circulation and after discussion with my committee it was placed in the reference room for issue only to those who appeared to be genuine students... I do not know how the book has been dealt with by other libraries but if it has been unwittingly thrown into general circulation to be the prey of prurient curiosity, harm has been done."

The *Daily Graphic* launched a wholesale "enquiry" into the "true nature" of psycho-analysis, on 11 January 1921. It turned out to be more balanced than one had a right to expect from a lurid popular daily, but on 13 January it said:

"Among the cases of victimization already recorded in the *Daily Graphic* [is] the following which can be fully vouched for: A fashionable woman suffering from a hopeless love for the husband of a friend consulted a psycho-analyst. Under hypnosis she imagined herself to be a man, Napoleon, and made love to the consultant whom she imagined to be Josephine."

Psycho-analysis became a new Aunt Sally for the press and finally one newspaper challenged the General Medical Council to look into its standards. The GMC shrugged its shoulders. Some members recalled historic precedents where respectable medical pioneers had been malignantly destroyed by ill-informed medical enquiries, but the British Medical Association was at last driven out of its inertia to conduct such an enquiry. Psycho-analysts emerged completely vindicated, but something of a smear remained in the public eye.

In America, matters became more complicated. Various pirated editions of Freud's work were circulating in the States and a series of cover addresses and nominee shareholders made it very difficult to pin down the culprits. One publisher had three addresses in New York, Boston and Philadelphia. Both Jones and Rank were involved in endless wrangles with international lawyers and correspondence reached mountainous proportions.

Freud at first sympathized with the London publishers who were prepared to accept money in compensation for the infringement, but Jones insisted that all these pirated works should be with drawn and Freud at last agreed with him.

One has to sympathize with Jones. He became the centre of a series of hostile communications, lawyers' letters, complaints and fierce exchanges, quite apart from his troubles with Rank and Freud, but a new development suddenly brought the Rank quarrel to the fore.

Rank began to intervene in the actual editing of the *Journal*, a role strictly outside his province. He became the spearhead of the attack on papers written by American analysts and developed a strong anti-American prejudice. It reached a point where he simply did not print papers which he referred to as

"American rubbish", and this was the beginning of a prolonged conflict between the Austrian and American schools which remained a simmering crater, volcanically erupting from time to time, over the following fifteen years. Jones tended to take the Americans' side because he wanted to make the Journal different from the Zeitschrift, and Freud tended to see Rank's point of view, because he had now become very suspicious of Jones. There were occasions when Jones found himself in the embarrassing position of having invited a contribution from the President of the New York Psycho-Analytic Society, only to find it mediocre when completed. Refusing the paper would have meant creating fresh hostility in New York, and Jones proceeded on the principle that since every third paper had the possibility of being a good one, he should print the others in the interests of Anglo-American amity. Unfortunately that meant upsetting the Viennese who still tended to regard the Americans as rootless intellectuals dabbling in matters which really required a European tradition. Freud, in fact, wrote to Jones criticizing the contents of the International Journal and this, combined with Rank's occasional and arbitrary usurpation of the role of editor, added to the stresses which made matters steadily more difficult for Jones.

Worse trouble now arose over the English translation of Freud's work. At first, Freud seemed indifferent to the English edition, but when he fully appreciated the scope of Jones' plan to reproduce the whole of his papers in English, his enthusiasm revived and very soon he was pressing for more speed, driven by the ghost of a premature death which he so frequently saw looking over his shoulder. Once again Rank and Jones clashed. Printing problems were further complicated by the constant chopping and changing about what precisely should be included in the four volumes of the Collected Papers, and Rank would arbitrarily issue final instructions which Jones point-blank refused to accept. Similar complications arose over copyright. In cavalier spirit, Freud would grant the English copyright to Jones, and then treat the American rights as something distinct, which his nephew, Edward Bernays, could dispose of at will, while Rank, in America, busily negotiated an American edition.

By 1922, Freud, with Rank at his side, had fastened the guilt for ever-growing delays on Ernest Jones. "I had to find out that you had less control of your moods and passions, were less consistent, sincere and reliable than I had a right to expect of you..."[2]

The reference to his passions completely bewildered Jones, until he connected it with a patient he had sent to Freud who misunderstood a "couple of kindnesses I had shown her as proofs of personal affection on my part". Explaining the situation to Freud, Jones remarked that she made "a declaration of love [to him] and a friend had misunderstood this as a declaration of love by Jones". Later Freud discovered his mistake and withdrew his charge.

Less personal, but more exasperating, differences now burst into the open. Constant frictions and delays in the publication of the English edition of Freud's work renewed his fear that he would not live to see its appearance. Once more inspired by Rank, he came to believe that Jones was deliberately creating the delays by unnecessary interference.

"Another wheel in the machinery seems to be wrong and I imagine it is your position in the middle of it and the ceremonial that prescribes your personal interference in every step…"

No less than five men, Freud said, seemed to read the proofs before the final copy went back to him, and at this rate he would hardly live to see the appearance of "two poor pamphlets". "I don't see why you want to do it all alone and suffer yourself to be crushed by the common drudgery of the routine work." The whole process, Freud concluded, could be accelerated enormously if only Jones would not insist on supervising every minute detail. His letter concluded with a remark which evoked in Jones what he described as "a mirthless laugh". Freud said: "Pardon my meddling with your affairs but they are ours and mine too and Rank is too meek to oppose you in these quarters."

Someone had clearly misinformed Freud about the nature of the relationship between Rank and Jones and all the evidence pointed in the direction of Rank himself. In reply Jones said that it was eighteen months since Hiller, installed on the spot in Vienna, had seen to it that only the final proofs came to Jones. Of course he could give up seeing the final proofs if Freud found that desirable. "On this matter of proofs", Jones wrote, "Rank's information seems very out of date and probably relates to the beginning of the Journal…"

As for the fate of the two pamphlets, Jones had revised one of them over a year ago and sent it to Vienna for printing as far back as May. Repeated enquiries about its fate since then had elicited the reply from Hiller that lack of type and paper was making matters very difficult. "So much", Jones commented, "for my interfering with details." After all, he concluded, it was for Freud that they were all working and if he, Ernest Jones, could feel that he had produced a sound Collected Edition of Freud's work in his lifetime, he would die a reasonably satisfied man.

This protestation moved Freud deeply. He replied immediately with a postcard. "Thank you so much for your kind letter. Afraid I am growing old and moody. You spared me all criticism."

Relations with Freud now passed through a series of fluctuations to improve on the whole but Rank, possibly because Freud remonstrated with him, turned an even more bitter eye on Jones.

Whatever scepticism one brings to bear on Jones' account of the whole affair, there is no questioning the fact that Hiller resigned from his job and left Vienna in March 1923. The psycho-analytic press was then separated off from Vienna and began an independent existence in London, helped by the newly founded Institute of Psycho-Analysis. Freud seems to have doubted its ability to survive, and cannot have had too much faith in Jones' business acumen because he reserved the American rights in his books and handled them separately.

A whole network of relationships within the main committee had now developed, with Rank and Ferenczi remaining very close, Freud sharing something of their intimacy and Jones, away in London, largely condemned to rely on correspondence. He makes no reference to the fact that his prolonged wrangle and open quarrelling with Rank had its counterpart in another battle with Ferenczi. Rank and Ferenczi had been working together for two years on a new book and each exchanged confidences with the other about Jones.

Clearly, by now, they did not like Jones, and Rank remarked to Ferenczi: "He doesn't really belong to us. He sits there away in London writing instructions to everyone about the Press as if we were children."[3]

Ferenczi and Rank went off to the Tyrol together in July 1923, to collaborate on a book which was itself to have cataclysmic repercussions. Simultaneously, they discussed what they should do about the ubiquitous Jones whose hand, they claimed, was appearing in far too many places for their peace of mind. By now, Rank had reached a point where he proposed demanding that Jones be expelled from the Committee but Ferenczi, who had no great love of Jones, restrained him.

By August 1923, Rank came into possession of the facts about the serious illness which had attacked Freud and since he depended on Freud for a living it changed his whole outlook. No one else at this time knew that Freud had cancer and Rank was sworn to silence.

It not merely encouraged him to strike out on his own, but made independence imperative. In this mood, he joined the last meeting of the Committee which took place at San Cristoforo on the beautiful Lake Caldanozzo towards the end of August. By now, Ferenczi and Rank had co-ordinated their forces, and Jones had to face the formidable pair in person. It quickly became evident that no reconciliation was possible.

Anxious to avoid the brunt of the first encounters and diplomatically adroit in the face of a very difficult situation, Freud remained aloof at Lavarone, higher up in the Dolomites, waiting hopefully for news of a *rapprochement*. He explained his absence to Jones by saying that if they could first achieve harmony without him, that was much better than any intervention of his own. Jones, unaware that a casual remark of his about Rank would be thrown down in the Committee like a bombshell, still had the highest hopes of reaching a reconciliation. I have tried to establish what precisely this remark was, but all three protagonists were, at this time, saying in private a number of things about one another, and at least two comments from Ferenczi were no less explosive than Jones'.

A tense scene now took place while the Committee was in session. Rank, white and anxious, insisted on stating his case against Jones, and Jones at once apologized for any unintentional pain he had caused Rank. Still more angry, because he could not accept the word "unintentional", Rank rejected Jones' apology and dramatically demanded that he be expelled from the Committee. It speaks volumes for the regard in which the Committee as a whole held Jones that most of its members would not countenance such a move. Rank's anger ran over. He stormed out of the room in a fury with Ernest Jones holding himself back "in puzzled silence".

Afterwards, as if a royal privilege had been granted, Jones wrote in his biography: "Freud agreed to receive us and I shall never forget the kindly forbearance with which he made every effort to bring about some degree of reconciliation."

The Committee members went their separate ways full of disillusionment and no one quite knew what would happen next, until suddenly Ferenczi and Rank published their new book with out any warning to Jones. Such was the understanding between Committee members that Rank and Ferenczi could be charged with a mild kind of treachery. No one except Freud knew the exact nature of this book and now its contents, when revealed, were regarded by several members of the Committee as revolutionary enough to involve sinister possibilities. Had the book received the imprimatur of Freud or was it published against his will?

Called *The Developmental Aims of Psycho-Analysis* the book brilliantly adumbrated "the propensity of patients to live out their unconscious impulses in action". Already familiar with this process, Freud had explained the conflict between it and the analytic aim of penetrating to the childhood sources of repressed impulses. Now, however, the authors seemed to suggest that discussion of contemporary situations might be sufficient, without probing deeply into the childhood roots from which they sprang. In consequence, at least two members of the Committee saw the book as a near repetition of the heresies of Jung.

A second book followed, written, this time, independently by Rank. Called *The Trauma of Birth*, it maintained that patients spent no small part of their lives in complicated endeavours to readjust to the trauma caused by the shock, and in some cases prolonged pain, of the actual birth processes. According to Rank, psycho-analytic treatment should set out to repeat the birth experience in the transference situation and if a rebirth could be achieved, the patient would be freed from the *angst*, the hidden terrors which had haunted him or her ever since the ruthless machinery of labour had expelled the patient into the outer world. Once again the dangers implicit in the book were transparently clear. If Rank, in practice, claimed that they were wrong to stop at the Oedipus complex and that the preceding birth trauma was even more fundamental to psycho-analysis, then the immensely complex elaborations from the Oedipal constellation, and indeed the kernel of psycho-analytic dogma, were replaced in a most revolutionary manner.

A discussion had taken place at the Berlin Congress in September 1922 between Rank and Freud when Rank enthusiastically outlined his new theory to Freud, but not his clinical practice, and Freud in turn discussed it with Ferenczi. Abraham has recorded that Freud's first comment to Rank had been made half-jokingly: "With an idea like that anyone else would have set up on his own."[4] Freud did not then know that Rank intended writing an elaborate book on the subject but later he revealed to Freud that he was well launched into it. The situation became complicated when Rank published the book without allowing Freud to read the manuscript, and the first step towards his own independence, consciously or unconsciously, was taken.

A tremor ran through the psycho-analytic world and more particularly the Committee. Sachs visited Freud in Vienna during the Christmas of 1923 and discussed the two books with him. Freud expressed some doubt about their contents without appearing too deeply disturbed. Sachs then wrote to Abraham in Berlin and received what was to him the reassuring reply that Berlin shared his fears. There followed the extraordinary incident when Ferenczi read a paper based on *The Developmental Aims*, to the Vienna Society, with Freud present, and did not mention the main theme of the book: "the tendency to live out memories instead of recalling them".

By January 1924, mounting criticism from Berlin served to revive the doubts Freud seemed to have stifled, and he wrote a mildly critical letter to Ferenczi which brought a passionate ten-page reply declaring that Ferenczi would never dream of departing by a hair's-breadth from Freud's teaching.

Freud, in turn, sent a balanced reply which said that Ferenczi and Rank had every right to explore any new avenue and Freud was the last man to challenge that right, but, "I know that I am not very accessible and find it hard to assimilate alien thoughts that do not quite lie in my path." It was his habit to suspend judgment, he said, because the process of evaluation tended, with him, to be prolonged. If he treasured Ferenczi's faithfulness as an expression of friendship he did not demand agreement as the proof of it, and still less thought agreement easily attainable.[5]

At this stage Freud preserved, in the steadily mounting international tension, an admirable detachment and constantly resisted pressures to take drastic action, but at last his hand was forced and he wrote a long circular letter which was a model of restraint. Dated 15 February 1924 it went to all members. Following a preamble about unpleasant agitation in Berlin and a demand from one member of the Committee for clarification of Freud's attitude, he came, by a series of highly diplomatic paragraphs, to this statement: "Our harmony, the regard for me that you have so often proved, should not hamper any of you in the free exercise of his productivity."

Freud made it clear that he saw the dangers inherent in the two books which might lead to a change in analytic techniques, but there a weakness occurred, he thought, because the authors had not set out the new techniques in detail. If it was imperative to "guard against condemning any such undertaking as *a priori* heretical", he could not himself believe, on the evidence available, that the deeper layers of the unconscious would yield up their secrets under a mere four-to-five months' analysis and "bring about lasting mental changes".

As for the second "and incomparably more interesting book", The Trauma of Birth, he regarded it as an important work but had not arrived at any final assessment of its true worth. The letter then analysed Rank's ideas with great ingenuity, in an attempt to make them fit Freudian dogma. Perhaps that exaggerates Freud's intention, but he certainly sought to show how what others regarded as heretical could be reconciled with Freudian terminology.

One big difficulty remained. The desire to return to the womb was common to Rank's interpretation and his own, but the barrier in his case was the incest barrier, whereas Rank refused to enter the phylogenetic field and saw the barrier as a direct repetition of the horror of birth. Detailed comparison, from this point onwards, revealed similar disparities. Neurotic regression was brought to an abrupt halt in one case by the repulsion of the birth trauma and in the other by fear of incest. Finally, Freud added: "It is not clear to me how prematurely informing a patient that his transference to the physician represents attachment to the mother can lead to a shortening of his analysis." A last sentence was characteristically graceful. Perhaps this long-winded analysis, he wrote, would in future deter his friends from encouraging him to write circular letters, especially on matters which they could easily resolve themselves.

One very important member of the Committee found the letter unconvincing. Abraham wrote to Freud from Berlin-Grunewald on 26 February 1924. "After very careful study I cannot help but see in the *Developmental Aims* as well as in *The Trauma of Birth* manifestations of a regression in the scientific field, the symptoms of which agree in every small detail with those of Jung's secession from psycho-analysis."

Abraham went on to say that it was very difficult to tell Freud the truth as he saw it, and certainly in other respects – the pleasant character of Ferenczi and Rank – the situation bore no comparison with "Jung's deceitfulness and brutality". None the less, three dangers were likely to ensue from these publications. First, two of their best members threatened "to stray away from psycho-analysis"; second this was symptomatic of the "falling apart within the Committee"; and third, both books would damage the image presented by the psycho-analytic movement. Abraham reminded Freud how he had warned him about Jung during their first Congress in Salzburg. "At the time you dismissed my fears and assumed that my motive was jealousy. Another Salzburg Congress is before us and once more I come to you in the same role – a role which I would far rather not play."[6] Ernest Jones shared the fears of Abraham: "To me this was reminiscent of the charge I had brought against Jung at the Munich Congress of 1913..."

Abraham firmly believed and bluntly told Freud that there was no question of hunting heretics, but the response to his circular letter disturbed Freud, and he wrote again to Abraham on 4 March: "The situation", he said, "was quite different from that which had existed with Jung." There was no malicious intent, no hidden hostility. Ferenczi and Rank were friends who were merely concerned with "the secondary concomitants of scientific work", and even if they were forced by scientific conviction to replace the sexual etiology of neurosis by physiological chance, it would merely lead to certain analysts modifying their techniques while remaining under the same roof "with the greatest equanimity". Freud added: "When Jung used his first independent experiences to shake himself free of analysis, we both knew that he had strong neurotic and selfish motives that took advantage of the discovery." This was not the case with Ferenczi and Rank. They were, in fact, quite different people. He had been forced to say of Jung that "his twisted character did not compensate me for his lop-sided theories". The theories of Rank and Ferenczi carried no such burden.

When he wrote this letter, Freud was in bad health and knew that he would never be able to sit through the new Congress at Salzburg listening to no less than fifteen threatened papers. It was equally certain that he could not attend the ceremonial dinner or read a paper of his own. The slowly developing cancer, with one operation following another, had sapped his reserves of energy and "efforts I should not have noticed before my illness are now obviously too much for me".

By the 31st of March, Freud, in a state of some depression, wondered whether he would be able to join the Salzburg Congress at all, and now he faced up to the fact, which was not at all clear to other members, that the Committee had already virtually ceased to exist. He complained of Abraham's handling of the situation. "To whatever extent your reaction to Ferenczi and Rank may have been justified…the way you set about things was certainly not friendly." A far worse accusation followed. Not only the Committee, but the whole psycho-analytic organization was in jeopardy, and Abraham's exaggerated anxieties over the dangers of the new theories might themselves "cause the collapse of the international association and everything that depends on it".

"Thank goodness", Freud said, he was selfish enough and too frail to be expected to absorb and pass an opinion on all the details of the "new squabble".

By 3 April 1924 he had definitely decided not to attend the Salzburg Congress and wrote a brief if not curt note to Abraham, Jones and Eitingon, bluntly stating the fact. Abraham replied on 4 April more or less evading the decision and suggesting that the Congress could be organized on lines which would not tire or distress Freud in any way. "For the rest your letter expressed a distrust of me that I find extremely painful… I must however state that your letter has not evoked even a shadow of guilt in me." The reason why he had not approached Ferenczi and Rank independently, Abraham said, in an endeavour to clear the air personally with them, was because of Freud's circular letter which obviously called for a reply direct to Freud. "*At your express desire* [my italics] I then wrote more extensively…'guilt' does, therefore, not exist."

As for the virtual disintegration of the Committee, Abraham claimed that it would certainly have collapsed the previous year in San Cristoforo had not he, Abraham, "kept it together". Freud's last charge about the International Association seemed ludicrous to Abraham and he had no intention whatever of splitting it into factions. He had merely tried to draw the Professor's attention to the dangers which seemed to him to threaten psycho-analysis and he fully realized how painful it would be to have this brought home to him.

Rather than split the Association he had devoted himself to strengthening its organization and "during the last few months I have borne practically the whole burden of preparation for the Congress, in the hope of making it particularly harmonious."

The letter, interwoven with affectionate references to "dear Professor", ended with the somewhat surprising statement that he was conscious of "having behaved with loyalty to everyone."[7]

Sachs and Jones meanwhile had not been quiescent. Sachs wrote to Freud on 1 March 1924: "I have tried with some success to soften Abraham's opinion but Rank and Ferenczi will also have to show themselves more amenable to his criticisms." By 10 March, Sachs' reaction had hardened considerably and he wrote saying that if psycho-analytic thinking, under pressure from the Rank–Ferenczi theories, replaced their causal psychological point of view with a few months' treatment of a patient which set out to explain the trauma of birth, "then…to co-operate with such a tendency would be just as little fruitful as that with the Jungian and Adlerian school".

The gathering storm really broke not because of Abraham's suspicions about Rank and Ferenczi, but because Freud, in an amazingly tactless moment, revealed to Rank the analogy which Abraham had drawn with the early history of Jung's defection. Rank promptly communicated the facts to Ferenczi and as Jones recorded: "it was hard to say which of the two became angrier. Ferenczi wrote denouncing the 'limitless ambition and jealousy' that lay behind Abraham's 'mask of politeness' and declared that by his action he had sealed the fate of the Committee."[8]

Many years later, Erich Fromm stated that Freud saw no sign of serious neurosis in Ferenczi, but in fact, at this stage of the quarrel, when all members of the Committee were accusing and counter-accusing one another, Freud "reproved Ferenczi about [the] re-emergence of his 'brother complex' "[9]

Abraham had been wise to avoid employing a circular letter when presenting his suspicions to Freud and could be cleared of the charge of deliberately fomenting trouble but now – although Jones does not admit it – Freud brought the fire down on his own head. Jones, Abraham, Ferenczi and Rank were locked in a hopeless struggle to sort out their difficulties and a whole turmoil of letters and talk boiled over. In an attempt to pacify the infuriated Ferenczi, Freud wrote a sadly conciliatory letter to him on 20 March, which began by saying that after seventeen years of family loyalty it would be terrible to find oneself a victim of deception. He was now an invalid whose "enfeebled frame of mind" diminished his power of working. Perhaps it would come to pass that just when ill-health had reduced him to his lowest ebb for many years, he would be "left in the lurch". He did not intend to move Ferenczi by this complaint to take any step to retain the lost Committee. That was immutably lost. He had survived the Committee that should have been his successor: "Perhaps I shall survive the International Association. It is to be hoped that psycho-analysis will survive me. But it all gives a sombre end to one's life."

Rank, meanwhile, had been in close touch with Freud, and ten days before the Salzburg Congress of 1924, a circular letter, backed by Freud, Rank and Ferenczi, reached all members of the Committee announcing, without any further equivocation, its dissolution. According to Jones, an attack of influenza made it impossible for Freud to attend the Salzburg Congress, but it is possible that his state of health only reinforced his distaste for all the feuds which centred on him.

The opening of the Congress took place in a tense atmosphere, but few of the general members were aware of the feuds disrupting the Committee and indeed, momentarily, the Committee itself came to terms with the situation in a highly civilized manner. On the second day of the Congress, Jones and Abraham put their heads together and decided to tackle Ferenczi directly. Speaking with that combination of cool deliberation and genuine concern for humanity of which he was such a master, Abraham told Ferenczi that the path he had chosen "would take him altogether away from psycho-analysis". Abraham's words carried such conviction that Ferenczi accepted the statement fairly calmly, but absolute incredulity echoed in his voice as he interjected such comments as: "You don't really believe that – but that's impossible – can you really mean what you are saying?" The conversation which followed was enlivened by the presence and wit of Sachs and the four men found themselves brought back to a degree of harmony which had proved impossible in correspondence.

The situation with Rank was quite another matter. When Abraham, elated by his success, turned his attention to Rank, he encountered a pale, intense figure, in such a state of prickly defence that however tactfully he presented his case, it was taken amiss. For nearly an hour, Abraham struggled with Rank, but it was like the blind colliding with the blind. That evening the incorrigible Hitschmann, who could never resist the temptation of a witty after-dinner speech, apostrophized Rank as the famous author of "The Myth of the Trauma of Birth". (The phrase combined elements from the titles of Rank's two books.) Rank sat, trying to smile lamely, but he was obviously in no mood to admit the solvents of wit. The following day he left hurriedly for America. Later he explained his departure to Freud on the grounds of not being able to face Abraham becoming President. After Rank had gone, Ferenczi made a splendid gesture of conciliation towards Abraham. He took it on himself to propose him as President, and the motion was carried unanimously. In Rank's absence, the Birth Trauma came under analysis and the Berlin contingent made special efforts to discuss it dispassionately, with considerable success. In the end, at least five of the six members of the Committee had achieved sufficient harmony to work together again and the Congress broke up in a quietly satisfied mood – with the exception of Rank. What had threatened to become open and destructive warfare had cooled to the point of creative compromise.

By now, Freud's doubts about Abraham and his views had diminished, and his early enthusiasm for the work of Rank suffered a setback. He wrote to Abraham on 28 April, saying that he now agreed with his judgement of the facts but could not share his view of the different personalities. By 4 May, tragically aware of the seriousness of his illness, he wrote again saying that if Abraham could imaginatively identify with his condition, he would avoid being so cross with him. "Though I am supposed to be on the way to recovery there is deep inside a pessimistic conviction that the end of my life is near." The scar from the second operation caused him constant torment and an "irrational love of life", was in determined battle with "a more sensible resignation", which led to a state of depressed tension.

Both Freud and Ferenczi now attempted some empirical application of Rank's theory of the Birth Trauma, and for the first time Freud admitted the relevance of statistical analysis which, until then, he had rejected. It seemed ironically convenient to pick up a weapon from which he normally recoiled in distaste in order to explore and expose the theories of an opponent, but at least he made an authentic use of statistics. Before Rank's theories could be seriously countenanced, he said, it was necessary to accumulate comparative data between those who had known a prolonged and difficult birth, those born in comfort via a Caesarean operation, and those who were first and third-born. In his own practice Freud now applied these categories but the analytical results were unsatisfactory and did not confirm Rank's presuppositions.[10] As if to underline the terrible difficulties of proving any psycho-analytic theory in practice, Ferenczi, in sharp contradiction to Freud, found Rank's technique highly successful and the correlation between neurosis and birth seemed to him established.[11]

Away in America, events were moving to a different climax. Richard Ames, President of the New York Society, had invited Rank to lecture there for six months, and Rank took advantage of this to propagate his own psycho-analytic theories. The old technique of long-drawn-out analysis, which Freud regarded as imperative before the secrets of the unconscious could be brought to the surface, had been superseded, Rank said, by his own short-term method, lasting possibly only a few months.

Brill, in America, received this dramatic shortening of analysis sceptically, but it came as a relief to many younger disciples who quailed when confronted with the prospect of treating one patient, week in week out, for three whole years. Once again, Freud received this news at first with great tolerance and restraint. The detailed identity with the events which had led up to the break with Jung, does not seem to have occurred to him.

Within a few weeks he dramatically reversed his view of Rank. Jones pointed out that eighteen months before, Freud had remarked: "In the fifteen years I have known Rank, I scarcely ever had the idea of Rank needing analysis." Now, suddenly, an explanation of Rank's conduct had to be found, and he began, for the first time, to talk of Rank's psycho-neurosis. Freud argued with Ferenczi about the exact nature of this neurosis, and Ferenczi fell back on common-sense terminology, claiming that it was due to a swollen head. Freud, following classically correct psycho-analytic lines, deplored that Rank had never been analysed.

Since the Jones biography of Freud was published, we have had the advantage of Erich Fromm's evidence and the statement given by Dr Harry Bone, a New York psycho-analyst, who was in frequent personal contact with Rank for years: "In all the numerous times and all the quite various situations in which I had the opportunity to see him in action and in repose I sensed no indication of psychosis or any mental abnormality whatsoever."

Despite his descent into the neurotic depths in search of an explanation of Rank's conduct, Freud determined to greet him warmly when he returned from America.

On 25 August 1924, he sent a curiously ambivalent letter to Rank in New York which admitted, for the first time in writing, that he had changed his view of the Trauma of Birth. The whole letter was permeated with the goodwill of the peacemaker, but in one of those bursts of tactlessness which sometimes shattered all his good intentions, he explained that Eitingon and Abraham had visited him. Both admired Rank's work, he said, but regretted the abrupt manner in which Rank had broken away. Rank, he knew, felt that he, Freud, had been exposed to influences hostile to Rank, but his changed view of the Trauma of Birth amounted to nothing more than a theoretical difference. He did not quite so easily come under the influence of others, nor did he take their difference of opinion too seriously. Either Rank or Freud would prove right in the long run and one or the other would have to modify his view.

The letter remained, up to this point – certain diplomatic ambiguities apart – very tolerant and rational. Then came this phrase: "I know that your discovery does not lack applause, but you must remember how few people are capable of passing judgement and how strong in most of them is the desire to get away from the Oedipus whenever there is a chance." This could be read to mean that much of Rank's applause came from people who were incapable of passing judgment or those anxious to over throw Freud's theories. No wonder Rank's reaction, on reading it, was one of dismay. The phrase which followed converted that dismay into outright anger. Even if his book contained "many misconceptions", Freud said, he did not have to be "ashamed of [his] brilliant and substantial production".

Ashamed! It had never occurred to Rank to be ashamed. Perhaps what Freud's unconscious meant was — ashamed of his deviation. I have not been able clearly to establish whether a letter from Rank mentioned by Jones in the biography[12] reached Freud before or after this one. At all events, it finally dashed Freud's hopes of any future reconciliation. It was an "extremely unpleasant letter", and Freud wrote off to Ferenczi on 29 August 1924 in complete bewilderment. "Which is the real Rank, the one I have known for fifteen years or the one Jones has been showing me in the past few years?"

This last comment needs emphasizing. In the biography, Jones did not evade responsibility for exacerbating Freud's view of Rank. Many years later Erich Fromm wrote: "In the next years, fantastic rivalries and intrigues between Jones and Ferenczi seem to have continued. Ferenczi suspected Jones of lying and of ambition, based on financial motives, to unite the Anglo-Saxon nations under Jones' sceptre."

Certainly Jones himself admitted that as a result of his frankness in appraising the new developments, and the direct way in which he told Freud what he now thought of Rank, "Freud was thereby influenced against me".

There is, in fact, a note of objectivity running through Jones' account which some of his calumniators sadly lack, but he certainly omitted any reference to his preliminary quarrel with Ferenczi, possibly for reasons of tact. As we shall see, quite new evidence is also available about Ferenczi, but for the moment, Rank dominated the scene and Ferenczi was one of the conciliators.

Rank, at this stage, tried to rationalize his growing hostility towards Freud as a result of his (Freud's) listening to the sustained and malicious criticism coming from Abraham, but Freud in stantly pointed out that it was an odd way of criticizing Abraham to follow the very path of which Abraham complained. Mean while Freud, corresponding at length with Ferenczi, admitted that it looked as though Jones had been right about Rank, and he was disturbed that Ferenczi should have become so involved with Rank. He now compared Rank to Adler, and said that Rank had been carried away in just the same manner, but if he came to his senses, it would be time to "recollect his extraordinary services and his irreplaceability and to forgive him…"

Whatever carefully organized picture of a ruthless dictator insisting on detailed observance of Freudian dogma may emerge from opposing camps, time and again, in a very complex correspondence, Freud at the outset showed great tolerance and restraint. Invariably, in the early stages, he emerged as a wise peacemaker searching for compromise, and only when he had finally made up his mind that no hope remained, did the iron fist descend; but then, woe betide the deviant. However, the question has to be asked – no hope of what? – and the answer – of undeviating loyalty to Freud's theories – did involve, in the final analysis, the imposition of a psycho-analytic discipline.

On 9 September 1924 he wrote again to Ferenczi. "It looks now as if, from the very beginning [Rank] had the intention of establishing himself on the basis of his patent procedure which he kept secret and wanted you to join him." Freud expressed astonishment at the degree of Ferenczi's collaboration with him. Freud sent one of Rank's letters to Ferenczi and after reading it, with great surprise, Ferenczi wrote to Freud saying that he had finally decided to break off relations with him.[13] By 20 October Abraham addressed another letter to Freud which said: "If a complete break should come about between Rank and yourself, there would be nothing to prevent us others from re-establishing the Committee."

In the same month, Rank decided to call on Freud personally in Vienna, and from all the evidence it cost him great anguish to make up his mind to face the Master. Indeed, he almost missed the train and as he jumped aboard at the last moment he "collapsed into a kind of melancholic-coma".[14] Three hours' sustained talk with Freud merely repeated old charges against Abraham and even Freud himself. The fact that Freud had been prepared to listen to Abraham's criticisms and suspicions had forced Rank to believe that Freud was about to disown him, and since he depended so much for patients upon Freud he had to think of his own survival and strike out alone. This explanation prefaced an embarrassed confession that he was on his way back to America once more.

A coincidence, shattering for Freud, now followed. Deeply disturbed by the thought of breaking away from a Father-figure who represented towering strength and a whole life experience of psycho-analysis, Rank called once more on Freud on 19 November, to say goodbye. They expected this to be the final break. Both men were heavy in heart, but Freud took the situation with a rationalist's calm. And then, that afternoon, he received a letter from Brill in America, which vividly described the wide spread heresies disseminated by Rank on his last visit to New York. He had, it seemed, brushed aside sexual etiology, removed the necessity to analyse dreams and limited interpretation to the basic birth trauma. In short, Rank had slowly grown in stature in his own eyes until his theories had obliterated those of the Master and Rank in person had replaced him. Freud now circulated Brill's letter to all members of the Committee, and that seemed certain to consign Rank to outer darkness for the rest of his psycho-analytic life.

Erich Fromm has described Ernest Jones' account of this quarrel as "rewriting...history" which "introduces into science a method...thus far we have expected to find only in Stalinist 'history'. The Stalinists call those who defected and rebelled 'traitors' and 'spies' of capitalism. Dr Jones does the same in psychiatric parlance with Rank and Ferenczi." [15]

Certainly there was a clear distinction between Freud's suspicion of Rank's neurosis and Jones' conviction of Rank's psychosis. Jones' tendency to overplay his hand in the biography, led Fromm to claim that "in the end Jones was to win out over his rivals". There were others who felt that Jones, like Freud, could not bear any serious rival, and that many of these new struggles were irreconcilable in consequence. Personally I gained a different impression of Jones. Intrigue was not a part of his nature, he gave no sign of overweening ambition and, in conversation at least, he remained objective about many contentious events. If he had the ability to precipitate quarrels by insisting on his own interpretation of the facts, no strong-minded, intellectual man, with a highly developed personality, could become a cypher.

Fromm seemed nearer the truth when he said:

"If what Jones writes was true it was indeed a most amazing oversight on Freud's part that not until the moment of manifest conflict did he see the psychotic development in two of his closest pupils and friends. Jones makes no attempt to give objective proof for his statement about Rank's alleged manic-depressive psychosis. We have only Jones' statement, that is, only the statement of a man who had been intriguing against Rank and suspecting him of disloyalty for many years in this fight within the court around Freud." [16]

Once again "intriguing against" has to be distinguished from "suspicion of disloyalty". The first was untrue and the second true. As for the image of a royal court, with courtiers seeking special favours – there is an element of truth in it although Freud himself would have recoiled from any such image.

The remaining details of Rank's final defection have been spelt out carefully by Jones, in his biography, and there is no need to recapitulate elaborately. Suffice it to say that a miraculous but temporary realignment suddenly occurred which indicated, according to Jones, the depth of Rank's psychosis. In commonsense parlance, Rank was not yet ready to face up to the consequences of the final break, and he had only reached Paris on his way to America when remorse overtook him and he broke off his journey and returned to Vienna. Presently there was another interview with Freud and now Rank had shaken off his depression and behaved like a changed man. "He discussed the whole matter with Freud", Jones wrote, "as if in a confessional... Freud was deeply moved by it and overjoyed at finding again his old friend an adherent."

Still more remarkable, Freud now seemed to use and endorse the very heresy which had nearly caused "the tragedy" to explain, technically, his rupture with Rank. He wrote to Eitingon saying that Rank had played out his neurosis along the lines which he and Ferenczi "had described in their joint book and that the content of it was closely similar to the theories Rank had put forward in his book on the birth trauma".[17, 18]

Rank finally employed the device of the circular letter to all members of the Committee to humbly apologize for his comments on Jones and Abraham, and to ask their forgiveness for what he had done. Abraham remained unconvinced. He received the circular letter and Freud's enthusiastic news of reconciliation, with reserve, and Freud tried to explain to him that since he did not know "all the circumstances of the case" perhaps he could not get a balanced picture. He added: "I know about it all, know the whole sad story and can say that I am confident that he has been cured of his neurosis by this experience just as if he had gone through a proper analysis."[19]

The reconciliation was short-lived. Rank set off for America in January 1925 but, after a few weeks, he was back once more in Vienna, in a state of apathy and depression. Freud still regarded his condition as pathological but did not expect a relapse to his former hostility. Rank appeared at the Hamburg Congress in September 1925, and read an obscure paper at breakneck speed, making assertions which he did not pause to verify, because he said, he had to leave for yet another American visit.

Once more Freud was absent from the Congress, and Abraham sent him, on 8 September 1925, a long account of the proceedings which said that "Rank tried in a commendable way to come closer to us and we, on our part, have – I believe – helped him in this." Abraham agreed with Jones that Rank seemed a really sick man. Abraham talked at length in private with Rank, and busied himself behind the scenes trying to reassure the disturbed Americans who clearly did not welcome yet another visit by Rank. None the less, after the Congress he set off. Almost a trans-Atlantic commuter by now, he returned once more at Christmas 1925, but remained aloof for several weeks hardly communicating with his old colleagues and ignoring Freud. Then on 12 April 1926 he paid a last visit to Freud and Freud's hopes of a warm response from

Rank were finally dashed. He looked pale and ill, he spoke haltingly and he seemed very uneasy. Freud's tone and manner quickly changed. When he realized that this was a final break and a last visit, he suddenly saw no reason "for expressing my special tenderness. I was honest and hard. But we have certainly lost him for good." [20]

Very much later in the year 1937, when he was an old man close to death, and the feuds and tensions no longer mattered to him, Freud wrote of Rank: "It cannot be denied that Rank's train of thought was bold and ingenious but it did not stand the test of critical examination..." Freud believed, in the end, that Rank's heresies were partly the product of a conflict between Europe's post-war misery and America's prosperity and that the ruthless foreshortening of the analytic process was a sop, carefully devised by Rank to meet the speed of the American way of life.

NOTES
1.   11 February 1921.
2.   7 January 1922.
3.   Verbal evidence from Dr Clara Thompson.
4.   Letter to Freud, 4 March 1924.
5.   4 February 1924.
6.   Letter dated 26 February 1924.
7.   Letters of Sigmund Freud and Karl Abraham: edited Hilda C Abraham and Ernst L Freud, pp. 356–9.
8.   Sigmund Freud: Life and Work: Ernest Jones, Vol. III, p. 68.
9.   Ibid.
10. Freud to Ferenczi: 4 February 1924.
11. Freud to Ferenczi: 14 February 1924.
12. Sigmund Freud: Life and Work: Ernest Jones, Vol. III, p. 12.
13. 21 September 1924.
14. Verbal evidence from Jones.
15. The Dogma of Christ: Erich Fromm, pp. 93–94.
16. Ibid., p. 95.
17. Sigmund Freud: Life and Work: Ernest Jones, Vol. III, p. 76.
18. Eitingon, 29 December 1924.
19. 29 December 1924.
20. Ferenczi, 23 April 1926.

Chapter Fourteen

The Breach with Ferenczi

Dr Michael Balint, the closest living friend of Sandor Ferenczi, believes that the ebullient, lovable Ferenczi preserved elements of the child in his character all his life. "It took some time for his critical faculty to catch up with his enthusiasm," Dr Balint said.[1,2] It was this temperamental inability to examine in depth the brilliant ideas which his ever-fertile mind constantly produced, and his skill at leaping to the conclusion that hypotheses were verifiable facts, which led to the first trouble with Freud.

Twenty-one years Freud's junior, unlike Abraham's, Ferenczi's career was not a steady, rising curve of success. Temperamentally opposites, the two men followed different paths, but Ferenczi found it hard to believe that Abraham, a man born to be president of whatever intellectual group he joined, was as Balint put it, "unswervingly fair". Analysts, Balint said, admired Ferenczi for "his freshness, originality and fertility", but they rarely understood him. He was "seldom studied thoroughly, seldom quoted correctly, often criticized more often than not erroneously". It had been his fate on at least one occasion to have his ideas "rediscovered later, and then attributed to the second discoverer". The entirely unknown and unpublished battle with Jones bears some small witness to this, although it eventually became clear that Ferenczi had misunderstood Jones, and later analysis cleared up yet another unecessary quarrel about priorities.

Ferenczi's relationship with Freud remained more spontaneous than that with Jung. It was, indeed, in its intensity, much more a repetition of the relationship with Fliess, and in Ferenczi's case reached a sometimes embarrassing pitch. He also had one similarity with Jung when he revealed a gullibility about occult "evidence". In the beginning, Freud, who was then much more sympathetic to the occult, came under Ferenczi's influence. On the way home from their joint American trip, they visited a woman who claimed to be a soothsayer capable of reading letters while blindfold. Freud rejected these magical powers, but both came away believing that she had telepathic gifts of a high order. Writing to Ferenczi later, Freud still refused to believe in the occult and explained away Frau Seidler's gift as a question of thought transference. A prolonged exchange of letters produced fresh examples of what we now call extra-sensory perception, some not easily explained away, some transparently charlatan. Ferenczi finally overreached himself by discovering that he, himself, was "an excellent soothsayer", not to say thought reader, and believed that this might make a revolutionary difference to psycho-analysis. According to Ernest Jones, he laughingly said he would present himself in Vienna as the Court Astrologist of Psycho-Analysts, but much more seriously, he wanted to publish his experiments and conclusions in the *Jahrbuch*. Freud gently indicated that perhaps it might be wise to wait a couple of years to digest and confirm his new theories.

In December 1910, Freud met Bleuler and Jung in Munich, and when he discussed Ferenczi's findings with them Jung at once said that he had long believed telepathy to be a possibility. From thought reading and telepathy, Ferenczi proceeded to the famous episode of the "talking" horse known as Hans, in Elberfield, which did not literally speak, but was said to be capable of making simple mathematical calculations, drawing circles and generally behaving, at some levels, rather like a child.

This markedly increased Ferenczi's enthusiasm for the subject. He decided to consult the Berlin soothsayer once more and to spend a week studying the behaviour of the horse in order to write a brochure for Freud's *Schriften zur angewandten Seelenkunde*. Freud agreed to this, provided that Ferenczi first spent at least a fortnight studying the literature on the subject. When Ferenczi discovered what a vast jungle of books, articles and pamphlets had been written already, his enthusiasm waned. In November 1913, he read a paper to the Vienna Society and produced a real live soothsayer, "Professor" Alexander Roth, who, unfortunately, did not perform according to expectations.

The whole prolonged excursion by Freud and Ferenczi into the realm of extra-sensory perception revealed Jungian characteristics in Ferenczi which presaged some of the difficulties to come. When Ferenczi told Freud that he wanted to give another paper on his telepathic experiments at the next Congress, Freud replied on 20 March 1925: "Don't do it...you would be throwing a bomb into the psycho-analytical house which would be certain to explode."

Ferenczi's final difficulties with Freud began in 1931, a year full of big and small disasters for Austria and Germany. The Viennese attempt to contain the economic situation with the *Creditanstalt* had failed, unemployment in Austria and Germany had reached catastrophic proportions, and the horrifying situation of a loaf of bread costing as much as a suit of clothes had begun to make money meaningless. Depression hit the analysts no less than the ordinary worker, and many could not afford to attend that year's Congress, which was finally cancelled.

Freud himself still underwent the torments of cancer and the unsatisfactory prosthesis, although he spent six thousand dollars to have it readjusted by Professor Kazanijan of Harvard, a man said to possess magical powers. The Nobel Prize continued to elude him. Several times, eminent men in many walks of life had put forward his name to the Nobel Committee and as far back as 1920 he had written to Abraham: "I got over the Nobel Prize passing me by for the second time excellently, and have also realized that any such official recognition would fit not at all into my style of life."[3]

It was in May 1931, that Ferenczi sent Freud a copy of a paper in which he "claimed to have found a second function of dreams – dealing with traumatic experiences". Freud replied that years before, he himself had pointed out that this was their first as well as their second function. A certain sophistication now informed his tolerance and he could, at last, detect heresy on the air even before his disciples. Freud first became aware of a change in Ferenczi when a gap of three months occurred in their correspondence. Ferenczi at last wrote to say that a wealth of new ideas had introduced a bewildering confusion into his methods, and Freud replied: "There is no doubt that by this interruption in our contact you are becoming more distant from me. I do not say more estranged, and hope not…"

Ferenczi set off to Capri for a holiday, and on his return, decided to visit Freud in Vienna where they talked far into the night. Once again, Freud felt that personal contact had achieved what correspondence so often complicated, and he said goodbye to Ferenczi in good spirits. On 5 December 1931 Ferenczi wrote a letter which showed that there had, in fact, been no change in his attitude to Freud.

Freud's concern over Ferenczi sprang as much from some startling elements in his new technique as from his growing sense of distance. One aspect of these techniques could only be seen in perspective by examining the theory surrounding it. Dr Balint, many years later, stated that "Psycho-analytic thinking is now beginning to re-examine Ferenczi's ideas about the paramount importance of the adult's actual libidinous behaviour towards children in the pre-Oedipal times."⁴ This was to take a much less anxious view than Freud now adopted. Ferenczi had come to the conclusion that when a patient, during the course of analysis, regressed to an infantile stage as a means of escape, the best way to treat him or her, was to play the part of the loving parent, thus breaking into the classic detachment which maintained a certain distance between patient and analyst. Dr Balint was later to distinguish between malignant and benign regression and to argue that Ferenczi's quarrel with Freud really crystallized around a distinction which neither, at that time, clearly understood. Jones put the matter somewhat differently: "In connection with his recent ideas about the central importance of infantile traumas, particularly parental unkindness, Ferenczi had been changing his technique by acting the part of a loving parent so as to neutralize the early unhappiness of his patients."⁵ Because she was more consistently associated with an image of loving-kindness, Ferenczi had chosen to play the role of the mother, relegating the father to a shadowy background in a manner alarming to orthodox analysts.

In order to achieve the maximum identity with a loving parent which many patients had never known, Ferenczi allowed the patients to kiss and caress him, and returned these attentions when it was desirable to establish a completely convincing reaction. The drums of taboo beat up from years of medical tradition to protest deafeningly against any such behaviour, but instead of referring to "this monstrous perversion of treatment", Freud received and analysed it with complete scientific detachment. On 13 December 1931, he wrote: "I see that the differences between us come to a head in a technical detail which is well worth discussing. You have not made a secret of the fact that you kiss your patients and let them kiss you..."

Difficulties among his colleagues would certainly arise, Freud said, when Ferenczi came to give a full account of his treatment and had to decide whether to reveal or conceal this factor. Concealment lacked integrity and was in any case difficult to achieve. Patients talked, and sooner or later it would leak out, as in fact, the "secret" had already leaked to Freud via a mutual patient. Freud was not a person bunkered by bourgeois convention to the point of condemning automatically minor erotic exchanges of this kind, and he fully appreciated, he said, that in the new Russia, sexual liberation had reached a point where such behaviour might be socially acceptable; unfortunately they were not living in Russia.

What would be the result if psycho-analysis assimilated these techniques into general practice and someone then said – why stop at kissing?: "...Soon we shall have accepted...the whole repertoire of *demi-viergerie* and petting parties..." No doubt a tremendous rush of new interest in psycho-analysis would be one result, but younger colleagues might find it very difficult to resist each new temptation as it arose and, "God the Father Ferenczi, gazing at the lively scene he [had] created [would], perhaps, say to himself: maybe after all I should have halted my technique...before the kiss."[6]

Freud did not want to enter into a discussion of the fresh calumnies this might bring down on the head of psycho-analysis because they were self-evident, but it certainly seemed to him a "wanton act to provoke them". The letter concluded: "I do not expect to make any impression on you. The necessary basis for that is absent in our relations. The need for definite independence seems to me to be stronger in you than you recognize."

Long after this letter was written, and many years after Jones completed his biography, Dr Michael Balint, who had access to Ferenczi's papers, spelt out the theoretical side of this new quarrel in much greater detail. Summing up the theory of regression as a mechanism of defence and a pathogenic factor, Freud distinguished between three aspects of regression – the topographical, the temporal and the formal.[7] In a later paper[8] "formal regression" has vanished from the list and regression as a part of the actual transference taken its place. Regression played a double role in analysis. In its "adult" form it became an "ally of analytic treatment" but it could also become, in another form, a very serious danger.

As Michael Balint put it with such concise clarity: "...certain patients could not remember some parts of their emotional past but must act them out in their relationship to the analyst, that is, that transference must be understood also as a repetition of the patient's forgotten past which had become inaccessible to any other means."[9]

Freud advised all analysts to treat this reaction with great caution, and proceeded from a simple warning that sympathetic interpretation was the best course of action, to recommend the more severe discipline of deliberately subjecting the patient to "privation".

This, of course, was in sharp contradiction to the course Ferenczi now pursued, with, he argued, no small success. In his fascinating Rado Lecture, Dr Balint has given an explanation of Ferenczi's successes and Freud's failures with regression techniques, which carries some conviction. It is necessary to recapitulate some of the earlier history to see the whole theory in perspective. It was shortly after he had undergone analysis with Freud that Ferenczi began his experiments with regression, backed, in the beginning, by Freud himself. Today ECT or electric-shock treatment is familiar enough in cases of chronic depression and it was a psycho-analytic equivalent of this technique which became the "guiding principle" of Ferenczi's work. At a certain, carefully chosen moment, the patient was either deliberately led into or asked to expose himself to recollections which. would increase tensions and come as something of a shock to him. The choice of the right moment might be dictated by a prolonged stalemate between patient and analyst, when the patient's associations had dried up, but it must also be qualified by the state of "sensitivity" of the patient. Someone already quivering with apprehension was not a suitable subject for shock treatment, but someone in a state of confused stalemate might, like the chronic depressive, be brought to life again and the associative currents set flowing once more. More important, the shock could easily produce "a break through into consciousness of a hitherto repressed instinctual urge, changing an unpleasurable symptom into a pleasurable satisfaction".[10]

Ferenczi had not, himself conceived this technique, nor did he claim to have done so, but Freud was at some pains to explain at the Budapest Congress of 1918 that the original idea came from experiments which he, Freud, had undertaken. In such experiments, the "shock" administered, might consist of warning the patient that treatment would be terminated on a fixed day. In another instance, a patient suffering from agoraphobia was, at the right time, deliberately exposed to the situation he most dreaded. Freud confirmed Ferenczi's findings that a shock of this kind sometimes reanimated treatment. Unfortunately, in the majority of cases, the breakthrough did not have sufficient momentum to last very long, but in others, the exceptional few, it carried over until the end of treatment. The results of several years' work convinced Freud that what had seemed to have revolutionary possibilities at first sight, proved to be too elusive and unpredictable to convert into an accepted part of psycho-analytic technique. When he saw Ferenczi carried away by enthusiasm, and watched him extending the new technique into ethically dangerous fields, he first sent him a long, chastening letter, and then tried to talk him out of what he privately regarded as the small madnesses inherent in the worst extremities of Ferenczi's treatment.

Developing shock treatment into active intervention, Ferenczi had discovered that when the infantile pathogenic traumas were reactivated by analysis, they revealed what he called a bi-phasic structure. In the first phase, it showed that the child's parents had subjected him to traumatic over- or under-stimulation, and in the second that their conscious or unconscious guilt feelings made it impossible to respond to the child's attempt to get "comfort, reparation or understanding". The parents were driven by guilt to deny their "participation in the preceding period and had to show...that they really did not know what all the fuss was about".[11]

Ferenczi's next step, seemed to him logically inescapable. If the original trauma had been brought about by what he called "over- or under-stimulation", and subsequently the parents had been forced to become indifferent to the patient's appeals, then therapy should replace the missing response. The analyst's reaction was, according to Dr Balint, to be reduced to three parts.

1. To help the patient to regress to the traumatic situation.
2. To watch carefully what degree of tension the patient will be able to bear in this state. 3. To see to it that the tension will remain at about that level by responding positively to the regressed patient's longing, cravings or needs.[12]

Disagreement with Freud intensified at this point, whether because Ferenczi had now built a therapeutic system of his own, or because Freud felt him to be scientifically in error, was open to question. Certainly Freud's fear that any improvement brought about in the patient's condition – by actively playing the role of the mother – would vanish as soon as the analyst withdrew, proved accurate in a number of cases. His second prediction, that patients would never independently maintain whatever mental health they had recovered, also had some validity, although Balint was later to question this.

Dr Balint, in fact, saw the whole disagreement in somewhat different terms. He distinguished very carefully, from his own clinical experience, between malignant and benign regression. "I think that Freud in his early psycho-therapeutic years encountered almost exclusively cases of malignant regression and these encounters left a deep impression on him. Ferenczi on the contrary had some remarkable successes with a few benign cases of regression as well as some failures with malignant ones."

As late as 1930, Ferenczi summed up the essence of his new techniques under the name of the "principle of relaxation". By now, active participation in regression which aimed at increased tension, had been replaced by intervention to avoid increased tension. Most of Ferenczi's patients came to him with more than "a decade of treatment by other analysts behind them" and many admitted quick and remarkable improvements. Any suggestion by Freud or Jones that Ferenczi failed to understand the problems raised by his technical innovations, is contradicted by his own notes and papers published since his death. The one aspect where he remained comparatively blind, involved his apparent inability to see that, when the analyst was so closely interlocked with the patient, he could never expect to set the patient free as an independent, self-sufficient entity, but would be forced to continue, *ad infinitum*, to gratify his cravings. This blind spot was probably the result of his intense relationship with Freud and the need to win his approval at any cost. Time and again, in his papers and in private conversation, he returned in bewilderment to the fact that Freud — did not understand. Lack of understanding in Freud promoted a reaction of lack of understanding in Ferenczi. Freud's inability to see the "major step forward" taken by Ferenczi produced a defence against accepting Freud's main criticism, which in turn involved abandoning his theory. A simpler factor persisted in the background. Nothing, Freud knew, was so calculated to throw psycho-analysis into disrepute as the appearance in the press of a story that kissing patients had become an accepted part of technique.

By the following year, the breach between Freud and Ferenczi had widened and Freud wrote to Eitingon on 18 April 1932: "Isn't Ferenczi a tribulation? Again there is no news from him for months. He is offended because one is not delighted to hear how he plays mother and child with his *female* patients." [13] This letter made clear another dangerous element in Ferenczi's treatment.

Despite the frictions, disputes and growing alienation Freud, with his tolerant self in the ascendant, now announced that he favoured Ferenczi's nomination as President of the Society in succession to Eitingon, but he qualified this in a way which displeased Ferenczi's friends. He implied — quite falsely according to those close to Ferenczi — that his condition had pathological elements and that becoming President would act as "a forcible cure". Ferenczi hesitated to accept the honour on the grounds that his practice now absorbed all his attention and he had so little time to spare for the heavy administrative and organizing work involved in the Presidency. [14] Ferenczi wrote protesting that there was nothing pathological in his reaction, but he himself oversimplified the situation when he said that it was entirely due to concentration on work. From all the evidence he wanted to maintain his distance from Freud, even if it still did not amount to an open break. [15]

By August, he much more frankly admitted the underlying motive for his refusal. He wrote to Freud withdrawing from the nomination and now he confessed that he found his own views so much in conflict with classic psycho-analytic principles, that it would be false for him to become President. [16]

In the background of this new quarrel, other matters were not going well for Freud, and his reaction seems reasonable when the growing pain of repeated operations, the agony caused by the clumsy prosthesis and a steadily diminishing practice, are taken into account. He wrote to Marie Bonaparte[17] saying that his four patients would be reduced to three in the following month and there was no sign of any newcomers: "They are, of course, quite right;

I am too old and working with me is too precarious." Freud now wrote to Ferenczi refusing to accept his explanations and claiming that there need be no conflict with the Presidency unless he intended developing a quite new form of psycho-analysis. This could be read as an attempt to bring Ferenczi back into conformity by repeatedly flourishing the prize of the Presidency. Moved by the persistence with which Freud was trying to keep their relationship intact, Ferenczi replied that he had no intention of founding a new school, but he had constantly doubted whether Freud really wanted him to become President. Now that this doubt was at last removed, he had brought himself to reconsider the whole situation. Ferenczi next telegraphed Eitingon asking him to suspend negotiations for the Presidency until he had personally talked the whole matter over afresh with Freud, and at this point, the American analyst A A Brill came into the picture.

He visited Ferenczi in Budapest, found him bristling with suspicion, and was disturbed to hear him exclaim in the middle of an argument about Freud's capacity for insight that: "He's got no more insight than a small boy." [18] Brill and Jones reported this remark but made no allowances for Ferenczi's temperament. Such a spontaneous outburst came naturally to him in the middle of a heated argument. Whether he would repeat it in cold blood, is another matter. However, the phrase certainly carried loaded implications because it reproduced almost word for word Rank's exclamation at the time of his defection.

A student and friend of Ferenczi's, Mrs Izette de Forest, went to see him before his last visit to Freud. Ferenczi "told Mrs Izette de Forest how sad and hurt he had felt at the harsh and hostile way Freud had treated him". When Ferenczi returned from his visit to Freud, Dr Clara Thompson accompanied him in the train from Vienna to Germany. He described the visit to her as "terrible", and said that Freud had told him he could read his paper at the psycho-analytic congress in Wiesbaden if he promised not to publish it. [19]

According to Ernest Jones, the visit developed somewhat differently. Ferenczi came striding into Freud's study and without any preliminary burst out, "I want you to read my Congress paper." Once again, this was not unexpected in a man of Ferenczi's temperament in that situation. He felt that his paper contained the best argument in favour of his views and he vainly hoped that when Freud had read it, his resistance would diminish if not vanish. Alas, it did not work. Worse still, in the middle of the interview, Ferenczi suddenly learnt that Brill would be joining them at any moment and when, some minutes later, Brill did appear, Ferenczi felt too embarrassed to continue discussing their very private quarrel. He left shortly afterwards in a disturbed state.

Now came the very unpleasant discovery that he was suffering from pernicious anaemia and thenceforward Jones explained the growing bitterness between Ferenczi and Freud as the result of this disease exaggerating his latent psychotic trends. At least two witnesses who knew Ferenczi well, and visited him frequently during 1932, deny that any such psychotic trends were evident. Dr Clara Thompson states: "...except for the symptoms of his physical illness, there was nothing psychotic in his reactions which I observed. I visited him regularly and talked with him, and there was not a single incident, aside from memory difficulties, which would substantiate Jones' picture of Ferenczi's psychosis or homicidal mood." [20] After a long discussion with Dr Michael Balint about Ferenczi's condition I came to a similar conclusion. "I saw him several times towards the end of his life", Dr Balint told me. "He was paralysed but there was no sign of mental disturbance." Dr Balint still treasures a collection of 2,000 letters from Ferenczi to Freud, and he told me that the correspondence ends on an exchange in which both men are revealed as "in a bloody-minded state".

Immediately following their last meeting, Freud telegraphed to Eitingon: "Ferenczi inaccessible – Impression unsatisfactory." Eitingon thereupon invited Jones to stand as President and there were those in the early psychoanalytic movement who saw something sinister in this nomination. Jones had quarrelled not so very long before with Ferenczi and had been accused of political manoeuvring to bring the Viennese group under the aegis of the Anglo-Americans with himself as President. He did, now, become President, but after long talks with Jones, Dr Balint and others involved in the situation, I cannot accept the charge that he manoeuvred himself into the position. Jones had worked desperately hard for the cause of psycho-analysis and if he had now emerged as President that was nothing more than his due. If Jones remained too reverential towards Freud the overwhelming pressure of Freud's immensely strong personality and his determination to maintain the "purity" of psycho-analysis, would automatically reduce the critical defences of all but the toughest person. Whatever the exact truth, Jones for the next twenty years, found himself burdened with the weight of an office which made extravagant demands on time and energy, and never failed to serve the cause with unflinching devotion.

When Ferenczi next wrote an angry letter accusing Freud of deliberately introducing Brill as a witness, he also complained of the attempt to delay publication of his paper for one year. Freud replied that this delay was in his, Ferenczi's, interests, but to the outside observer, it could also be seen as in the interests of maintaining psycho-analytic discipline if not what Fromm refers to as the Party Line. An important question has, at long last, to be asked. Was psycho-analysis now contained within a political party, the leader of which could cast out any deviant simply by disapproving of the line he took? That was the claim later made by Erich Fromm. Freud told Ferenczi in his letter of 2 October 1933 that he, Ferenczi, had systematically turned away "from him and had probably developed a personal animosity which goes further than you have been able to express". He added: "Each one of those who were near me and then fell away might have found more to reproach me with than you, of all people." This was his first admission that he harboured any feeling of guilt in the case of earlier defections.

Extraordinarily, against such a highly charged background, the Wiesbaden Congress went off reasonably well, but the whole question of intellectual freedom seemed in some danger when Eitingon decided to forbid Ferenczi to read his paper. Jones, too, remarked that "it would be so offensive to tell the most distinguished member of the Association, and its actual founder, that what he had to say was not worth listening to". Moreover, to prejudge a paper before the whole Congress had heard it came, in these special circumstances, close to censorship. Even more important, Freud himself was not against the paper being read and Jones felt that its contents were too vague to do any real harm.

Between the stormy exchanges, Ferenczi finally sailed home to read it with a panache made more dashing by an edge of anger. In the end, all their worries and anxieties proved ill-founded. The paper received a warm welcome and to Jones' astonishment Ferenczi responded to him personally in a most friendly way.

Following the Wiesbaden Conference, Ferenczi and Freud never discussed their differences again. The relationship dwindled away into a series of short, warm and friendly letters from Freud which carefully avoided any reference to past conflicts and Ferenczi replied in a similar vein. One Ferenczi letter revealed a combination of insight into future events and profoundly sane advice to Freud, which, as late as 1933, a few months before Ferenczi's death, showed no sign of the mental disturbance of which Jones and Freud complained. Ferenczi entreated Freud to flee from Austria while there was yet time to escape the Nazi persecution, and Jones, at last, had to admit that their might be some "method in his madness" – a phrase of unconscious ambiguity?

Freud's last letter to Ferenczi, dated 2 April 1933, was full of warmth and consideration for his very old friend, and said that any discussion of technical and theoretical novelties could wait for a more auspicious moment.

Ferenczi wrote on 3 May, opening his letter: "Dear Herr Professor", in marked contrast to Freud's "Lieber Freund". "Only a few short lines to tell you that the date of your birthday is continually in our mind. Let us hope that this next year will not bring forth such unpleasant events as the last has done."

His health was much the same he said and he tried to share his doctor's optimism.

Ferenczi's last letter – a few lines of birthday congratulation – was written the following day, and three weeks later his condition rapidly deteriorated and he died. Jones recorded that "towards the end came violent paranoic and even homicidal outbursts", but Ferenczi's friends deny the statement. It remains true that some patients with pernicious anaemia suffer brain damage which produces symptoms similar to those described by Jones.[21] As for Jones, he was moved to re-emphasize Ferenczi's mental imbalance in unusually colourful language: "The lurking demons within, against whom Ferenczi had for years struggled with great distress, conquered him at the end…"

Without exception, everyone rose above the quarrels and recriminations to regret the death of a distinguished colleague who, whatever his personal shortcomings – and who was without them? – had worked for over thirty years as a pioneer in the arduous techniques of analysis, and had himself made a number of brilliant contributions.

Freud wrote to Oscar Pfister: "My warmest thanks for your letter of condolence on Ferenczi's death. I deserve it for the loss is very distressing." There followed a reference to the pernicious anaemia and the deep psychological changes in Ferenczi's makeup. Freud concluded: "We will continue to remember him as he has been for the past twenty years. I believe some of his achievements, his Genital Theory, for instance, will keep his memory alive for a long time."[22]

Dr Balint, who saw Ferenczi shortly before his death, said that Ferenczi deeply regretted his differences with Freud. What had begun as near love between the two men ended in professional jealousy and personal recrimination. For the rest, some of Ferenczi's patients, who are still alive, remember him with great affection and there are those among them who still swear that his "activist" treatment gave them back the precious gift of mental health. As one man put it: "I shall never forget his warmth, animation and courage – he took risks with his patients – moral risks because he could be so easily misunderstood – but he never took advantage. I am what I am because of what he did."[23]

Thus, in the end, there was no open and definite break with Ferenczi but with his death, the Old Guard seemed on the point of disintegration. Jung, Adler, Stekel, Rank, Ferenczi, one after another they had broken away, defected, or deviated from the Freudian circle, and the persistent erosion disturbed the whole group. Even the sworn bonds of blood brotherhood symbolized by the Order of the Ring, had not proved strong enough to hold them together. It remains to say that Dr Balint does not believe that Ferenczi's theories are dead.[24]

One further question requires attention. Was the psycho-analytic movement debased from a profound theory of the nature of the human psyche with a brilliant therapeutic technique, into a political party, subject to all the petty feuds, disciplines and manoeuvring which are characteristic of politics?

Erich Fromm has pointed out that while Freud was at high school he had a considerable interest in politics and a close school friend, Heinrich Braun, was to become a leader of the Socialist movement. "By that time," Fromm wrote, "Freud had become greatly interested in a future as a political leader, and he intended to study law as a first step in this direction."[25] Later, Fromm claimed, Freud tended in various written and verbal comments to identify to some extent with Moses "who led a mass of ignorant people into a better life".

Fromm was obviously searching for evidence to fit the theory of a psycho-analytic party boss with a messianic vision. Of course, politics did enter into the struggles of psycho-analysis, but Freud was not, as we have seen, by nature or conditioning, a born political leader.

There are other explanations, not only of the feuds and quarrels themselves, but of the particular character they acquired, which belong in another and later place.

NOTES
1. Verbal evidence from Dr Balint.
2. *International Journal of Psycho-Analysis*, Vol. XXX, 1949, part 4.
3. 31 October 1920.
4. *International Journal of Psycho-Analysis*, Vol. XXX, 1949, part 4.
5. *Sigmund Freud: Life and Work*: Ernest Jones, Vol. III, p. 174.
6. Letter 13 December 1931.
7. *A Metapsychological Supplement to the Theory of Dreams*, 1915, p. 227; *The Interpretation of Dreams*: Sigmund Freud, p. 548 (1914).
8. 'The Benign and Malignant Forms of Regression', Sandor Rado Lecture (24 and 25 May 1963).
9. Sandor Rado Lecture (24 and 25 May 1963).
10. *Ibid.*
11. Sandor Rado Lecture (24 and 25 May 1963).
12. Sandor Rado Lecture (24 and 25 May 1963).
13. The italics are mine.
14. 1 May 1932.
15. 21 August 1932.
16. 19 May 1932.

17. 14 April 1932.
18. Evidence from Brill and Sigmund Freud; *Sigmund Freud: Life and Work*: Ernest Jones, Vol. III, p. 184.
19. *The Dogma of Christ*: Erich Fromm, p. 97.
20. *The Dogma of Christ*: Erich Fromm, p. 99.
21. This is disputed by one school. Vitamin B12 deficiency may cause psychotic states but not violent paranoid or homicidal states.
22. 28 May 1933.
23. Personal communication from a patient.
24. *The Journal of Psycho-Analysis*, Vol. XXX, 1949, part 4.
25. *The Dogma of Christ*: Erich Fromm, p. 100.

Chapter Fifteen

After the Dissolution

What happened to these men as, one by one, they left Freud and his circle and developed professional lives of their own? Adler, after his defection, continued a successful career, with a number of well-known people becoming his patients, but a continuous need to firmly establish a school of his own comparable with Freud's remained a powerful part of his ambition. Among his patients there unexpectedly appeared the English actor, playwright and wit Noël Coward. Coward did not undergo analysis by Adler, but he happened to read one of Adler's books one day while suffering from a breakdown, and according to his own account some mysterious alchemy produced a dramatic effect tantamount to a cure. When Adler came to lecture in England, Coward invited him to see *The Astonished Heart*, a play which he had written almost as part of his therapy. Coward took the lead himself and Adler said: "I think that he may have felt for this one moment, 'an old man sits up there who knows what I am up to', but he soon forgot since he is a real artist."[1]

Like all other ex-members of the Freudian circle Adler under went many hardships during the First World War, but one, at least, differed from the account given by Phyllis Bottome. It is sometimes assumed – quite wrongly – that any analyst or psychiatrist worth his salt should be capable of curing his own family troubles on the principle, physician heal thyself; but Adler, like most other analysts, had his share of domestic trouble which culminated in Raissa, his wife, suddenly uprooting herself with all her children and hurrying back to her beloved Russia in a storm of homesickness and bitterness. Adler, bereft of his children, the most prized of his possessions, was shattered but he quickly sent a peremptory telegram demanding their immediate return. Raissa telegraphed back "Shall wait". According to Dr John Moore, who knew Adler well, Adler himself now decided to ignore the risks of war-torn Europe and rushed off deep into Russian territory in an attempt to bring her back. To everyone's surprise he successfully accomplished, in record time, a mission full of hazards.

Phyllis Bottome's account explains Raissa's dramatic return to Russia as the result of homesickness, intensified by misunderstandings with her husband. In fact, Raissa's own evidence shows quite clearly that far more serious dissension had temporarily broken up the Adler family circle. When she returned from Russia, Raissa's closest friend told Phyllis Bottome,

> "that she had gone away wretched, like a human being who had lost his [sic] way in the world; and she came back having fought out her battle in her own soul like a human being that has found the way to live under whatever difficulties or provocations. I don't say that Raissa was any happier with Adler, for I saw no reason to suppose that she was until later…

Behind the façade of a respectable marriage, terrific tensions, quarrels and reconciliations converted family life into a series of dramatic explosions, interwoven with long spells of passionate and sometimes tearful response. It could hardly be otherwise. Raissa was politically a revolutionary and her extreme thinking must have disturbed the much more liberal Socialism of Adler. No fiercer strife exists than that between different shades of left-wing thinking. Worse still, they were almost forced into taking different sides during the First World War, with Adler, an intransigent Viennese supporting the Germans, and Raissa of Russian birth, embracing the Allied cause.

The family reunion did not last long. Adler was suddenly conscripted and served for two years as a military doctor near the Russian front, first at Cracow and then at Brno. When he returned to Vienna once more, in 1916, he went back to the old Café Central to find some of the original Individual Psychology group dead, some far away in other lands and a mere remnant still waiting to hang on his words. "Adler was never the same again after the war," an old friend said of him. "He was much quieter and stronger."

Now, at these meetings in the Café Central, another storm within a storm blew up to reveal volcanic troubles disturbing the Adlerians no less than the Freudians. When one of their number asked what the world needed today, Adler answered: "It seems to me that what the world chiefly wants today is *Gemeinschaftsgefühl*."

From the height of his wisdom and intelligence, from the depth of his experience and imagination, Adler, the great Individualist Psychologist, had decided that what the world wanted was good will. No wonder that the hard-bitten journalists, the finicky intellectuals, the positivist scientists, sitting round him in the Café Central, looked at him with some bewilderment. Was this the great message he brought back from the turmoil of war?

The Nietzscheans among his disciples were first puzzled, then dismayed and finally angry. As Phyllis Bottome put it: "They had gladly accepted his 'inferiority sense'...the family constellation was no difficulty for them; even the teleological rather than a causal aim they had swallowed...but this tame ethical stress upon a vague word..."

Neuer, one of the disciples in the group, re-echoed the word: "*Gemeinschaftsgefühl!*" he exclaimed. "What a word to use – it doesn't even exist in philosophy."

"It is what the world wants," Adler repeated quietly.[2]

His disciples Neuer, Schrecker and Freschel, all burst into argument and slowly the atmosphere became tense. As good Nietzscheans, Schrecher and Freschel could not possibly accept this sentimental generalization in place of their realistic will to power and in the end they quarrelled openly with Adler and dramatically, that night, left his circle. The analogy with Freud and his circle was not very close. These café discussions were bohemian gatherings where men sharpened their wits on one another, and they bore little resemblance to a disciplined group with an appointed Chairman which read and seriously discussed scientific papers.

It is a sad thought that Phyllis Bottome's biography which sets out to re-create a great man only succeeds in smothering him with a dangerous kind of idolatry. "From this moment, in the Café Central," she wrote, "and with those men who sat around the table, Adler was prepared to alter the history of mankind. Because he had told them that he was, and because they had learned to rely upon him, they threw in their lot with his new idea."[3]

In the early 1920s Adler developed a circle in his Vienna flat which duplicated in some respects that of Freud. A group of twenty members came and went in the flat until with increased numbers, again like Freud, they were forced to move out of Adler's large drawing-room into a hired hall. As Lewis Way wrote: "The intimate discussions became lectures, although after they were over the friends would still congregate in the Café Siller down by the Danube Canal." Adler was invited by the President of the City School Council to help create child-guidance clinics attached to state schools. He took charge of the clinic at the Kaiser-Franz-Josef Ambulatorium and in due course –

according to Lewis Way – no less than thirty similar clinics were functioning in Vienna "under the direction of his co-workers".

In 1934, with Hitler in the ascendant, Adler decided to abandon the country of his birth and to make a permanent home in America. From boyhood onwards he had always cherished a dream of settling there. He first visited the States in 1926 on the strength of a slender invitation to give three lectures through a commercial agent and his difficulties were intensified by his poor English. Listening to Adler struggling with the English language could produce as much anguish in the listeners as it did in the speaker, but by 1929 he had become much more proficient and was appointed a visiting professor to the College of Physicians and Surgeons at the Medical Center of Columbia University. His main difficulties in America arose not from language or a certain resentment among some psychiatrists about the intrusion of this alien Jew with the thickest of accents, but from the same old internecine psycho-analytic strife. Adler now seemed to some Americans to commit the very crime of which he had complained in Freud. The American approach was frequently eclectic, absorbing elements from Freud, Jung and Adler, but Adler now refused to compromise with any other school. He expected his colleagues to accept his own exclusive Adlerian gospel, and they expected him to admit the value of some points in the approach of Jung and Freud. Phyllis Bottome put it this way: "They asked and expected Adler to 'mix' his psychology with theirs; but this, to him, was to 'divide' the individual... It would have seemed as reasonable to St Paul to join the teachings of Christ with those of the prophets of Baal."⁴ Adler made constant approaches to his American colleagues, and tried to persuade them to accept his point of view but whether he persistently attempted co-operation with them is another matter. According to Mrs Bottome: "After a time Adler settled down into an intellectual loneliness tempered by friendships without professional understanding, or professional understanding without friendship."⁵

If anyone had dared to suggest to Adler that he had tried, like Freud, to set up an exclusive school of his own, with himself as the Master, and that any individual who did not accept and swear by the whole creed was doomed to rapid expulsion – he, Adler, would have exploded into that wonderfully dramatic anger which made him such an exciting person to encounter. There were, none the less, elements of truth in this. A prophet unrecognized in his own land he had gone to a far country expecting the recognition and honour traditionally rendered to exiled pundits, only to find a qualified admiration which refused to accept his key to the Universe as that exclusively cut by the Almighty with Adler's assistance.

In May 1937, he lectured at Aberdeen University in Scotland, and the night before he died he went to the cinema with Phyllis Bottome's husband, to see the film *The Great Barrier*. He returned home, wrote letters for a couple of hours and went to bed. Always an early riser, Adler got up the next morning, ate a good breakfast and went for a short walk. A young girl observed him striding vigorously along the street and said to herself, "What a vigorous old boy that is! He steps out like an athlete."[6] At that very moment he slipped and fell. A young theological student dashed to his aid, and heard him mutter the one word – "Kurt" – the name of his son, and then he relapsed into complete unconsciousness. The student desperately tried a form of heart massage but it was useless. So it came about that Alfred Adler died on the street with no one near who knew him, but it was a quick, painless death of which he knew nothing, and in the many discussions on death he had indulged, that was always the way he had hoped fate might choose for his personal extinction.

The greater tragedy was perhaps Raissa's, his wife's. She had torn herself out of two different cultures at great cost to her spirit, first from her beloved Russia where her many friends were now completely cut off and living in a forgotten past, and then from Austria, where her new friends were left behind as she reconciled herself to living in America. She had recently readjusted herself to married life with Adler, and was beginning to adapt to the American way of life when suddenly – her husband fell dead on a far-distant, chilly, Aberdeen street.

She flew from Paris to London and thence on to Aberdeen, and she was present with several members of the family at King's College Chapel, Aberdeen, for the memorial service. The whole faculty of Aberdeen University appeared in their robes, with the Lord Provost, representatives of Individual Psychology groups from London, Chicago, Germany, Belgium and Holland, and the Rev. Mr Linton, Adler's translator. As the chapel vibrated to Adler's favourite Bach Chorale one at least among the audience found her grief overwhelming.

In terrible contrast, Freud added a few words as an obituary on Adler's death: "For a Jew-boy out of a Viennese suburb, a death in Aberdeen is an unheard-of career in itself and a proof how far he had got on. The world really rewarded him richly for his service of contradicting psycho-analysis."[7]

The story of Wilhelm Stekel ran very differently. Shortly after his final quarrel with Freud and the break with Jung, he took over from Alfred Adler the neuro-psychiatric section of the War Hospital in Vienna. According to Stekel, Adler "had been transferred to a provincial town, although he had done excellent work. His examinations were profound, his histories of the diseases were blameless, he was a model physician." None the less, Adler had been moved to what could only be regarded as lower-ranking work in a provincial town. Not that the War Hospital in Vienna could be considered a medically desirable place if you were a wounded soldier: "I have seen", wrote Stekel, "terrible examples of the work of these executioners. Convalescents still in pain, their wounds unhealed, were marched off to their regiments. In many hospitals, they were tortured with a faradic brush so that they preferred the terrors of war to the terrors of hospital."[8]

It was not difficult for Stekel to establish a reputation for loving-kindness in such an atmosphere but his spectacular ability to hypnotize patients at will and send them off into profound sleep, won him fame as a veritable magician of medicine. He claimed that his real satisfaction came from work and especially from writing his book *Onanie und Homosexualität*. Masturbation, he argued in this book, freed men and women or boys and girls, from the "social obligations of gratitude". The masturbator gave himself or herself great pleasure with an organ which society expected him to employ exclusively in marriage. Children, he claimed, sometimes masturbated out of defiance towards the parents. "The drive to masturbate becomes most deeply fixated when the child feels that in this way he acts against his parents' wishes..." There was a great deal more detailed and intelligent analysis of masturbation in the book, but in Freud's eyes it did not justify its title.

After the war, Stekel successfully practised as a psycho-analyst, but he developed a defiance towards Freud in his own success. "Freud", he said to a friend, "fondly believed that I would not be able to earn a decent living without his help." Strictly speaking, Stekel first supported himself after his break with Freud by articles in newspapers, lectures and books, and these in turn presently drew many new patients into his net. He was also at one stage – during the first weeks of the war – forced to live on his savings. Some Freudians called him "a mere journalist" but he commented: "I wasn't disturbed by their often venomous animosity." An important letter from Freud to Stekel has come to light since Stekel wrote his autobiography. It certainly reveals hostility from Freud but it was hostility far removed from hatred. Dated 13 January 1924 it said: "You are mistaken if you think that I hate or have ever hated you. The facts are that after an initial sympathy I had reason for many years to be annoyed with you while...having to defend you against the aversion of everyone around me..."

Stekel's letters, Freud complained, failed to mention the central fact in their relationship, that he, Freud, was forced to break with Stekel after he had deceived him "on a certain occasion in the most heinous manner". This referred to the editorship of the *Zentralblatt für Psychoanalyse* which Stekel, according to Freud, had refused to relinquish when their relationship broke up. Stekel gave a vague but quite different account of this: "After our separation Freud was confident that he would get the editorship of the *Zentralblatt* for himself and Tausk, but Bermann [the publisher] did not co-operate. I remained the sole editor of the *Zentralblatt*."[9]

Freud's letter, written with withering coolness, went on to dismiss Stekel's "repeated assertion" that the break between them occurred on scientific grounds. It might sound very good in the ears of the wider public to provide such an alibi, Freud said, but it was far from the truth. He could only repeat that Stekel's character and behaviour first made any collaboration with Freud and his friends impossible and then precipitated the break. "As you most certainly will not change – you don't need to for Nature has endowed you with an unusual degree of self-complacency – our relationship stands no chance of becoming any different..."

Stekel had suggested that his psycho-analytic and literary success would probably annoy Freud but Freud quietly denied this and admitted that Stekel had both helped psycho-analysis "and done it great harm". A last piece of advice concluded the letter: if Stekel couched his polemics in more polite terms, Freud's colleagues might begin to read his publications more objectively.[10]

I have not been able to trace Stekel's letters to Freud, but it was almost as if after a long interval, Stekel desired to become friendly once more with Freud. However, neither side made sufficient concessions.

Like most of the early analysts, Stekel presently looked to the rich, new, ever-accommodating America for fresh pastures and when Dr Samuel Tannenbaum, a New York doctor, came to Vienna, he immediately brought up the possibility of a lecture tour for Stekel. Dr Tannenbaum was already a disciple of Stekel's and now, in Vienna, he revealed that he had one great ambition in life: to attempt a reconciliation between Freud, Adler and Stekel. Stekel smiled ironically as he listened to the eager outpourings of Tannen-baum. When Stekel told him of his recent correspondence with Freud, Tannenbaum remained undismayed and insisted that reconciliation should first be attempted between Stekel and Adler, proceeding by easy stages to the more remote Freud. He then booked a box at the Opera in Vienna, and invited Adler and Stekel to join him for a performance of *Don Giovanni*. Stekel gave a brief and direct account of what followed in a simple, revealing sentence: "We accepted but there matters remained." Frustrated in the early stages of his high mission, Tannenbaum insisted that Stekel could establish a new future in the United States and strongly advised him to master the rudiments of English.

Stekel was grappling with another problem at this time which absorbed every penny of the money he possessed. His relations with his wife had finally broken down, another woman had appeared in his life and he had determined on divorce, despite the crippling expense involved under Viennese conditions. In the end, the expenses for the American trip were provided by Tannenbaum and one day Stekel received a curt cable: "I am sending the money."

Stekel's expectations on arrival in New York have not been recorded, but Tannenbaum met him at the pier and almost at once wafted him away to address one of those groups of middle-aged American ladies who represent a formidable hazard to any visiting lecturer. "I had expected a reception committee. Instead I entered a small room where I was introduced to four elderly women who wore large spectacles." The usual formalities were fulfilled with almost unseemly haste and then, without more ado, "these women fired off" a barrage of questions about conditions in Vienna, about the unconscious, about transference. In no time, the trapped Stekel confronted by all four of his unrelenting audience was restless, bored and unhappy. The situation became crucial when some bladder trouble made a toilet an urgent necessity. Tannenbaum later and rather heartlessly advised him, "America is a country where you have to be master of your bladder."

This unauspicious opening to Stekel's visit to America was followed by further surprises. He had what he referred to as other "tedious engagements" and when he travelled by night to Chicago to fulfil one of these he was astonished to find the lower berth occupied by a "pretty young lady". She seemed quite self-possessed and quickly informed him that this was normal in America. Once again in Chicago he suffered from the suffocating attention of clouds of "elderly ladies, wearing horn-rimmed glasses, in urgent search of information". Finally, he refused to accept any more invitations to dinner parties unless they ceased to harass him with torrents of superficial questions. Stekel's last lecture, delivered at Chicago University, was called "Psycho-analysis: Its Limitations and Its Abuses". This had a very special reference to the conflict in Chicago between the preoccupation with psycho-analysis of the upper-middle and intellectual classes, and the quacks who exploited it.

Despite Stekel's attempt to cloak his visit to America in evasive terms it could not be considered a success. He gave a last lecture to the staff of St Elizabeth's Hospital in Washington and returned with a sigh of relief to his beloved Europe. Stekel now followed a pattern which had an interesting uniformity among exiled members of the Freudian circle. Like princes in exile they each sought to establish a court of their own, reproducing within it the rituals and sometimes intolerance of which they accused their former monarch. Invited by the famous psychiatrist Kretschmer to deliver an introductory lecture on "compulsion diseases" at a psychotherapeutic congress in Baden-Baden, Stekel wrote: "The congress would be dedicated to the study of this abnormality. It was not only a great honour, it was the first official recognition of my work. Simultaneously twelve of my pupils announced lectures on the same theme. My school came before the public for the first time as a group."[11]

If it did come before the public as an organized school, it did not prosper for long, and there was something pathetic in what really amounted to a challenge to the now internationally widespread acceptance of Freud and the permeation of his name and doctrines into everyday life.

Stekel, of course, had been subjected to all manner of hazards and hardships in his lifetime and it was not unexpected that he should exaggerate his success. His health, too, now showed serious signs of deterioration. Not only a constant state of nervousness and the persistent bladder disorder troubled him, but new symptoms suddenly warned him, as a doctor, that he might be suffering from diabetes. A urine analysis showed a seven and a half per cent sugar content and he immediately consulted a specialist who put him on a rigid diet. Freud's complaint that Stekel's personality, not his work, caused disruption was partly borne out – on this occasion at least – by his nurses and doctors. The doctors "complained that they had never seen such a nervous man". This, of course, had a physiological basis, since the rapid reduction in his blood-sugar content had produced hypo-glycaemia.

When he recovered, Stekel set out to realize his long-standing ambition to start his own clinic. He rented four rooms where he and his pupils treated and analysed patients, and founded the quarterly periodical *Psycho-Analytic Practice* with his friend and pupil Dr Ernst Bien as editor. Unfortunately, the same journalistic streak of which many Freudians complained, broke into his activities to create, under his direction, a "Clinic for Jealousy", where he devoted one evening a week to "the victims of morbid jealousy and to jealous individuals in general".

Not unexpectedly, the journalists of the day immediately fastened on this and Stekel was inundated with telephone calls, requests for interviews and a desire on the part of the more persistent to "sit in" at the work of the clinic. The ferment of publicity reached a peak when a humorous journal published a sketch in which Othello was seen entering the Stekel Jealousy Clinic as dark-skinned and malignant, and leaving it as fair-skinned and smiling. One can visualize the cool fury with which Freud would have received any such representation of psycho-analytic work. It seemed to justify his worst fears about Stekel. The whole balloon of talk, novelty and publicity was finally pricked in the most ignominious manner when the expected crowd of jealous people turned out to number two only, and both were women "who claimed to be victims of their husbands' morbid jealousy". The clinic died from inanition.

As the Nazi movement gained momentum, Stekel's German publisher decided that it would be unwise to continue publishing the ten volumes of his work and a refugee publisher bought the remaining copies at a shilling a volume. On the very day Hitler marched into Austria, Stekel was still hesitating whether to leave the country or not, and only the urgent persuasion of the American writer, John Gunter, finally drove him to uproot himself, abandon his home, furniture, musical instruments and library and take one of the last trains, with his wife and three patients, to Switzerland. Travelling from Switzerland to England he fell in love with London at first sight and wrote: "If I could only stay in this wonderful place for the remainder of my life!"

His wish was unexpectedly granted. He had intended to cross the Atlantic to the United States, but a successful lecture at the Tavistock Clinic inspired the staff to organize a petition to the Home Office claiming that English psychology would benefit if Stekel were allowed to remain in England. His wife had been seriously ill and he himself was in frail health. The Home Office, despite tightening restrictions on the increasing number of refugees, gave him the necessary permit.

Stekel settled for a time in Tonbridge where he drifted through the days weeding the garden, reading, playing the piano and working on his autobiography. He sat in the garden one high summer day writing his last words about Freud: "In my writings I have pictured the pettiness and the foibles of one of the greatest geniuses of our time...but the last thing I want is to produce the impression that I intended to belittle the greatness or deny the merits of this singular personality." [12]

Slowly, the lack of intellectual stimulation began to distress a man accustomed to the bustle, activity and gaiety of Vienna, and Stekel found himself forced to take a room in a London hotel. His wife, still recovering from a serious operation, was not fit enough to accompany him, and remained at Tonbridge.

One day, in March 1940, Mrs Hilda Stekel was called urgently to the London hotel to find her husband in a state of apathetic collapse. The doctors said he had fallen into a hypoglycaemic coma from self-injection of too large a dose of insulin. Mrs Hilda Stekel wrote: "I suspect that this was his first suicide attempt – made with conscious or unconscious intent."

It now emerged that Stekel had developed diabetic gangrene of the foot, and as a physician he knew that the prognosis was very bad. By June, the condition of his foot had seriously deteriorated and his depressed mental state was much worse because news of the fall of France had shocked him profoundly. The old energetic, jaunty, Stekel who always needed vigorous employment, who had once been nicknamed Quicksilver and never knew an idle moment, was reduced now to a thin, haggard, yellow-hued person who slowly lost interest in the external world.

A few days later, Mrs Mundy Castle, a close friend of the Stekels, went to see him in his hotel and found him beautifully dressed in grey and white, looking very distinguished with silver hair and a well-trimmed beard, but his face was unrecognizable as that of the old Stekel. "He had passed into a new dimension," she said. "A sense of stillness and of resolution emanated from him…" A week later, a friend of Mrs Mundy Castle's telephoned him saying that Mrs Castle had recommended Dr Stekel to her and she wished to become his patient. "Dr Stekel," he repeated after her. There was a long silence and then he said: "He is dead," and put the receiver down.

Mrs Stekel saw him on one last occasion. She offered to stay in London to nurse him but he vigorously opposed it. "When we parted I cried bitterly," she wrote.[13] Four days later he did not answer when the maid knocked on the door of his room and after many attempts to make him hear, they finally broke in to find him dead in bed.

From the letters he left it was clear that he had planned his suicide several months before. A splendid flourish occurred in his last note: "I am passing away like a warrior. Guns and cannons are only temporary. The greatness for which England stands will put right all wrongs."

Ironically, the newspapers reported his death as the act of an "unbalanced mind", but no man ever made his exit from this life in a more deliberate and rational manner.

NOTES

1. *Alfred Adler*: Phyllis Bottome, p. 88.
2. *Alfred Adler*: Phyllis Bottome, p. 115.
3. *Alfred Adler*: Phyllis Bottome, p. 115.
4. *Alfred Adler*: Phyllis Bottome, p. 223.
5. *Ibid.*, p. 224.
6. *Alfred Adler*: Phyllis Bottome, p. 277.
7. Letter to A Zweig, 22 June 1936.
8. *The Autobiography of Wilhelm Stekel*: p. 159.
9. *The Autobiography of Wilhelm Stekel*: p. 145.
10. *Letters of Sigmund Freud*. Selected and edited Ernst L Freud, p. 352.
11. *The Autobiography of Wilhelm Stekel*: p. 238.
12. *The Autobiography of Wilhelm Stekel*: p. 285.
13. Introductory Note by Mrs Hilda Stekel to *The Autobiography of Wilhelm Stekel*.

Chapter Sixteen

The Last Years

Long after his troubles with Freud were over Jung set out to build a house of his own beside the beautiful upper lake of Zurich "because", he said, "I wanted to make a confession of faith in stone". In 1923, the first round house at Bollingen was built, and at intervals of four years he added fresh structures until finally, in 1931, with dark symbolic intent he extended the tower-like annexe because, "I wanted a room in this tower where I could exist for myself alone." Jung kept the key to the room exclusively himself and this second tower became for him a place of spiritual concentration where he spent long hours alone, either in the deepest contemplation or painting the walls with many strange pictures. His anthropomorphic view of the house developed very remarkable characteristics which, when Freud heard about them, drew from him the comment: "I would never have believed my old colleague could have persisted in his eccentricities quite so long – or elevated them to the importance of a philosophy."[1] The apotheosis of Jung's mood was reached when he wrote: "I suddenly realized that the small central section which crouched so low, so hidden, was myself."[2] He could no longer hide himself behind the "maternal and spiritual" towers, he wrote, and was forced to add another upper storey which became for him his "ego-personality".

Every new utterance about the house at Bollingen brought it closer to the human psyche, and however poetic or mystical the observer, there were times when his words read like those in the case history of one of his own patients. "At times I feel as if I am spread out over the landscape and inside things and am myself living in every tree, in the plashing of the waves, in the clouds and animals that come and go."[3]

Calling upon Jung at Bollingen, one first confronted and knocked on a heavy wooden door set in a thick stone wall which in turn seemed to have grown out of the earth. The wall, the door and the oddly shaped towers rising beyond it all, seemed medieval. It was not uncommon, as you waited outside, to hear the ringing sound of an axe falling upon wood because there was no coal, gas or electricity in this strange house and Jung lit his own oil lamps and chopped his own wood.

Elizabeth Osterman was one such visitor and she recorded: "There, beyond a second doorway, was the strong-backed, white-haired, eighty-three-year-old man in his green workman's apron, seated before the chopping block. Behind him was a large square stone carved by him in earlier years when he was attempting to give form to his emerging realizations."[4]

Everyone who visited Jung came away with the impression of a man whose powerful personality and intellect had come to terms with the natural life and whatever mysterious forces underlay everyday turmoil. Certainly by now Jung was something of a sage, an oracle, living out his last years in distinguished isolation, and famous men and women came from all over the world to pay homage as they might to a holy man, or to pose questions which he alone, they believed, was equipped to answer. A certain disposition and temperament were prerequisites to such reverence. Those who followed the coldly scientific paths of Freud found it difficult and at least one distinguished Freudian crinkled his nose with distaste when he heard of the medieval towers, the Yoga exercises, the extravagant personifications of wood and stone, and said: "Every man to his own taste."[5]

Whereas most of Freud's early circle are now forgotten, Jung sustained an international reputation and left an imprint which seems likely to last as long as Freud's. Certain religious or mystical predispositions are necessary to appreciate the finer points of Jung's collective unconscious, individuation and his excursions into the occult.

Jung's career, after his break with Freud, differed widely from that of Adler or Stekel. In 1920 he set out on a series of expeditions to unexpected places like Tunis and Sousse, and in Morocco he carefully studied and claimed to have penetrated the Oriental mask of calm and apathy. He visited London in 1925, and a wonderful exhibition of tribal life under British rule in the famous Wembley Exhibition of that year made him resolve to take a trip to tropical Africa. In the autumn of the same year he set out for Mombasa. Whereas the enormously powerful Jung survived the hazards of tropical malaria, amoebic dysentery and pneumonia, several of his fellow travellers fell sick and died.

Later came visits to India and Italy. In the 1930s, as we know, he was mixed up in the unfortunate business with the German Society for Psycho-therapy then directed by Reichsführer Dr M H Göring, and subsequently challenged the charge of fellow-travelling with the Nazis. His work as a psychiatrist and psycho-analyst was brilliant but he did not resign his co-editorship with Goring of the *Zentralblatt für Psychotherapie* until 1940.

Serious illness attacked him at the beginning of 1944, but he saw no psychosomatic symptoms in the heart attack which followed a broken foot. The heart attack was serious and, "hanging on the edge of death", he had to be given oxygen and camphor injections which carried him into phantasmagoric experiences of a remarkable kind. When his nurse told him afterwards that "it was as if you were surrounded by a bright glow", he seemed to take this statement at its face value. He absorbed, literally, the illusion that he was floating high in space observing "the globe of the earth, bathed in a gloriously blue light" and commented: "Later I discovered how high in space one would have to be to have so extensive a view – approximately a thousand miles!"

He still firmly believed – indeed until his death – that there was at least part of the human psyche not subject to the normal laws of space and time and constantly invoked the name of J B Rhine as proof of these experiences, apparently unaware that Rhine's experiments have been subjected to severe qualification.

A brilliant linguist, with a very easy, natural manner, he could talk most entertainingly in five languages, and in 1936, at the tercentenary of Harvard University, he gave an oration which was long remembered for its erudition, grace and insight. Popular in American university circles he revisited that country again in 1937 to give the Terry Lectures at Yale. His visits to England were no less frequent than those to America. He became Chairman of the International Congress of Psychotherapy at Oxford in 1938, and at last, in his fifties, responded to a persistent demand to resume systematic teaching at university level. The C G Jung Institute now grew into an organized body, where those interested in analytical psychology could attend seminars and lectures. The London Society of Analytical Psychology was formed, and the Institute of Psychiatry at the Maudsley Hospital gave systematic lectures on Jungian psychology.

In his eighties, Jung wrote that remarkable book *Memories, Dreams, Reflections*, which combined a great deal of confused metaphysical, and very revealing biographical material. It was one of thirty books and scores of papers which he wrote in his lifetime – many of them important works, some of major significance – and not unexpectedly it contained a long and interesting dissertation on life after death.

"...while the man who despairs marches towards nothingness, the one who has placed his faith in the archetype follows the track of life and lives right into his death. Both to be sure, remain in uncertainty, but the one lives against his instincts, the other with them."[6]

Jung underwent other experiences of the "evolution of the soul after death" when he woke one night convinced that he had spent an entire day with his dead wife in the South of France. Before she died she had been engaged on a long study of the Holy Grail and now "the thought that my wife was continuing to work on her further spiritual development – however that may be conceived – struck me as meaningful and held a measure of reassurance for me".[7]

Clearly Jung went to his death with considerable hope that somewhere concealed within the awe-inspiring imponderables of the Universe lay a gleam of hope for the hereafter, which might eventually illumine the everlasting darkness of death and extinction.

As for the charming and implacably honest Abraham, he did not live long enough to fulfil all that his talents promised. Born in Bremen in 1877, he died forty-eight years later, and Jones wrote of him in a brief memoir: "He was always hopeful, however irksome or sinister the prospect and his buoyancy, together with the confidence that went with it, often contributed materially to bringing about a more successful issue than at first seemed possible."[8] Throughout the course of the First World War he was chief physician to the Psychiatric Station of the Twentieth Army Corps, which gave him wide experience of war neurosis and left him with a disastrous legacy of ill-health. Dysentery became a recurrent trouble over the years until the spring of 1924, and then, in May 1925, he picked up a virus and within a fortnight developed an alarming attack of broncho-pneumonia. A local bronchiectasis troubled him for the rest of his life, and although he presided at the Hamburg Congress, he obviously found it a strain. A brief recovery was followed by another relapse, and in November he underwent a serious operation which failed to bring about the expected cure. His strength slowly diminished until he lost consciousness and died on Christmas Day 1925.

Abraham's most systematic and important contribution to psycho-pathology were his three works on manic-depressive in sanity, but Jones has said that if he were asked to select Abraham's most distinguished single piece of work "it would probably be that on anal erotism".[9]

The most horrifying and dramatic death among Freud's early circle was that of Tausk. When Lou Andreas-Salomé terminated her brief affair with him, it was a bad shock to Tausk who tried to control the situation by throwing himself desperately into work. He became a neurologist and during the war served as chief physician to a field hospital, working with the determination of the damned. When he returned to Vienna after the war, he attempted to rebuild his medical practice under impossible conditions, and became engaged to be married, but the horrors he had witnessed in the war preyed on his mind and within a week of the marriage, in the midst of a black hell of depression, he killed himself. According to H F Peters' biography: "Rumour has it that he died a particularly gruesome death by first castrating himself." [10] He too died young – a mere 42 years old. Lou Andreas-Salomé wrote on the news of his death: "Poor Tausk. I loved him. I thought I knew him and yet I would never have thought of suicide..." [11]

What of the subsequent career of Ernest Jones? In one sense the fates were kind. He had the warm response and loving care of his wife, Katharine, a woman who shared his life at all levels for many years.

Jones undoubtedly made important contributions to psycho-analytic theory, and a complete list of his writings would cover many pages. Most of his papers are collected in two books, *Papers on Psycho-Analysis* and *Essays in Applied Psycho-Analysis*, but he is better known for his books *On the Nightmare* and *Hamlet and Oedipus*. As President of the International Psycho-Analytic Association from 1920 to 1924 and again from 1932 to 1949, he was involved in complicated diplomatic work, a vast correspondence, world-wide journeys and the responsibility for preparing the biennial Congress. Between the two World Wars, Jones edited the *Journal* and the International Psycho-Analytical Library, and when he retired from the Presidency, he was made honorary President of the Association for life.

His son Mervyn has written of him: "Even as a child I was aware of the prodigious amount of work my father got through. For years he saw ten or eleven patients a day. His hours were too long for the Harley Street house where he had his consulting room; so one patient came to York Terrace before breakfast and others on Saturday morning." [12]

I, too, remember him as a man whose very quick wits were allied to a positive gluttony for work and a responsibility for whatever he undertook which almost qualified him as an obsessional character.

As early as 1907 Jones felt himself getting into the habit of undertaking more work than he could satisfactorily perform: "At first this was dictated by eagerness or ambition, in later years by a sense of duty; in either case there always seemed to be some irrefutable reason why the next task had to be accepted." Jones frequently revealed a clinical honesty about his own life and motives but, like most of his colleagues, whenever physical symptoms attacked him without any sign of organic cause he did not consult his own psycho-analytic gods. Possible psychological roots to his illnesses were not discussed in *Free Associations*. Instead, with almost fanatical relentlessness he pursued possible physical causes. Surgeons were employed with remarkable frequency, first for a septum operation, then the removal of tonsils, next an appendectomy, and finally the removal of many teeth. These operations may have been necessary in themselves but they were exploited in search of a cure for neuritis. When it became impossible for Jones to use a pen or hold a telephone receiver for six months at a time, the paralysis of two of his main means of communication with the outside world looked suspiciously psychological, and when one at least of these periods coincided with great stress in his own life, it certainly required psycho-analytic investigation. Instead Jones wrote: "I tried of course to get at the source of the trouble. Vaccines made from my own germs or other people's had no effect. My body was so healthy that it was hard to think of any septic focus." Jones regarded himself as a supremely sane, fair-minded person and on the whole he realized this image.

There were two interpretations of his work for the International Psycho-Analytic Association. One group believed that psycho-analysis would not have been the same without it. Those organizational chores which Freud found so distasteful he – reluctantly rather than readily – embraced and carried out, with a thoroughness of which perhaps no other member of this very complex group of men was capable. He became a major force in shaping psycho-analytic history. The second interpretation said that far too much power was concentrated in the hands of one man, and his elevation to the honorary presidency was a question of being "promoted upstairs" in order to modify his dominance. This group believed that Jones was very much involved in the struggle for power.

Towards the end of Freud's life Jones performed the most romantic and spectacular feat in his whole career, assisted by men like Sir Samuel Hoare. He went to Vienna to persuade Freud that he must take the last chance of leaving Austria before the Nazis overwhelmed it. Planes were operating only as far as Prague at the time, but the indefatigable Jones managed to conjure up a small monoplane to complete the journey to Vienna. When he arrived, he at once made his way to the publishing house to find the stairs and rooms "occupied by villainous-looking youths armed with daggers and pistols". He had no sooner spoken than he was put under arrest and all his protestations that he must be allowed to communicate with the British Embassy were met by obscene remarks about the nature of the English. A combination of modesty and concern for the essentials gave Jones' account of this episode a matter-of-fact air, but it must have required considerable courage to face what were, in effect, young Nazi thugs, under such circumstances and demand one's rights. They released him after an hour and he at once made his way to Freud's home, to find a remarkable drama being played out there. A gang of young Nazis had invaded the house and were beginning to ransack the dining-room where Mrs Freud confronted them with the dignity of someone accustomed to civilized behaviour. She first invited the sentry to take a seat "instead of standing so uncomfortably", and when they demanded to see any money or valuables she placed the household money on the table and said: "Won't the gentlemen help themselves?" They next insisted on opening the safe in another room, and as they were gathered round it, counting the loot, they suddenly heard the door click open and there stood the frail figure of Freud, white-haired, gaunt, an apparently helpless old gentleman, incapable of thwarting their slightest wish. How ever, the sight of the clumsy marauders suddenly brought Freud to his full height with his eyes blazing like any prophet out of the Old Testament, and such was the impact of his distaste and authority that the SA suddenly changed their minds and announced that they would call again another day.

A prolonged wrangle between Freud and Jones followed. Freud made it quite clear that he wished to stay in Vienna, even when Jones pointed out that he was not alone in the world "and his life was very dear to many people". "Alone," Freud said, "ah, if I were only alone I should long ago have done with life." How could he, a man too weak to climb the high steps of Continental trains, leave Vienna he said, and assuming he survived the journey which country would take him in anyway?

One by one, Jones wore down his arguments and overcame the complicated problems of exit visas, of persuading the Nazis to release a sick but obviously Jewish old gentleman, of getting the British Home Office to issue permits for entry, residence and work in Britain. Jones certainly saved Freud from the terrible persecution, humiliation, brutality and death which overtook so many Jews, no matter how distinguished they were, or advanced their age, but Jones himself made no such claim. Once again, he recorded the facts in a business-like, non-heroic way.

And thus it was that on 6 June 1938 a fragile, death's-head figure, dressed almost gaily in a green hat and green top-coat, walked with the aid of a cane into the house at No. 20 Maresfield Gardens, Hampstead, London. One of the first letters Freud wrote was to Havelock Ellis, the English sexologist, saying that after all these long years they had at last a chance to meet. Ellis replied on

14 July regretting that it was very difficult for a permanent invalid to arrange a meeting, and later mutual friends explained the situation more exactly to Freud.

They never did meet. The two figures who had so deeply contributed to our understanding of the human psyche, who had, between them, broken down the conspiracy of silence about sex and invoked a moral revolution, were now within a few miles of each other, both facing death, Freud with the cold courage of the scientist, Ellis with a detachment which did not break down for ten years. It was said that Freud seldom revealed the agony he underwent. So it was with Ellis. Both men died with a rationalist's disdain of death.

As for Jones, he made no fuss, no ceremony, no sentimental journey of leaving this world. His last years were largely given up to writing his three-volume biography, an undertaking which took rather less than the ten years he anticipated. In many respects it was a remarkable book, which unfolded in wonderful detail the life and work of one of the greatest men of our time, reconciling personal and technical knowledge with great skill, and if occasional chapters suffered from a partisan approach, it still stands today as by far the most authoritative and comprehensive account of Freud's life.

In 1956, Jones underwent an operation for the removal of a growth in the bladder and immediately afterwards carried out an exhausting lecture tour in America. He hurried back to London to give four Centenary Addresses on the anniversary of Freud's birth, and in June 1957 was suddenly attacked by a coronary. He had survived a worse coronary as far back as 1944, but the second attack undermined his general health. By October, he fell seriously ill with what seemed to be gastric trouble, but his sheer sense of efficiency didn't permit him to remain in bed for the double anniversary of Christmas and his seventy-ninth birthday. Frail and tired, he left his bed, dressed and was moving about the house busying himself with one task or another. Some residue of the enormous energy which had driven him through a rich, burdened, complex life, came to his aid for the next few days, but early in the New Year he was forced back into bed again. Suddenly it became clear that something very different from gastric trouble or the coronary threatened him at last with death, and now cancer of the liver was diagnosed. His son later wrote: "He knew that death was not far, and faced it with the keen regret of one who had greatly loved life, but entirely without fear, and of course without any change in [his] view of the universe..."[13]

The end came in University College Hospital, which brought him back to his first beginnings. He had trained there as a medical student. Cremated at Golders Green, his ashes lie close beside those of the man whose life and career overshadowed his. Perhaps, among many distinguished achievements, Ernest Jones will be remembered as much as the Boswell of Freud as anything else, and it is fitting that he should lie close beside him in death.

NOTES
1. Verbal evidence from Ernest Jones.
2. *Memories, Dreams, Reflections*: C G Jung, p. 213.
3. *Memories, Dreams, Reflections*: C G Jung, p. 214.
4. *Contact with Jung*: Edited Michael Fordham and Elizabeth Osterman, p. 219.
5. Ernest Jones.
6. *Memories, Dreams, Reflections*: C G Jung, p. 284.
7. *Memories, Dreams, Reflections*: C G Jung, p. 287.
8. *Selected Papers*: Karl Abraham (introduction by Ernest Jones), p. 37.
9. *Selected Papers*: Karl Abraham (introduction by Ernest Jones), p. 35.
10. *My Sister, My Spouse*: H F Peters, p. 181.
11. *Ibid.*
12. *Free Associations*: Epilogue, Mervyn Jones, p. 260.
13. *Free Associations*: Ernest Jones, p. 264 (Epilogue, Mervyn Jones).

VINCENT BROME

H G WELLS

To some, author of *The Time Machine* H G Wells was an icon. To others he was intolerable and bad tempered. His demonic life once drove a whole generation along new and daring paths, and even in old age he insisted that people 'run the gauntlet of his iconoclasm'.

In this seminal biography, Vincent Brome recounts the rich fantastic cauldron of Wells' life – from his politics and writing to his complex and torn emotional life, and his painful, lingering death. Here was a man 'whose greatness lay in his ordinariness', but who was never truly ordinary.

J B PRIESTLEY

'See him sweep dramatically into the Savile Club, a burly man with a black hat set at a slightly rakish angle, an old-fashioned cape encompassing the broad shoulders, and the heavy-jowled face full of brooding purpose, and it became clear at once that this was a man to be reckoned with'.

This delightfully readable biography of the author of over fifty hugely popular books, not to mention plays, journalism and essays, paints a vivid portrait of a man who was almost as famous for his cantankerous grumbling and three marriages as for his writing. An international figure who made much of his Yorkshire origins, Priestley claimed not to give a damn about literary style, and was determined to write for ordinary people rather than for critics. Most of his books remain in print many years after his death.

Vincent Brome

Jung

Carl Jung was – as everyone knows – a famous psychiatrist. Vincent Brome's in-depth biography is the result of five years' intensive research in several languages. The result reveals his childhood love life, relations with Freud, alleged anti-Semitism and above all the immense range of his work. The result is essential reading to all those interested in the human mind and spirit.

'This book is a very readable account of Carl Jung's life and work. The author is steeped in his subject, admires Jung as a psychologist, though not slavishly...I thoroughly enjoyed reading Brome's book and I expect it will be indispensable reading for Jungologists for some time to come.'
R D Laing, *The New York Times Book Review*

'The best biography of Jung ever written...a rounded picture of...a man who was both troubled and inspired, both scientist and mystic...[Brome] has neither over-simplified nor become lost in trivial psychological analysis.'
Choice

'Brome has talked to lots of Jung's contemporaries and gathered anecdotes and bits of evidence that shed new light on Jung's relation to Freud, his alleged anti-Semitism, his boyhood, his love life. Brome's Jung is a very human, brilliant and passionate man.'
Christiana Robb, *The Boston Globe*

The Other Pepys

Samuel Pepys endures as one of the most famous figures in English literature. He was in fact two men, not one: the warm and supremely human confessor of the Diary and an extraordinary hypocrite. Previous biographers tended to rationalise the darker side of his characters or to explain away his conduct as socially acceptable in his day. Vincent Brome's biography is the first to face up to the contradictions in Pepys' personality. *The Other Pepys* is a gripping, frank yet sympathetic portrait.

Vincent Brome

Reverse Your Verdict

Ever since the private prosecution in the Stephen Lawrence case, there has been renewed interest in cases brought by British citizens against the police or the state. Until 1968, any person could serve an indictment for any crime, subject to the proviso that the Crown could intervene when it pleased. This book details six successful attempts to reverse the verdicts of the courts – including two convictions for murder – and was written as part of a campaign to safeguard the right of private individuals to seek justice.

Six Studies in Quarrelling

An entertaining introduction to the great debates of the *fin de siècle* era, from Darwinism to Socialism. Brome describes the 'quarrels' of some of the key literary figures of the time: George Bernard Shaw, H G Wells, G K Chesterton, Hilaire Belloc and the formidable Dr Coulton. Churchill and Henry James also put in appearances in this lucid and accessible guide to the big ideas of the age, which is as readable for its insights into the lives and characters involved as for the essentials of the arguments.

OTHER TITLES BY VINCENT BROME AVAILABLE DIRECT
FROM HOUSE OF STRATUS

Quantity		£	$(US)	$(CAN)	€
FICTION					
☐	THE AMBASSADOR AND THE SPY	6.99	11.50	16.95	11.50
☐	LOVE IN THE PLAGUE	9.99	16.50	24.95	16.50
☐	RETRIBUTION	9.99	16.50	24.95	16.50
NON-FICTION					
☐	H G WELLS	10.99	17.99	26.95	18.00
☐	J B PRIESTLEY	14.99	24.75	39.95	25.00
☐	JUNG	10.99	17.99	26.95	18.00
☐	THE OTHER PEPYS	10.99	17.99	26.95	18.00
☐	REVERSE YOUR VERDICT	7.99	12.99	19.95	13.00
☐	SIX STUDIES IN QUARRELLING	7.99	12.99	19.95	13.00

ALL HOUSE OF STRATUS BOOKS ARE AVAILABLE FROM GOOD BOOKSHOPS
OR DIRECT FROM THE PUBLISHER:

Internet: www.houseofstratus.com including author interviews, reviews, features.

Email: sales@houseofstratus.com please quote author, title and credit card details.

Hotline: UK ONLY: 0800 169 1780, please quote author, title and credit card details.

INTERNATIONAL: +44 (0) 20 7494 6400, please quote author, title and credit card details.

Send to: House of Stratus Sales Department
24c Old Burlington Street
London
W1X 1RL
UK

Please allow for postage costs charged per order plus an amount per book as set out in the tables below:

	£(Sterling)	$(US)	$(CAN)	€(Euros)
Cost per order				
UK	2.00	3.00	4.50	3.30
Europe	3.00	4.50	6.75	5.00
North America	3.00	4.50	6.75	5.00
Rest of World	3.00	4.50	6.75	5.00
Additional cost per book				
UK	0.50	0.75	1.15	0.85
Europe	1.00	1.50	2.30	1.70
North America	2.00	3.00	4.60	3.40
Rest of World	2.50	3.75	5.75	4.25

PLEASE SEND CHEQUE, POSTAL ORDER (STERLING ONLY), EUROCHEQUE, OR INTERNATIONAL MONEY ORDER (PLEASE CIRCLE METHOD OF PAYMENT YOU WISH TO USE) MAKE PAYABLE TO: STRATUS HOLDINGS plc

Cost of book(s): .... Example: 3 x books at £6.99 each: £20.97

Cost of order: .... Example: £2.00 (Delivery to UK address)

Additional cost per book: .... Example: 3 x £0.50: £1.50

Order total including postage: .... Example: £24.47

Please tick currency you wish to use and add total amount of order:

☐ £ (Sterling)   ☐ $ (US)   ☐ $ (CAN)   ☐ € (EUROS)

VISA, MASTERCARD, SWITCH, AMEX, SOLO, JCB:

☐☐☐☐☐☐☐☐☐☐☐☐☐☐☐☐☐☐☐☐

Issue number (Switch only):

☐☐☐

Start Date: Expiry Date:

☐☐ / ☐☐   ☐☐ / ☐☐

Signature: _____

NAME: _____

ADDRESS: _____

_____

POSTCODE: _____

Please allow 28 days for delivery.

Prices subject to change without notice.
Please tick box if you do not wish to receive any additional information. ☐

House of Stratus publishes many other titles in this genre; please check our website
(**www.houseofstratus.com**) for more details.